CW00539903

DICTATING TO THE MOB

Dictating to the Mob

The History of the BBC Advisory Committee on Spoken English

Jürg R. Schwyter

Great Clarendon Street, Oxford, OX2 6DP,
United Kingdom

Oxford University Press is a department of the University of Oxford. It furthers the University's objective of excellence in research, scholarship, and education by publishing worldwide. Oxford is a registered trade mark of Oxford University Press in the UK and in certain other countries

First Edition published in 2016

Impression: 1

Published in the United States of America by Oxford University Press
198 Madison Avenue, New York, NY 10016, United States of America

British Library Cataloguing in Publication Data
Data available

Library of Congress Control Number: 2015953855

ISBN 978–0–19–873673–8

Printed in Great Britain by
Clays Ltd, St Ives plc

Early days are crucial ones in either individual existence or corporate organisation. I repeat we had no precedent. Almost everything depended upon the personality of those to whom, almost by chance, this service had been committed.

J. C. W. Reith, *Broadcast over Britain*, 1924, p. 24

Contents

Preface

This book about the BBC Advisory Committee on Spoken English has been in the making for a long time. Crucially, I suffered a brain stroke in 2009 and was forced to pause in the writing of the book.

Originally it was triggered by Lynda Mugglestone's *'Talking Proper': The Rise of Accent as Social Symbol* (2003), where she describes, in passing in the chapter 'The Rise (and Fall?) of RP', the role of the BBC, John Reith, and the BBC Advisory Committee on Spoken English as the 'standard setting' institution for the pronunciation of English.

Historically, the Committee was conceived to advise the BBC on pronunciation, but soon the members took it upon themselves to prescribe rules for pronunciation and language at large. As a historically minded linguist, I find such attempts very interesting in view of the frequently failed or futile attempts to regulate and standardize spoken language. The role of spoken English in British society in particular is still evident in Britain's class system today, but it was much more so in the past. Since the First World War, great efforts have been spent on attempts to 'engineer' language. The BBC played a unique role in these attempts, as the rise of radio as a communication tool occurred at the same time. Even so, the BBC, through its Advisory Committee on Spoken English, had to experience its own learning curve to discover that standardization and regulation of spoken language is extremely challenging, bordering on the impossible.

This book attempts to document the process during the active years of the Committee from 1926 to 1939 and point out the legacy of the Committee, which still can be felt today and is, with a much reduced brief, embodied in today's BBC Pronunciation Research Unit.

The book addresses the history, sociology, and linguistics of the Advisory Committee on Spoken English and thus is aimed not only at linguists but also at historians and social scientists, as well as anyone interested in language policy or the role of the BBC in general. The first two chapters describe the linguistic aspects of the Committee's work, particularly after it had taken on the role of standardizing spoken English, a task well beyond its mandate and the BBC Charter. The challenges encountered in assuming their prescriptive role resulted in a structural crisis for the Committee, and an attempt was made to solve this through a reconstitution, the subject of the book's third chapter. The recognition that language evolution is highly dynamic led to a variety of changes to linguistic policies, such as using the International Phonetic Alphabet and attempting to define new words—the focus of the fourth chapter. These and other difficulties in reaching consensus, described in Chapter 5, were indicators that the Committee would have run out of steam long before its official suspension at the beginning of the Second World War. Yet the legacy of the Committee, the subject of Chapter 6, still lives on today in the Home Service (BBC national, regional, and local radio and TV stations) and the World Service (though in fewer areas and with a much limited scope).

The International Phonetic Alphabet (IPA) and BBC Modified Spelling

The International Phonetic Alphabet (IPA) and Modified Spelling as used by the BBC (adapted from Trudgill and Hannah 2008; *Broadcast English III* [1932] and *VII* [1939])

1. The International Phonetic Alphabet (IPA)

Vowels (long vowels are indicated by a colon (:))

ɪ	as in	*big, mirror*
ɛ	″	*bed, merry*
æ	″	*bad, man*
ɒ	″	*pot, not*
ʌ	″	*putt, cut*
ʊ	″	*put, foot*
i:	″	*bee, see*
u:	″	*boot, too*
ɔ:	″	*saw, more*
ɑ:	″	*bard, hard*
ɜ	″	*bird, furry*
ə	″	the unaccented vowel in *above, about, sofa*

Diphthongs

ei	as in	*bay, day*
ai	"	*buy, my*
ɔi	"	*boy, choice*
ou	"	*boat, goat*
ɑu	"	*bout, now*
ɪə	"	*peer, near*
ɛə	"	*pair, square*
ʊə	"	*poor, cure*
ɔu	"	*pore, shore*

Triphthongs

aiə	as in	*fire, shire*
ɑuə	"	*tower, power*

Semi-vowels

j	as in	*yes*
w	"	*well*

Consonants

b, d, f, g (as in *get*), *h, k, l, m, n, p, r, s, t, v, z,* have their normal values

ŋ	the sound of	*ng*	in	*singer, long*
θ	"	*th*	"	*thick, thought*
ð	"	*th*	"	*then, that*
ʃ	"	*sh*	"	*she, ss* in *mission*
ʒ	"	*s*	"	*pleasure, vision*
tʃ	"	*ch*	"	*church, cheat*
dʒ	"	*j*	"	*jute, j* and *dge* in *judge*
x	"	*ch*	"	Scottish *loch*, German *Buch*

Word stress

Stress is marked with ′ before the stressed syllable.

2. Modified spelling

The modified spelling used by the BBC has been made as simple as possible by the BBC, and for the most part is self-explanatory, for example:

ī represents the long i-sound in *time, my*
ō represents the long o-sound in *no, home*

The intermediate vowel, the neutral mid-central vowel or 'schwa', as in the unstressed vowels in the words *arrange, colonize, industrious, succeed*, has been marked by the diacritic ˘ over the vowel (but usage by the BBC has been inconsistent). So has the short vowel sound of *look*, to distinguish it from the long vowel of *loot*. Stress is indicated by ′ over the stressed syllable.

Consonant letters have their normal values.

ch is always pronounced as in *church, cheat*
ch (underlined) represents the sound of *ch* in Scottish *loch*, German *Buch*
zh represents the sound of *s* in *pleasure, vision*
g is always hard, as in *get, go*
th is always pronounced as in *thin, thick* unless otherwise stated
u(r) represents the long vowel-sound in *bird*, without any following *r*-sound, and is the common English approximation to the sounds of French *eu*, German *ö*

o(ng) represents the nasalized form of the vowel in *not,* and is the common English approximation to the sounds in French *bon* and *banc*, which are not usually distinguished in the pronunciation of a native English speaker.

Naming Conventions

The BBC Advisory Committee on Spoken English (1926–1939) and its associated sub-committees are referred to in the primary sources at the BBC Written Archives Centre in a highly variable manner. I list for convenience the various names that have been used:

After 1934, the *BBC Advisory Committee on Spoken English* itself was also referred to as the *Full Committee* or the *Main Committee*, abbreviated to the *Spoken English Committee.* On occasion, ad hoc sub-committees were formed (for example, for place names).

Also after 1934, following the reconstitution of the BBC Advisory Committee on Spoken English, an additional layer of important sub-committees was established. One of them was the *Permanent Specialist Sub-Committee*, which was also known as the *Expert(s) Committee*, *Specialist Consultants*, *Specialist Members*, or the *Consultant Members.* And from 1935 to 1937, an additional *Sub-Committee on the Invention of New Words* existed, which was also known as the *Sub-Committee on Words.*

Chapter 1
Introduction

1.1 The BBC and 'BBC English'

The BBC, or British Broadcasting Corporation, has been an integral part of life in Britain and many other countries for more than ninety years. It would be difficult to imagine our media landscape without the BBC's ten national radio networks, over forty-five regional and local stations, eight national TV channels, the World Service with news in twenty-seven languages, seven partly commercial news and entertainment channels (among them BBC World News and BBC Entertainment, the former reaching more than 160 countries, the latter available in South Africa, Asia, Australia, Latin America, Europe, and the Middle East), and its vast number of other commercial activities, ranging from magazines on all sorts of topics like gardening and wildlife to books, tapes, CDs, DVDs, podcasts, and materials for education, training, and English Language Teaching.[1] And let's not forget the *Radio Times*, that BBC magazine which lists all its programmes and contains a host of other features—the *Radio Times* in fact has one of the highest magazine circulations in the UK, at approximately 1,000,000.

Dictating to the Mob. First edition. Jürg R. Schwyter

Today the BBC's UK domestic services are largely financed through licence fees paid by television owners, whereas the World Service was funded by the Foreign and Commonwealth Office (FCO) until 1 April 2014. Now the World Service is also financed through the licence fee. BBC Entertainment is part of the BBC's commercial group of companies. In 1922, however, the BBC's founding year, the situation was very different. The Post Office invited the manufacturers British Thomson-Houston, General Electric, Marconi's Wireless Telegraph, Metropolitan-Vickers, Radio Communication, and Western Electric Companies to contribute £10,000 each to initiate the service. By July 1924, the number of member firms had risen to 1,700, and the BBC, no matter how large its revenue, paid a maximum dividend of 7½ per cent interest on the investment. John Reith, the BBC's first managing director, countered the argument that the BBC should be under the direct control of the state by emphasizing

> the extreme difficulties which prevailed in 1922 before broadcasting could be inaugurated. A number of companies wished to operate independently, and the patent position was serious. But it is more important to review the manner in which the responsibilities have been discharged, and to inquire whether they show any taint of interested bias, and whether in any single respect the interests of the public have been subordinated to those of the trade. There are occasions on which it is well to allow performance and results to justify means, even if the means be not generally understood or appreciated. (Reith 1924: 58–61, at 60)

This form of funding, however, was soon to end: on 1 January 1927 a Corporation was created, initially for a period of ten years (for details, see Briggs 1995a: 297–371).

In short, the BBC is a British *institution* par excellence—and not just when it comes to entertainment and reliable coverage of news from around the globe, but also when it comes to spoken English. 'The influence of the BBC', the social historian and former Provost of Worcester College, Oxford, Asa Briggs wrote, 'both on education and the pronunciation of "standard English" has been noticed by almost all the people who have described its work' (Briggs 1995a: 222). Burnley's (2000: 316) and McArthur's (2012: 452) comments in this respect are fairly typical:

> The rapid development in public broadcasting after about 1920 led in England and abroad to the establishment of BBC English as *de facto* spoken standard. The standard, alternatively known as Received Pronunciation, is that of a social and educational elite, originally developed from the manner of speech approved by the nineteenth-century public schools, and concurrently by the universities of Oxford and Cambridge.

> *BBC English* and *BBC accent* gain[ed] prestige nationally and internationally as the BBC itself acquired a reputation for both a clear, measured style and dispassionate, authoritative broadcasting.

Received Pronunciation (RP) is thus a hallmark of the BBC, or at least the early BBC. Andersson and Trudgill (1992: 9) found that '[t]he language of the BBC has *prestige*; voices with accents like these are associated with power, education and wealth. These things are highly valued and this explains why so many people strive to acquire the official language.' Although this may no longer be strictly true for the United Kingdom, where only news reading and presentation remain dominated by RP or near-RP, 'the use of RP remains strong in the World Service, and for many overseas listeners the traditional BBC voice is equated with good English' (McArthur 1992: 109). Interestingly enough, the term 'BBC English' originally had a rather negative connotation and was used 'among regional BBC staff resentful of the better prospects of speakers with public-school accents' (McArthur 1992: 109). The fact that in the 1920s the two terms 'BBC English' and 'public school accent' were perceived as largely synonymous speaks volumes about the public image and composition of the early BBC.[2]

It will be the aim of this linguistic and contextual history of the BBC to describe—with the help of historical BBC documents, linguistic examples, and, at times, newspaper articles—the language policy of the BBC, or more specifically, of the BBC Advisory Committee on Spoken English during the period 1926–39, and also to give some impressions of the public's reaction to that policy. Although the book will end with a brief look at the BBC's pronunciation guidelines after the end of the Second World War, its main focus is on the early days, as 'early days are crucial ones', to quote Reith (1924: 24); and indeed, whatever changes in language policy the BBC has introduced in more recent years, the influence of the Advisory Committee on Spoken English can still be felt. Hence the book should appeal not only to scholars of the BBC, but also to a wider body of researchers in the fields of linguistics, social sciences, and history.

1.2 The problem of 'standard': A linguistic approach

In a *Radio Times* article in 1931, A. Lloyd James, a Welsh phonetician at the School of Oriental and African Studies and Honorary Secretary of the BBC Advisory Committee on Spoken English, argued that even sentimentalists should realize that 'progress demands a standardized speech'. He tried to strengthen his argument with the following comparisons:

> Is speech the only thing that modern conditions tend to standardize? What about railway gauges, wavelengths, units of heat, length, weight, capacity and money, the pitch of screw-threads and the pitch of musical notes? Standardization is the antidote to chaos. Increased communication means an increase in standardizing the *means* of communication, and Speech, whatever man wants to make of it, is fundamentally his principle means of communication. (*Radio Times*, 6 November 1931)

What then is 'standardized speech'—or 'Standard English' for that matter? Can a linguistic standard really be compared to pound and penny, yards and inches, nuts and bolts? And does the absence of a linguistic standard necessarily mean communicative chaos? Before returning to Lloyd James and the BBC Advisory Committee on Spoken English, it is worthwhile looking into these questions, particularly since so much confusion, among linguists and non-linguists alike, surrounds the term 'standard' with respect to language issues.[3]

If we take a diachronic view (Haugen 1966), we can say that a language undergoing standardization passes through several stages, namely selection (that is, a particular variety is chosen so that a norm can be derived), elaboration of function (the selected variety becomes used for a much wider range of purposes, from central government and the law to literature and the sciences), codification of form (for example, in the form of grammars, dictionaries, or a language academy), and acceptance by a body of users (a linguistic community accepts the selected variety and frequently even sees it as synecdochic of their language as a whole). The standard may thus have a unifying function among both standard and non-standard speakers of that language, as well as a separating function vis-à-vis speakers of other languages; and it also takes on a kind of frame-of-reference function for its users—that is, it serves as a 'yardstick for correctness' (Garvin and Mathiot 1956). These very basic factors are widely accepted by linguists, with some modifications, and are by and large uncontroversial. Bex, for example, lists similar stages of standardization, but prefers to see the process as a perpetual cycle:

> Because language is always evolving to meet new needs and express new purposes it is more appropriate to see these processes as a continuing cycle rather than as something which can ever be complete. (1996: 26)

Whether we accept the standardization process as a perpetual cycle or not is really a matter of degree; of course, elaboration of function presupposes, for example, massive expansion of the lexicon (the Early Modern English period, spanning the period roughly from 1450 to 1750, illustrates this rather well), but this may not necessarily mean that an entirely new variety had to be selected. A new variety was, however, chosen early on in the history of English, when the standardization process of the previously selected variety, Late West Saxon,[4] was interrupted by the Norman Conquest; so, for example, the chancery clerks writing after about 1430, and Caxton when he introduced the printing press to England in 1476, had to select new varieties for their endeavours (see Smith 1992, 1996: 68–73, 2012: 173–6; Bex 1996: 32–4). But this was not the case, say, in the sixteenth and seventeenth centuries: the writings of authors such as Puttenham, Palsgrave, Coote, Wallis, and Cooper all seem to indicate that selection of a particular variety had already taken place.

Puttenham further attests to 'a codifying stage in the standardisation of English', that the standard 'has yet to penetrate beyond the River Trent', and that 'it signals the existence in towns of a class structure correlating with speech—including matters of accent' (Smith 2012: 169–70). 'This evidence shows', Dobson (1955: 30) commented,

> that from early in the sixteenth century there was in being an idea that there was a correct way of speaking English, which might be taught. . . . It was in general the speech of the South of England and was not current in the North or West; it was in particular the speech of London and was in use among well-bred and well-educated people in the Home Counties. But merely to define a geographical region was not enough; hence the more precise observation that it was the language of the Court, i.e. of the highest social classes and of the administration. Again it was the language of clerks, of learned men, of scholars, and as such it was the language of the Universities . . . [5]

The Reformation, various Bible translations, the growth of science, as well as nationalism and colonialization, led to the expansion of English into disciplines previously the reserve of Latin, for example, religion, philosophy, medicine, botany, and so on; and with it came a radical expansion of the English lexicon, mostly by means of borrowing and derivation.[6] It was not the case that a new variety had to be selected, but rather that the previously selected variety was rapidly elaborated so as to allow it to take on new functions. That is why the Early Modern English period 'exhibits the fastest growth of the vocabulary in the history of the English language' (Görlach 1991: 136).

In very simplified terms, it could be said for the standardization history of English that selection took place in the fifteenth century, elaboration of function in the sixteenth and seventeenth centuries, and codification of form through prescription by various grammarians and dictionary writers in the seventeenth and eighteenth centuries. 'There is general agreement about the central importance of the first sixty years of the eighteenth century in creating the conditions under which an "ideology of linguistic prescriptivism" became the dominant conceptual framework for setting up the notion of a national standard language' (Watts 1999: 40). Note that this does not necessarily apply to spoken language, as will be discussed later.

I shall argue that the story of the early BBC and its Advisory Committee on Spoken English shows a widespread acceptance of the idea of a standard by the 1920s and 1930s, which in fact goes back to the nineteenth century, the great public schools, and a form of linguistic insecurity as language became increasingly marked by social class and education. The latter can be found as early as George Puttenham's *The Arte of English Poesie* (1589); but it was, as Lynda Mugglestone has pointed out, 'the prescriptive tradition of the late eighteenth and nineteenth centuries [that] had catered for (and fostered) linguistic insecurity' and that 'the increasingly non-localized intake of a major public school [was] often presented as particularly important since—at least in the ideal world—it was able to purge speech of those regional forms which were regularly perceived, and depicted, as inherently "statusless"' (2003: 263, 227; see also Tiekken-Boon van Ostade 2012; Mugglestone 2012b).

But this still does not answer the question of what a standard language is (except to say that it has undergone the standardization stages already outlined and discussed), nor whether standardization is desirable and necessary at all; that is, whether a system of non-standard dialects necessarily results in communicative chaos. The answer to the second question is a simple and straightforward 'No'. Take Norway, for example, where everybody speaks in regional dialect and extremely few communication problems have emerged. So there is no *spoken* standard Norwegian, though Norway's 5.1 million inhabitants (as of 2013) use either of two *written* official standards, *Nynorsk* and *Bokmål*, which not only differ between each other but also allow internal variability (Trudgill 2000: 137–44). Or take the dialects of Swiss German: there is no 'standard' Swiss German, just a large variety of regional dialects, which does not mean that conversation between a German-speaking Swiss person from (say) Berne and one from Zurich would be difficult. And although most written business communication in Switzerland is—as in Germany, Austria, and Liechtenstein—conducted in Standard High German, Swiss German dialects are frequently used on radio and TV—several private radio stations and local TV channels even use Swiss German in all (not just local) news broadcasts.[7] As these two examples from outside the English-speaking world show, standardized speech as postulated by Lloyd James is by no means necessary to avoid communicative chaos.[8] And the fact that a speech community uses a variety of non-standard dialects can also serve as a unifying and distinguishing factor. This is certainly the case for the Norwegians or German-speaking Swiss: the one linguistic experience they share is that they all speak dialect. One could therefore just as well ask: Why should anyone want to standardize speech?

Turning now to English, what then are the attributes of Standard English? Or put differently, what is Standard English? James Milroy (1999: 26–8) lists the following characteristics of any variety, not just of English, which has undergone standardization:

1. The chief linguistic consequence of successful standardisation is a high degree of uniformity of structure.
2. Standardisation is implemented and promoted through written forms of language.
3. Standardisation inhibits linguistic change and variability.

Points (1) and (3) are the direct consequences of codification; point (2), however, needs further discussion in the case of English. For it is precisely the confusion or the equating of written and spoken standards that has clouded much of the debate surrounding Standard English.

Traditionally, standard grammars, which in turn form the basis for judgements of correctness in any medium, have been based on written or literary data only; but spoken discourse differs from written language in a number of features, including back-channelling, false starts, hesitations, lexis, and—often overlooked—grammar (e.g. phrasal heads '*This friend of ours, Carol, her daughter*, she decided to buy one'; ellipsis: 'Interesting, isn't it?'; word-order: '*That's what she said* was the biggest shock') (Carter 1999: 151–6). Recent definitions of the spoken standard also all *exclude* accent. Trudgill (1999) therefore has defined Standard English as not a language, not an accent, not a style, not a register, but simply a dialect,[9] one variety among many, albeit with some unusual characteristics:

- Standard English . . . is . . . by far the most important dialect in the English-speaking world from a social, intellectual and cultural point of view; and it does not have an associated accent. (p. 123)
- There is really no continuum linking Standard English to other dialects because the codification that forms a crucial part of the standardisation

process results in a situation where, in most cases, a feature is either standard or not. (p. 124)

- Unlike other dialects, Standard English is a purely social dialect. (p. 124)

Crystal's definition of Standard English (SE) is very similar (2003a). There are five principal elements in his definition. First, Crystal states that 'SE is a *variety* of English' and that '[s]ome people call it a "dialect" of English'. However, it is unique in that there 'is nothing in the grammar and vocabulary of a piece of SE to tell us which part of a country it comes from'. Secondly, Crystal argues that the 'linguistic features of SE are chiefly matters of grammar, vocabulary and orthography (spelling and punctuation)'. Importantly, he notes that 'SE is not a matter of pronunciation: SE is spoken in a wide variety of accents (including of course any prestige accent a country may have, such as British RP)'. Thirdly, from a sociological point of view, he states that 'SE is the variety of English which carries most prestige within a country'. He quotes a US linguist, who views SE as 'the English used by the powerful'. Fourthly and as a consequence, there is an impact on education. Crystal asserts that the 'prestige attached to SE is recognized by adult members of the community, and this motivates them to recommend SE as a desirable educational target'. Thus it is the preferred variety in formal communications such as 'government, law courts, and media'. And finally, and also highly relevant to this study, Crystal notes that although 'SE is widely understood, it is not widely produced. Only a minority of people within a country (e.g. radio newscasters) actually use it when they talk' (Crystal 2003a: 110).

One of the consequences of Standard English being considered *the* prestige social dialect is language-based inequality;

and it is therefore simply taken as a fact of life that 'lack of competence in Standard English is a barrier to social advancement' (McGill 1998: 11).[10] We saw that the elaboration process led to maximal variation in function of the standard variety, but all these functions are associated with central government and the law courts, bureaucracy and administration, scientific and literary writing—in short, with 'high culture'. Standard English, therefore, does not so much have an equalizing function, as parents and school teachers so often claim, but rather a gatekeeping function.

Although Standard English does have a local origin in the 'golden triangle' of London–Oxford–Cambridge (Lesley Milroy 1999: 184), it is no longer a geographical dialect (this is quite contrary to the Advisory Committee's claim that Southern English should naturally serve as *the* standard; see Chapter 2). Absolutely crucial, therefore, is Trudgill's and Crystal's exclusion of accent from their definitions of Standard English.

The close relationship between social class and dialect/accent has been described by many sociolinguists. In the case of English, one can say, somewhat simplified, that the higher up the social scale one happens to be, the less likely one is to exhibit any local features, and the more likely to employ standard English/the RP accent. In Trudgill's famous social and regional variation triangles (see e.g. Trudgill 2000: 30–2), the dialect variation triangle has a flat top (allowing for alternative linguistic forms, for example *I haven't done it* vs. *I've not done it* in certain relative clauses),[11] whereas the accent variation triangle goes to a point because of the special role of RP in the United Kingdom. However, there *is* variation within RP as well, although this tends not to be geographically determined (for examples, see Wells 1982, II: 279–301). An example that kept the Advisory

Committee on Spoken English busy for years is the (in)famous word *golf*, which can be pronounced with the 'l' [gɒlf] or without [gɒf].[12]

One main reason for the confusion surrounding the notion of Standard English is, as we have seen, the equating of written and spoken modes of standard language:

> In the written mode it refers to the fixity of spelling, lexicon and grammar which derives from the work of the prescriptivist writers of the eighteenth century. To use written Standard English is to signal competence in a set of established rules enforced by a normative educational system . . . A frequent definition of standard spoken English is that it is a prestigious system of grammar and lexis which can be used by any speaker in communities where English is the first language, available for any register of language (as opposed to varieties which are often termed 'restricted' or 'dialectal'). In the British Isles, it can be, but need not be, expressed in Received Pronunciation, a prestigious accent of English associated with, but not restricted to, the South-East of England. Thus it is possible to speak Standard English with a Scottish, Welsh, American or Yorkshire accent. (Smith 1996: 65)

It went without saying for the Advisory Committee on Spoken English that grammar and vocabulary would be those of spoken Standard English. But as we shall see, the Advisory Committee incorrectly applied Received Pronunciation, an accent, 'to set a standard' for isolated and often rather irrelevant expressions and words. Part of the uncertainty surrounding the notion of Standard English is actually caused by 'transferring written-mode notions of fixity to the spoken mode without modification' (Smith 1996: 65). The confusion continues when accent is included in the definition of spoken Standard English, and when notions of discrete choices in the written standard are extended to pronunciation. The problem lies in the fact that RP, as we saw, represents more of a gradient (for example *again* [ə'gen] and [ə'geɪn] are both RP) rather than consisting of a set of binary either–or rules (for example 'I say' is Standard English, whereas 'I says' is not):

> One of its [RP's] defining characteristics is that it is not a clear-cut set of fixed shibboleths, but rather what the nineteenth-century scholar A. J. Ellis, who first described it, called 'a sort of mean': a kind of prestigious magnet of pronunciation towards which prestige-seeking accents tend. . . . Received Pronunciation may be defined, therefore, as an abstraction, rather like the phoneme; individual speakers may produce utterances which tend towards or deviate from this 'mean'. It is therefore perhaps better to consider Received Pronunciation in terms of focus rather than fixity; in other words, individual speakers tend to a greater or lesser extent to conform to Received Pronunciation usage, but no one of them can be said to demonstrate every characteristic of the accent. Thus Received Pronunciation may be considered to be *standardised* or focused rather than *standard* or fixed: a centripetal norm towards which speakers tend, rather than a fixed collection of prescribed rules from which any deviation at all is forbidden. (Smith 1996: 65–6)

John Reith was well aware of variation among educated speakers of English; that is why he set up the BBC Advisory Committee on Spoken English: to fix what had only been focused. This story—and whether he and the Committee succeeded or not—will be told in the remainder of this book.

NOTES

1. See <bbc.co.uk/radio>, <bbc.co.uk/tv>, <bbc.co.uk/news/world_radio_and_tv/>, and <bbcentertainment.com> (last accessed on 26 April 2013).
2. Note that Lloyd James, the Honorary Secretary of the Advisory Committee on Spoken English, in a paper entitled 'The Spoken Word' published in 1936 in *The Magazine of the English Association*, speaks of 'the so-called BBC English' at which 'arm-chair critics rail' (p. 60, R6 / 196 / 9).
3. A pertinent example is Honey 1997, the many confusions, inconsistencies and shortcomings of which have been pointed out by Crowley 1999.
4. For useful discussions of the Late West Saxon 'standard', see Gneuss 1972, Hofstetter 1988, and Gretsch 1999.
5. The crucial distinction written *versus* spoken 'standard' is introduced and discussed further down in Section 1.2.
6. For details, statistics and examples, see e.g. Görlach 1991: 136–210, Barber 1997: 219–43, and Algeo 1998.
7. For Swiss diglossia, see Ferguson 1959; more recent accounts in English of the language situation in German-speaking Switzerland can be found in e.g. Barbour and Stevenson 1990 and Clyne 1995.
8. Other sociolinguistically interesting examples of non-uniformity from Europe are: Breton, which has never been standardized; Irish, which was only standardized (*An Caighdeán*) after the Irish Republic left the British Commonwealth in 1948 (Tristram 2001: 21–3); and the five linguistic regions of the Romantsch-speaking Grisons, although an artificial standard was created in 1982 in order to save the language from extinction and increase the viability of Romantsch radio and print media (Steinberg 1996: 147–50).
9. Note that British linguists tend to exclude accents from their definitions of dialects (which differ only in grammar and lexis), whereas many American linguists include differences in accent in their definitions of dialect (Trask 2000: 89).
10. Interesting in this context is Lesley Milroy's (1999) observation that language and standard ideologies differ from speech community to speech community: in the UK, language ideologies manifest themselves mainly along social class divides, but in the USA largely along racial and ethnic lines.
11. For further examples of variation within Standard English, see Hughes, Trudgill, and Watt 2005: 18–23.
12. For the International Phonetic Alphabet and BBC Modified Spelling, see the preliminary matter of this book.

Chapter 2
In the Beginning

2.1 'The Responsibility'

The BBC started life as the British Broadcasting Company (note: Company not yet Corporation) in 1922. From very early on the BBC was meant to be a tool to entertain, in the most positive sense, and to educate 'the masses'—though John Reith, the BBC's first managing director, never used the word 'masses' himself but preferred 'the public' or 'the great multitude' instead. In his 1924 *Broadcast over Britain*, Reith described the main aim of the Company as follows:

> As we conceive it, our responsibility is to carry into the greatest possible number of homes everything that is best in every department of human knowledge, endeavour and achievement, and to avoid the things which are, or may be, hurtful. It is occasionally indicated to us that we are apparently setting out to give the public what we think they need—and not what they want, but few know what they want, and very few what they need. (Reith 1924: 34)

One can observe that Reith assumes—although with best of intentions—that some people are indeed authorized to decide

Dictating to the Mob. First edition. Jürg R. Schwyter

what is 'best' for 'the great multitude', a behaviour that reflects a benevolent yet somewhat patronizing attitude.[1] He made it quite clear that to use 'so great a scientific invention' as radio 'for the purpose and pursuit of "entertainment" alone would have been a prostitution of its powers and an insult to the character and intelligence of the people'; instead it should be 'part of a systematic and sustained endeavour to re-create, to build up knowledge, experience and character' (Reith 1924: 17–18). Reith sought to delicately balance the educational and entertainment functions of the BBC from early on. While entertainment 'was the stated function of the Company, and many apparently considered that all its operations and the whole of the time available should be confined to entertainment alone', Reith introduced short lectures, which were 'intended to cover a wide range of subjects of general interest, delivered in a popular manner'. By doing so, he broadened the scope of the BBC. These lectures were hailed, in certain quarters, as 'the most interesting part of the programme', thus vindicating Reith's view (1924: 147–8). Eventually 'three separate lines of educational activity' were set up:

> There is the broadcasting of talks of general information in the course of the evening programme; there is, secondly, the broadcasting of lectures in schools; and, thirdly, a line of activity which has not yet been started, but which will be begun in the coming winter—a systematic series of lectures for adults at some convenient hour which will not interfere with their normal work. (1924: 149–50)

Whether bringing 'the best of everything into the greatest number of homes' meant 'popularizing Shakespeare' (1924: 168), 'educating musically large numbers of people' (1924: 175), or making the 'wireless lessons...an integral part of [the child's] schooling' (1924: 182), 'it followed naturally', as Briggs (1995a: 218) has pointed out, 'that genuine differences of opinion would be expressed about what constituted "the best"'. Reith not only reinforced the conception of the BBC as a public service by employing outside programme advisers and critics, but he also tried to solve any 'differences of opinion' by creating a 'network of advisory committees which drew upon the services of experts in various fields' (Briggs 1995a: 218–19). Reith wrote under the heading The Responsibility: 'We have set out to secure and have succeeded in securing, the co-operation and advice of recognized authorities and experts in all branches of our work... either in the form of advisory committees or by more direct participation' (1924: 32–4).

Examples of such advisory committees are the Religious Advisory Committee (founded in May 1923), the Musical Advisory Committee (formed in July 1925), the Children's Hour Committee and the Women's Advisory Committee (formed in 1924, but these two committees soon lapsed), and the Central Educational Advisory Committee (appointed in August 1924).[2] One of the 'offshoots' of the Central Educational Advisory Committee, to which Reith himself attached the utmost importance, was the Advisory Committee on Spoken English, which was formed in April 1926 (Briggs 1995a: 219–28).

In fact, the language education role of the BBC was quite explicitly stated by Reith as early as 1924 in his chapter from *Broadcast over Britain* entitled 'The King's English'—which incidentally also deals with the possibility of teaching foreign languages to radio listeners. Reith was keenly aware that spoken language and social standing were intimately linked in early twentieth-century Britain. He remarked that he 'heard it said that one can place a man socially and educationally from the first few dozen words he utters. There is a measure of truth in the statement.' But Reith also held strong notions about 'correctness' in spoken English. He even went as far as stating that it 'is certainly true that even the commonest and simplest words are subjected to horrible and grotesque abuse. One hears the most appalling travesties of vowel pronunciation.' Reith, with a sense of missionary zeal, saw BBC broadcasting in this regard as an important tool for educating and elevating the masses. 'Pride in a local or national intonation is perhaps quite natural', he stated benevolently, and 'this is not necessarily mutilation'. Nevertheless, the BBC could help offset the perceived disadvantages of such speech, since Reith did not suppose that 'any man wishes to go through life handicapped by the mistakes or carelessness of his own pronunciation, and yet this is what happens'. Thus, the BBC and Reith, in their mission to educate the 'great multitude',

> have made a special effort to secure in our stations men who, in the presentation of programme items, the reading of news bulletins and so on, can be relied upon to employ the *correct pronunciation* of the English tongue. . . . I have frequently heard that disputes as to the *right pronunciation* of words have been settled by reference to the manner in which they have been spoken on the wireless. *No one would deny the great advantage of a standard pronunciation of the language, not only in theory, but in practice.* Our responsibilities in this matter are obvious, since in talking to so vast a multitude, mistakes are likely to be promulgated to a much greater extent than was ever possible before. There is now presented to any who may require it, an opportunity of learning by example. I am told that children particularly have acquired the habit of copying the announcer's articulation; this has been observed by their teachers, and so long as the announcer is talking good English, and without affectation, I think it is much to be desired that he should be copied. (1924: 161–2, my italics)

Not only can Reith's prescriptive notions of 'correctness' be traced back to the eighteenth century, but even his ideal of defining and spreading a spoken standard was explicitly expressed by Thomas Sheridan as early as 1780 (Mugglestone 2003: 15–21). Judging from the press during those early BBC years and the many Letters to the Editor in the *Radio Times* and other magazines and newspapers, the public in general was quite happy with the idea that announcers could or should be their teachers, as this fairly typical voice from the same year as Reith's *Broadcast English* (1924) illustrates:

> *Announcers as Teachers*
> Happily for us, the officials of our Broadcasting Company have been well chosen, and are all educated and refined men and women, who use cultivated language to which it is a pleasure to listen. Unlike in America, the very tones of our own announcers' voices are an indication of a background of education and culture. In America, it seems, one hears daily slips in grammar, faults in diction, and the mispronunciation of both English and foreign words. In England such slipshod broadcasting is unknown. We look upon our announcers as teachers. And they are.—William Le Queux in *The Scot's Pictorial* (*Radio Times*, 18 January 1924)[3]

The letter shares the commonly held sentiment that Received Pronunciation is the standard one should aspire to. Also noteworthy are the terms 'educated', 'cultivated', and so on in connection with language use. Such attitudes are a product of the nineteenth century, where '"culture", "refinement", status and superiority were, according to popular belief, all able to be conveyed within the nuances of a variety of pronunciation' (Mugglestone 2003: 258–9). This confusion of speech with cultural and moral qualities can still be found today.[4] In terms of the standardization phases we discussed in Chapter 1, one could argue that such unquestioning belief in one correct 'variety' of grammar and pronunciation, as evidenced by Reith's passage and William Le Queux's letter quoted above, reflect a stage of 'acceptance'. This is also mirrored by the fact that Arthur Lloyd James, 'who has always given most valuable assistance to the B.B.C. in the matter of phonetics, and who is a Lecturer in Phonetics at the School of Oriental Studies' (*Radio Times*, 16 July 1926; see Figure 1), gave a number of lectures to BBC announcers on 'good English' even before the Advisory Committee on Spoken English had been set up. His diary notes for 10 June 1925 what he told them: 'We are daily establishing in the minds of the public the idea of what correct speech should be, and this is an important responsibility' (quoted by Briggs 1995a: 268).

Two additional points, however, should be made here. First, 'the public image' of the BBC was very much 'an image drawn from upper-class or upper middle-class life' (Briggs 1995a: 167). The broadcasters, 'mostly young men', were to 'a large portion . . . University undergraduates':

> They are rather shadowy personalities to the average man; they are aloof and mysterious. You will probably not find them at garden parties or social functions; their names may not figure among the distinguished ones present, even if they do go; most likely they are much too busy to spend time in this way. They neither receive, nor do they desire the attention of the street and market place. (Reith 1924: 37, 51)

Formality was as important as anonymity: it was decided in 1925 that announcers 'should be required to wear dinner jackets' when on duty in the evening as 'an act of courtesy to the artist' (Briggs 1995a: 268); and they should speak, as we saw, 'good English and

The King's English.

A B.B.C. Advisory Committee on Pronunciation.

THE B.B.C. have long felt their responsibility in the matter of setting a standard of spoken English by means of the speech of their announcers. This is a responsibility which they are forced to assume whether they like it or no. However little they may wish to dictate or lay down principles of pronunciation for the country, they are aware that they must constantly be setting fashions.

For example, it frequently happens that their announcers are confronted with a word in print which is seldom or never heard in speech. Difficulty arises, also, in the case of foreign names, such as Marseilles, which are half acclimatized in this country. It would obviously be an affectation to speak of Paris as "Paree." Ought one to adopt the sailor's pronunciation of Buenos Ayres, or the Spanish pronunciation, or something in between?

Then again there are a vast number of doubtful words which have two or three alternative pronunciations even among educated speakers. The B.B.C.'s correspondence contains many complaints by Northerners against what they call the slovenly methods of Southerners, particularly in relation to the letter "r" and the aspirate in words like "which" and "when." There are also technical words, such as "aerial" and "acoustics," in which the professional people have adopted a pronunciation that can hardly be defended on logical principles, and then the question arises whether the announcer ought to use the technical pronunciation or the form to be found in the best dictionaries.

* * * *

Thus the problems are many and varied, and it seemed to the B.B.C. that it would strengthen their position in the face of criticism, and at the same time be of valuable service in maintaining the purity of our spoken language, if they could have a body of experts to whom they could refer for advice.

The experts in phonetics no longer, as in the days of the great Lindley Murray, lay down the law of right and wrong. As in the case of other inductive sciences, their business is to collect and record the facts. They may tell you, for example, that it is the practice of educated speakers of Southern English not to pronounce the "t" in "often," but they are very chary of saying *this* is right and *that* is wrong. They recognize that language is a living, growing, and changing thing, constantly being modified by the habits of practical people.

In the course of a preliminary conversation with Mr. Robert Bridges, the Poet Laureate, Sir Johnston Forbes-Robertson (one of the most distinguished speakers of the British stage), and Professor Daniel Jones, of the London University, the author of the standard pronouncing dictionaries in common use, it was decided to form a Committee and include, in addition to these three gentlemen, Mr. Logan Pearsall-Smith, as representing the Society for Pure English, and Mr. Lloyd James, who has always given most valuable assistance to the B.B.C. in the matter of phonetics, and who is Lecturer in Phonetics at the School of Oriental Studies. This Committee held their first meeting on Monday, July 5th, with the Poet Laureate in the chair. A first list of doubtful words was submitted to them. Most of these consisted of queries raised by the announcers. The following are some examples. We hope to print a full list with the decisions of the Committee in our next issue.

Word.	*Committee's decision.*
acoustics	a-coó-sticks
gyratory	jýratory
courtesy	cúrtesy
gala	gáhla
idyll	íddil
obligatory	oblígatory
Northants	Nórth-ámptonshire
Southampton	Soúth-hámpton
char-a-banc	shárrabang (s)
garage	garage (Fr.), *not* garridge
Mozart	Moze-art
Marseilles	Marsáles
Rheims	Reams

These decisions will be circulated to all the stations of the British Broadcasting Company for the benefit of the announcers. It can hardly be expected that all announcers will be able to comply at a moment's notice with all changes involved by the Committee's advice without fail, but these are the standards to which the Company's announcers will endeavour to adhere.

* * * *

It is realized that in many cases the recommendations of the Committee involve a dogmatic decision on points which might legitimately be arguable, but to prevent confusion uniformity has to be attempted.

Figure 1 Facsimile of *Radio Times* 16 July 1926, p. 126.

without affectation'. The most appropriate medium for this, it was agreed, was the *Public School Pronunciation*—eventually renamed by Daniel Jones as *Received Pronunciation* or RP—as this accent 'would convey a suitable sense of sobriety, impartiality, and impersonality' (McArthur 1992: 110).

The second point is that whether in fact radio and television can influence people's speech behaviour, and if so to what extent, represent two different questions altogether. Labov and Harris (1986: 20) have claimed that 'linguistic traits are not transmitted across group boundaries simply by exposure to other dialects in the mass media or [even] in schools'—with the exception of a few self-conscious corrections, sometimes hypercorrections, in formal styles. Trudgill (1986: 39–41) explains why: as accommodation seems to be the most likely explanation for the spread of linguistic features from speaker to speaker, that is the conscious or unconscious convergence of a speaker to the speech of his or her interlocutors, face-to-face contact is obviously a prerequisite for the linguistic diffusion to take place. It is thus clear that 'the electronic media are not very instrumental in the diffusion of linguistic innovations, in spite of widespread popular notions to the contrary', a fact supported by 'the geographical patterns associated with linguistic diffusion':

> Were nationwide radio and television the major source of this diffusion, then the whole of Britain would be influenced by a particular innovation simultaneously. This of course is not what happens: London-based innovations reach Norwich before they reach Sheffield, and Sheffield before they reach Newcastle. (Trudgill 1986: 40)

By contrast, neither the broader public nor Reith and his contemporaries at the BBC seemed to have doubted the Broadcasting Company's mission and success. Though Reith admitted that it was impossible to 'compute in concrete terms' the influence broadcasting would have on children, he insisted that 'there is an influence, and a great one' (1924: 183). He supported his notion of learning 'good English' by example from the radio, as we saw, with the claim that 'children in particular have acquired the habit of copying the announcer's articulation; this has been observed by their teachers' (1924: 162).[5]

On the one hand, then, Reith felt a great responsibility in this respect, particularly since, by the end of September 1924, the BBC already had 950,000 licence fee payers, calculated to represent an audience of 'over four million' and significantly advancing every month (Reith 1924: 81, 205). On the other hand, he was confronted with the problem already stated by A. J. Ellis and Henry Sweet, namely that 'even among educated London speakers' there are many words that 'are pronounced with differences'; that, in short, there is quite considerable variation 'from individual to individual, and more markedly from generation to generation' (quoted by Mugglestone 2003: 259, 261). These factors—combined with Reith's firm belief in the possibility as well as necessity of fixing, of standardizing pronunciation, and what Jean Aitchison has called a 'vintage wine year' view of language (2001: 13)—are very clearly reflected in the minutes from the preliminary meeting of the Advisory Committee on Spoken English, which took place at Savoy Hill on 25 June 1926.

Reith realized that the BBC had a vast reach into the population, since '[a]pproximately half the population of the country was at one time or another listening to broadcast announcements'. The BBC thus carried a 'great responsibility' in that its broadcasts might be taken 'as an example of how English should be spoken'. However,

> it was becoming increasingly apparent that large numbers of words in common use were pronounced by educated people in entirely different ways, and in many cases it was practically impossible to say which was best.

Further, in addition to the particular question of vowel sounds or accents in various words, there arose such general questions as the final and medial 'r' in southern English and various common usages by educated people which in some quarters might be regarded as being as wrong and unfortunate as the practices of (say) the Cockney.

Reith and the BBC were not only concerned with the varieties of pronunciation but also sought to remedy this undesirable state of affairs:

The Broadcasting Company felt that they should secure the most expert advice to the intent that, if possible, *a standard form of pronunciation for doubtful words should be settled* which would then be adopted at all Broadcasting Stations, and a ruling given as to *whether such modern customs of educated people as those mentioned above should be accepted as justified and authorised, or whether the Broadcasting Company should by their powerful example endeavour to stem modern tendencies to inaccurate and slurred speech*. (R6 / 201 / 1; my italics)

The following people were present: Reith himself, Robert Bridges (Poet Laureate since 1913), the actor Sir Johnston Forbes-Robertson, Daniel Jones (Professor of Phonetics in the University of London), and a number of BBC staff—Admiral Charles D. Carpendale (the BBC's Assistant General Manager), Mr Roger H. Eckersley (appointed Organizer of Programmes in 1925), J. C. Stobart (Director of the Education Department), and Mary Somerville ('a very clever and self-confident young lady', according to Reith, who worked with Stobart, 'with schools work as her special responsibility'; the minutes list her as Acting Secretary) (Briggs 1995a: 231).

In that Preliminary Meeting they further stated that the wireless announcers had a special responsibility regarding pronunciation and then formally decided on the formation of the Advisory Committee on Spoken English. All of the people present expressed their willingness to serve on it—to the great relief, one suspects, of Reith and Stobart. This was because the correspondence immediately preceding the Preliminary Meeting had revealed two problems. First, that not everyone invited was keen on the prospect of serving on the Committee, as they seemed to fear the additional workload and commitments that Committee meetings would bring. Daniel Jones, for example, was very reluctant initially to join the Committee, as a letter (23 April 1926, R6 / 196 / 1) from Lloyd James, who had approached Jones, to Stobart shows: not only was Jones 'busy and not well' and felt that he and Lloyd James 'would more or less duplicate each other', but he, Jones, emphasized that 'he has so often expressed his views in private & public. That there may be a danger of the opinion arising that he & he alone holds these views.' Lloyd James replied that he had 'invited Daniel Jones to act, on the understanding that he will not have to attend committees'. However, two months later Stobart invited Daniel Jones to the first official meeting of the Committee, 'at which we very much hope you will be present' (30 June 1926, R6 / 196 / 1). Because of his acting career frequently taking him out of London, Sir Johnston Forbes-Robertson was equally hesitant initially, as his reply to Stobart's invitations shows (20 June 1926, R6 / 196 / 1). But Stobart was equally persistent (21 June 1926, R6 / 196 / 1): 'I ought to have explained in my previous letter that it is not supposed that the Committee would have to meet personally except at rare intervals. Most of the points could be referred to them by correspondence', and invited him to the Preliminary Meeting anyway.

And secondly, there was the issue of whether recommendations on pronunciation should be restricted to England only and, if not, how this should be reflected in the membership of the Committee. Lloyd James made the following suggestion on 23 April 1926: 'The people mentioned by you [Stobart] are all speakers of one type of English, i.e. South-Eastern. It might be as well if you were to include a representative of some other type. Scotland would not take kindly to any recommendations of southerners.' Stobart replied (26 April 1926) that 'Scottish stations might possibly follow suit if desired; but the kind of problem I have in mind—e.g. the pronunciation of words like "gyratory" and "Chars-a-bancs"—is very much the same for them as for us, and we could at any rate inform them of our Advisory Committee's recommendations, leaving it to them to translate them into Scottish if they so desire' (R6 / 196 / 1).

For the additional members of the Committee it was

> . . . unanimously and cordially agreed that invitations be sent to the following gentlemen, asking them if they would be willing to join the Committee—Mr. George Bernard Shaw, Mr. Logan Pearsall-Smith (representing the Society for Pure English) and Mr. Lloyd James, Lecturer in Phonetics at the School of Oriental Studies, London, who would also be asked to act as Honorary Secretary. (R6 / 201 / 1)

A letter by Stobart to Lloyd James, in which he suggested that Lloyd James should act as Honorary Secretary, dated 25 June 1926 (R6 / 196 / 1) and written immediately after the Preliminary Meeting, indicates that H. C. Wyld, Merton Professor of English at Oxford and another Englishman, was also briefly under consideration for membership, but that it was decided to ask Shaw, born in Dublin in 1856, instead. Logan Pearsall Smith was a

Philadelphian who had spent most of his life in Britain as an English language and literary scholar and was, together with Bridges, one of the founding members of the Society for Pure English. No Scotsman was on the list.

Four days later, the formal letters by Reith to Logan Pearsall Smith and George Bernard Shaw were sent, inviting them to become members of the Committee. Shaw replied on 11 July, writing at the bottom of Reith's letter: 'I accept and suggest (off hand) the following additions to the list of recent problems. Cowardice, facile, fertile, isolate, Jacobean, exemplary.' The Committee could begin its work.

2.2 'The King's English'

The agenda that was being prepared for the first official meeting (R6 / 196 / 1) consisted of six items, among them the procedures of the Advisory Committee, the 'attitude of the Committee towards the modern tendency of slovenly speech', the 'consideration of a list of doubtful words submitted by the announcers and others', and the following resolution:

> That in the case of certain doubtful words it is necessary for the B.B.C. to adopt uniform standards of pronunciation for use by announcers and other officials of the Company in their work, and that the Committee, after due consideration of derivations and traditional usages, will decide upon the form to be adopted.

The (undated) front page of the Advisory Committee's minute book not only gives us again a brief mission statement but also illustrates what a most distinguished body this actually was (see Appendix I (a) for brief biographies of the original members):

The British Broadcasting Company, recognising their responsibility in setting a standard of spoken English, have appointed the following to act as an Advisory Committee:—

Dr. Robert Bridges,
Mr. Logan Pearsall Smith,
Mr. G. Bernard Shaw,
Mr. Daniel Jones,
Sir Johnston Forbes-Robertson,
Mr. A. [Arthur] Lloyd James

The Company will refer to this Committee for advice on the pronunciation of new words or imports from foreign languages which are becoming acclimatised.

The Committee will advise in respect of the London and Daventry stations, where the B.B.C. intend to maintain a standard of educated Southern English. It is not intended to impose this standard upon the Northern, Scottish or Irish stations. Pronunciations as adopted on the advice of the Committee will be made known to the Company's official announcers in the Southern stations. (R6 / 201 / 1)

Of special interest are the focus on the treatment of loan-words in English and the aim of maintaining 'a standard of educated Southern English'—precisely the variety that, according to Henry Sweet's 1881 *Elementary Sounds of English*, is 'approximated to, all over Great Britain, by those who do not keep their local dialects' (quoted by Mugglestone 2003: 258)—but above all the Committee's self-imposed restriction to advising the London and Daventry stations—whether out of respect for other regional varieties of English, golden-triangle centricity, the absence of a Scotsman on the Committee (at least in 1926), or out of a sense that everything north of Watford was a lost cause anyway, is anyone's guess; unfortunately the BBC files do not make clear how and when this decision had been reached. But below is a letter from 1926 making it clear that Southern English was accepted as the standard:

The B.B.C. Announcers are setting up a commonly accepted standard of Southern English speech. Their voices are penetrating into every nook of England and they are breaking down the linguistic barriers between county and county.—R. N. Plows, Kippax, Leeds (*Radio Times*, 16 April 1926)

Lloyd James was well aware of the difficulties that dialect and accent differences potentially could have caused for the reception of the Committee's decisions outside England. The official line taken in the end was that suggested even before the preliminary meeting: namely, that Scottish stations and, one assumes, by extension stations in Wales and Northern Ireland, 'might possibly follow suit if desired' (R6 / 196 / 1). Not all listeners, however, were happy with the choice of 'educated Southern English', as shown in an admittedly curious complaint, made in 1936 by a Scotsman living in Canada:

I am satisfied, after careful listening, that it is the cadence, and not the pronunciation, that sounds unpleasing to Canadian ears. The announcer tonight had a steady movement from D flat to G natural, or thereabouts, (with slight variants at each end). It was a very typical English movement; but to ears on this side [of the Atlantic] it suggests weakness—the last thing we want to suggest to Canada just now. Is it not possible to reserve such announcing for the earlier transmissions, and to give us something more rugged? Have you ever thought of using a Scottish announcer for this side?

A slight Scottish accent is greatly appreciated both in Canada and the States. (R6 / 196 / 9)

After the preliminary meeting there was a sense of urgency and excitement; consequently, things moved very rapidly. The first official meeting of the Committee was held on 5 July 1926, only ten days after the preliminary meeting. It was attended by Bridges (as Chairman), Forbes-Robertson, Jones, Pearsall Smith, and, representing the BBC, Reith, Stobart, Somerville, and a new face, Basil E. Nicolls, the London Station Director. Two points stand out from this 'official' meeting. First, the Committee established itself as the BBC's absolute authority in matters of 'doubtful words'. The resolution mentioned on the agenda was, according to the minutes, 'unanimously' carried by the Full Committee and thus found its way into the official minutes. This meant that the BBC would adopt a 'uniform pronunciation', at least internally, and that it was up to the Advisory Committee on Spoken English, 'after due consideration of derivations and traditional usages', to 'decide upon the term to be adopted' (R6 / 201 / 1).

The aim was not only to achieve consistency, but to do this through a rather prescriptive approach, certainly for announcers and, once pronunciation had been successfully standardized, eventually for 'most educated persons'. With hindsight, though, it was acknowledged that the public at large could not be forced to accept a standard as defined by the BBC. A brief, undated summary of the history and function of the Advisory Committee on Spoken English, probably written shortly after the Committee was suspended at the outbreak of the Second World War (the past tense is used throughout and references made to publications as late as 1937; R6 / 196 / 1), is quite explicit on these points. Through the Advisory Committee on Spoken English the B.B.C. hoped to lay the foundations of a standard pronunciation which would eventually be common to most educated persons, although it emphasized from time to time that is [*sic*] published lists of works were for the guidance of B.B.C. announcers and other officials, and were not an attempt to dictate to the general public how it should speak, as was so often alleged. It was not suggested that the chosen pronunciations were the only 'right' ones.

Secondly, a number of 'general principles' of pronunciation were agreed in the July 1926 meeting, so that rules for announcers could be drawn up:

Vowel sounds in accented syllables.	The Committee agreed that it was desirable to oppose any tendency towards the increase of homophones in the language, and that the announcers should therefore be instructed to differentiate the vowel sounds in such groups of words as shaw, shore, sure; yore, your; tired, tarred, etc.
Vowel sounds in unaccented syllables.	The Chairman demonstrated that it is possible to give all vowels in unaccented syllables a flavour of their original character without unduly stressing the syllable containing them, and that indeed the matter was merely one of good or bad articulation, e.g. the slovenly speaker uses a single sound (represented by 'eh') for all vowels in unaccented syllables. He says parehdy, parehsite, Julieh, Ehphelieh, where the speaker with good articulation says parody, parasite, Julia and Ophelia. It was agreed that the announcers should attempt the differentiation of such vowel sounds, but without becoming stilted.

Purity of Vowel sounds.

The Committee were in agreement that all affectations such as compaoused, for composed, m'yah for mere, nem for name, which definitely prejudice the purity of vowel sounds, should be opposed.

The 'h' in which, why, whale, etc.

After some discussion it was decided that speakers of Southern English would find difficulty in pronouncing which, whale, why, white, etc. with the aspirated 'w', and that no definite principle could be determined in this case, although differentiation between which and witch, whale and wail, etc. should be recommended in order to avoid homophones.

Untrilled final 'r' and 'r' between vowels.

The possibility of pronouncing the 'r' in fire, tower, sure, hour, poor, etc. without trilling, was demonstrated. It was felt, however, that Southern English speakers having come to be unaware that such 'r's' had any sound value whatever, would have considerable trouble in pronouncing an untrilled 'r'. If that were so, it was agreed that the untrilled 'r' should be treated as a separate vowel, though not syllabic, e.g. tired to be pronounced tired, not tahd.

It was agreed that an attempt should be made to give the letter some sound value, however slight.

The adoption of French 'age' sound into English.

The Chairman proposed that the broad 'a' (of father) in such words as garage, mirage, rajah should be recognised, and that an attempt should be made to adopt the sound of the French 'age' into English, rather than to add to the list, already too long, of words ending in the sound 'ehdge'. Agreement was not reached on these proposals, though it was later decided not to anglicise the word 'garage' as yet.

Foreign words. No definite rule was found possible as to the pronunciation of place names or of foreign words. It was agreed, however, that foreign words in common use should be Englished and that where their sounds approximated to English sounds the original sounds should be respected, e.g. chauffer, and in proper names, Shoobert, but Mose-art, Reams (Rheims). (BBC ACSE, Minutes, 5 July 1926; R6 / 201 / 1; emphasis in the original document)

Subsequently, a BBC internal memo from Reith was sent to all station managers ('Main and Relay') with the minutes of the first meeting enclosed, adding:

I shall be glad if you will make every endeavour to have the decisions of this Committee carried out by all station [*sic*] who announce or speak in any way at the microphone, I am not of course referring to outsiders or even to regular lecturers. We are only concerned with our own staff.

There will of course be no difficulty with the pronunciation of the 'r' in Scotland. The 'r' should be pronounced but we would probably be quite unable to have Englishmen pronounce the 'r' without exaggeration and we wish to avoid stilted announcing even in an attempt to become more accurate. (17 July 1926, R6 / 196 / 1)

English as spoken in much of England is non-rhotic, i.e. post-vocalic /r/ is not pronounced; words such as *star* are pronounced /stɑː/. However, in Scotland, for example, the older pronunciation /stɑr/ prevails (Trudgill 2003: 112).

It is clear that the Committee's decisions were not followed by all announcers all the time; it is a linguistic fact that there existed and still exist pronunciation variations even within RP or near-RP. A BBC internal memo from the Programme Executive sent to 'all regional and station directors' almost three years after the Committee's first official meeting, with a reprint of the 'general principles' enclosed, is ample testimony to this: 'I should be glad if all members of your staff who appear before the microphone would study it [the reprint with the general principles] and if you would impress upon them the importance that is attached to the adoption throughout the Corporation of a universal method of pronunciation' (7 March 1929; R6 / 196 / 3).

It should be added here that it is not always easy to interpret the Committee's 'decisions' without the use of phonetic script (see Chapter 4). While most of the examples of homophones, aspirated *h*, etc. given in the general principles are clear enough, this is not the case for their transcriptions for the words *composed* and *name*. It is likely, however, that 'compaoused' contains a rather bad attempt at showing a fronted o (that is, articulated as forward as the o vowel can be) and 'nem' shows a very narrow diphthong (that is, a single vowel that slightly changes its quality during pronunciation). Daniel Jones (1972: §162) discusses an 'almost monophthongal E', that is, an almost pure e, which 'may often be observed in the speech of BBC announcers'.[6]

During the next meeting (held on 8 November 1926), it was recognized that rendering unstressed vowels as 'eh' was unsatisfactory in light of the decision that vowels in unstressed syllables should have a 'flavour of their original character'; 'eh' was therefore replaced by putting the diacritic mark ˘ over the vowel. They decided not to use the phonetic alphabet (in this case a schwa, ə, as heard in the unstressed vowel in *about*), in order to make communications to the Press—and therefore the general public—as easy and straightforward as possible (R6 / 201 / 1).

Later on, the Committee's decisions were also published in the form of a number of hugely popular pamphlets called *Broadcast English* (see Section 2.4).

From a linguistic point of view, it is quite remarkable not only that most of the pronunciation features that appear in the Committee's first list of recommendations are 'old friends' going back to the nineteenth century,[7] but that they continued to raise fierce reactions—in the press and amongst the Committee members themselves—at regular intervals. There are dozens of letters complaining about the pronunciation of vowels in unstressed syllables, about the pronunciation of 'wh', the letter 'r' in all positions (postvocalic, linking and intrusive), and, of course, the treatment of foreign words. The following is an example of a letter dealing with the first three of those issues:

Announcers' English.
. . . The announcers seem to find a lot of difficulty with the letters 'r' and 'h'. Why should a word ending in 'er' be pronounced as if it ended in 'aw' or 'ah'? Why put in an 'r' when it isn't there? Such vulgarisms as 'Indiar' and 'Australiar rand Africa' are painful. Why say 'modden' when the word is 'modern'? . . . We also heard that the King had been 'weeled' in a bath-chair, when—I suppose—the announcer meant 'wheeled'. Also, is it the British Empire or the British Empiah? If the B.B.C. pronunciations in the above instances are the correct ones, then I apologize for my ignorance. If they are not correct, surely listeners are justified in saying so.—F. W. E. Wagner, Castletown Road, West Kensington. (*Radio Times*, 28 June 1929)

The 'wh' aspiration question, by the way, triggered months of controversy in the *Radio Times*, with quotations ranging from the *New English Dictionary* (that is, the *Oxford English*

Dictionary) to Anglo-Saxon. With respect to this pronunciation, Gimson (1984: 47) observed that 'the phoneme /ʍ/ as in *white*, although characterized as obsolescent by phoneticians a hundred years ago, was nevertheless often recommended as appropriate in more formal styles'.[8] As for foreign words, decisions on the pronunciation of foreign names were questioned regularly, particularly by listeners with some knowledge of the country or language in question:

I myself think the endeavour ultimately to make the pronunciation used by B.B.C. announcers the criterion an excellent one, particularly as we lack any official body to which appeals could be made. May I, therefore, as a musician, and one who has spent eight years in Austria—the home of Mozart—raise a protest against the mispronunciation of his name as given in your article, entitled 'The King's English'? It is, of course, impossible to put down phonetic equivalents in writing, but surely the German 'z' can be fairly adequately dealt with. A much more accurate rendering would be 'Mo-tsart', the accent falling on the first syllable. There seems to me to be no justification whatever for Anglicizing the name, since it has not become a household word. . . . —Ernest Whitfield, 67, Finchley Road, St. John's Wood, N.W.8. (*Radio Times*, 30 July 1926)

Though Lloyd James called on his audience in a radio talk, broadcast on 29 November 1926, 'to continue to take an interest in all the problems of our native tongue, and never to hesitate if they want the B.B.C. committee to consider any vexed question of pronunciation', he continued with the following pronouncement on who has the last say on 'foreign words':

Foreign words are a source of anxiety, and here the committee has one policy, which is, for better or worse, to anglicise as many as possible.

Whether a foreign word has lived long enough among us to be given papers of naturalisation is for the committee to decide. (R6 / 196 / 1)

It seems that by late 1930, 'garage' was given its UK passport, as the minutes of the Committee's tenth meeting record: 'GARAGE: The committee substituted GÁRREDGE for their previous recommendation.' However, *hors d'oeuvre* and *kursaal*, for example, were still to be pronounced 'as in French' and 'as in German' respectively (R6 / 201 / 1).

Interestingly enough, 'foreign words' often caused not only members of the general public to write in, but also members of the Advisory Committee themselves, as is illustrated, for example, in a letter by Pearsall Smith to Lloyd James, in which he questioned 'some pronunciations I have heard on the Wireless which seemed to me unusual', such as 'Eskímo' or 'Himálayan' [the accent mark indicates stress] (30 May 1929, R6 / 196 / 3). Pearsall Smith also wrote to Miss Somerville about 'Bízantine vs Bizántine' (26 December 1929, R6 / 196 / 3) or a year later again to Lloyd James: 'I have heard an announcer give a French pronunciation to Lyons & Marseilles, which I think should be pronounced as English words' (R6 / 196 / 4).

Even several years into the Committee's work, the complaints from listeners often were the same or similar, as was the misunderstanding that the BBC set itself up as a general pronunciation authority. That misunderstanding was, of course, if not fostered by the BBC itself in the late 1920s, at least tolerated or deliberately left ambiguous. On the one hand, it was emphasized time and again that the Advisory Committee's brief was to achieve consistency amongst the BBC's announcers. On the other hand, one could ask why their decisions were published if they were meant for BBC-internal consumption only. The following two examples are both from the spring of 1929:

Cockneyisms.
Paolo and Francesca was a very beautiful performance; but ought the B.B.C., which sets itself up as a fount of pure English for the education of the masses, to broadcast cockneyisms like 'Francescerrand her women' for 'Francesca and her women' and 'Malatesterrawaits' for 'Malatesta awaits'? It was the voice describing the scenes and action which was guilty of this. It is noticeable that the same people who perpetrate the above atrocities are quite capable in an access of refinement of such things as 'Paw out the tea'.—W. Walsche, 2B Bickenall Mansions, Gloucester Place. (*Radio Times*, 29 March 1929)

Our Mother Tongue.
I wish to add my note of condemnation to the way in which the English language is mutilated by speakers on the B.B.C. staff to whom we have to listen. Far from being a mirror of perfection as to pronunciation, it is positively exasperating to hear continually 'mod'n' for 'modern', 'gov'n' and 'gov'nment' for 'govern' and 'government', etc. This is surely not the way in which we wish our rising generation to talk, or foreigners to learn to talk our tongue.—A. F. Hole, Hillfield Gardens, Muswell Hill, N. (*Radio Times*, 12 April 1929)

As late as 1935, a letter by a listener triggered an internal debate as to the 'correct' pronunciation of the word *vegetable*. A BBC memo asks:

Shall we follow the modern tendency, or shall we go back to four syllables? The question seems to me to be complicated by the fact that I think at present it is more or less a class distinction. The middle and upper classes make the elision, whereas the working class pronounce all four syllables.

To which Miss Simond, the Committee's then Assistant Secretary, replied: 'I am afraid I must side with the lower classes: four syllables, please. Also I don't agree that it is a case of class distinction—I think it's merely one of... slovenly rapid speech by all classes' (7–13 September 1935, R6 / 196 / 8).

As for giving the postvocalic /r/ 'some sound value', it was not until 1934—more than eight years after the first official meeting and following numerous complaints—that the Committee finally realized that

Southern announcers cannot treat the r sound in the Northern manner, and very few English born speakers give to the unaccented vowels the flavour that Mr. Bridges recommended. But the B.B.C. very definitely concerns itself with checking ultra-modern tendencies in the language, and in carrying out the injunctions of the Committee with regard to the so-called 'purity' of English vowels. (Minutes, Enclosure A; 20 September 1934; R6 / 201 / 2)

This is, in fact, another important point about the working mechanisms of the Committee: in spite of the fact that 'in many cases the recommendations of the Committee involve a dogmatic decision on points which might legitimately be argued, but to prevent confusion uniformity has to be attempted' (*Radio Times*, 16 July 1926; Figure 1), the Committee actually increasingly sought the public's views and, not infrequently, took some of the criticism on board, and from the late 1920s onwards showed an increasing willingness to change some of its earlier decisions.

2.3 'What Say They?': A listening BBC?

Over the course of 1927, the Committee started drawing up its word-lists under two headings:

(a) Pronunciations definitely recommended
(b) Pronunciations suggested

The former were to be adopted by the announcers, for example:

zoology	zō-óllŏjy
zoological	zō-ŏlojjicăl, but Zoolójjicăl Gárdĕns

while the suggestions would be constantly reviewed in later meetings, when they might be revised in the light of criticism, for example:

again	The last syllable rhymes with either 'rain' or with 'then'. The Committee suggests the latter pronunciation.
cross	This, with other words like 'frost', 'cough', 'loss', is pronounced either with a short vowel as in 'boss', or a long vowel as in 'all'. The Committee suggests the former pronunciation.
explosive	Pronounced 'explousiv' and 'explouziv'. No decision.
golf	The pronunciation 'goff' is current in the South among players of the game. The Committee suggests the retention of the 'l' sound. (BBC ACSE, Minutes, 26 May 1927; R6 / 201 / 1)

Note, that both pronunciations of *again*, *cross*, *explosive*, and *golf* are examples of RP (or upper-class RP). Wells (1982: 295) states that '[t]here are several very common words . . . having two or more rival forms in RP', which he refers to as 'lexical-incidental variability'. Thus the preference of one over the other is an individual choice and not a matter of prescription.

The minutes of a meeting in the following year state that, after a lengthy discussion of 'doubtful words . . . it was decided that these pronunciations should be published in the "Radio Times", and that readers should be invited to submit their views' (29 November 1928; R6 / 201 / 1). The phrase 'lengthy discussion', in BBC parlance, appears to indicate severe disagreement. Reith, in a letter to Bridges, proposes to 'bring out decisions in "The Radio Times" and let them, so to speak, simmer for some months before putting them into the more or less permanent pamphlet form'. The vetting process, of course, encountered practical challenges. For example, when 'the first pamphlet was published it did not contain all the words which had previously been passed by the Committee and had been printed in the "Radio Times". Many were omitted because of subsequent correspondence in the press and otherwise' (R6 / 196 / 3). This procedure was confirmed in a document drawn up after the Committee's first six meetings in the autumn of 1929:

> The decisions of the Committee have been communicated to the Press, through the Radio Times, which has claimed the right of first publication. These decisions, as they appear in the Radio Times, are provisional, and are published in order to be exposed to public criticism; the Committee has always reserved the right to modify these provisional findings, and the final decisions are published in the Booklet only after they have been publicly criticised. (R6 / 196 / 3)

172 — RADIO TIMES —

Announcing and Pronouncing.

Some Decisions of the B.B.C.'s Advisory Committee on Pronunciation.

IT will be remembered that in our last issue we gave an account of the first meeting of the British Broadcasting Company's Advisory Committee on Spoken English, on which Mr. George Bernard Shaw has agreed to serve, and which met recently under the chairmanship of the Poet Laureate, and we promised to give a complete list of the words then discussed and the pronunciations advised.

These were merely a first selection from many hundreds of words noted as of doubtful pronunciation. Many of them had been submitted by the Announcers as being the subject of differences of opinion; others were words which had been challenged by correspondents; and others again were merely submitted as samples of the kind of difficulty that arises. One whole group of words, for example, consists of foreign names which are half-acclimatized in this country. Another consists of technical terms, where the practise of the specialist does not always conform to the lexicographer's pronunciation following the derivation or history of the word.

The pronunciations recommended in the following list are given here for convenience in ordinary printed type, and not as they should strictly be represented, in phonetic script. Probably our readers will be most inclined to dispute the section headed "Problems of Accent." The principle that the Committee had in mind in this section was that the accent should be thrown back as far as convenient, but it should not be thrown back so far as to involve the swallowing of later syllables.

Technical Words.

acoustics	acoóstticks
autogiro	autojýro
gyratory	jýratory
gyroscope	jýroscope

Doubtful Consonants.

humour	humour
often	off-en
soldier	sóle-jer

Doubtful Vowel Sounds.

courtesy	curtesy
finis	fýnis
gala	gáhla
idyll	iddill
opus	ó-pus
privacy	príve-acy
project	prŏ-ject
respite	réspit
precedence	pre-cédence
precedent	prĕcĕdĕnt
unprecedented	unprĕcĕdĕnted
via	vý-a

Problems of Accent.

allies	alíze
condolence	cóndolence
congratulatory	congrátŭlatory
despicable	déspicable
hospitable	hóspitable
indisputably	indispútably
indissolubly	indissólubly
inextricably	inéxtricably
obligatory	obligatory
sonorous	son-órous
vagary	vagáry
quandary	quándary

Place Names.

Northants.	North-amptonshire
Southampton	South-hampton
Towcester	Toaster

Words adopted unchanged from a foreign language.

carabiniers	carabineérs
char-a-banc	shárabang
chauffeur	show-fer
garage	gárage (" age " as in French)
liaison	leeáyzon
piano	p'yánno (instrument)
questionnaire	quést-yon-air

Foreign Place Names.

Boulogne	Boulóan
Calais	Cállay
Lyons	lions
Marseilles	Mar-sáils
Rheims	Reams

Accents :— ˘, short vowel ; ¯, long vowel ; ʹ, accented vowel.

Figure 2 Facsimile of *Radio Times* 23 July 1926, p. 172.

By 1930, the Committee even went so far as to state that *all* its decisions on pronunciation should be considered 'provisional and be published as such in "The Radio Times", being given as much publicity as possible' (as opposed to selective publication as in Figure 2). Then 'these provisional decisions should be reviewed at the following meeting, when they would be either confirmed as final, or altered in the light of criticism received'. Also important—and the cause of a great deal of controversy later—is the decision taken during the same meeting 'that no useful purpose would be served by the publication of alternative pronunciations' (17 January 1930; R6 / 201 / 1).

This new, pragmatic 'listening BBC' can be illustrated through two brief examples. The first involves place names.

The Committee decided as early as its meeting on 8 November 1926 to produce a pronouncing dictionary of English place names that would be 'of service to general learning, and of practical use to the B.B.C.' The need for such a dictionary arose as 'it was difficult to obtain information about the pronunciation of small villages, hamlets, etc.' These apparently were subject to some mispronunciation by BBC announcers which in turn led to 'adverse criticism in the country' (R6 / 201 / 1). Interestingly enough, it was in various letters to the editor of the *Radio Times* that the issue was first raised. In the letters page of the 30 July 1926 issue, two listeners questioned at least some of the Committee's decisions on the pronunciation of place names, but one, Edgar W. Wood, a Fellow of the Royal Geographical Society, may well have given the Committee the idea to get to work on the matter:

I would propose that, in the pronunciation of geographical names by your announcers, the recommendations of the 'Permanent Committee on Geographical Names' be adopted. This Committee had been formed by the Royal Geographical Society . . . and has already issued several pamphlets giving rules for the spelling and pronunciation of geographical names in various countries. It seems a matter of regret that already there is a difference between your Committee and this one. I give an example: the word 'Marseilles' mentioned by you. Your Committee give as the correct pronunciation, 'Marsales', but the P.C.G.N. say it should be 'Marseiy'.

In the spring of 1927, 'a card index of some nine hundred place names, with their pronunciations, had been compiled from information received from listeners in the country'. Reith suggested that the BBC should verify that information, so that announcers could be confident about consulting the card index for the pronunciation of difficult place names (26 May 1927; R6 / 201 / 1). The minutes of the December meeting of 1927 record not only that the Station Director at Edinburgh requested information about the place name index—thereby clearly reflecting its usefulness—but also that the Committee did in fact verify every single entry in the index (1 December 1927; R6 / 201 / 1); this was done by writing a circular to educated people in 'all villages the names of which were contained in the card index', such as postmasters and country vicars, and asking them for confirmation or correction of a particular pronunciation (17 May 1928, R6 / 201 / 1). At the time, country vicars in particular were considered to be beacons of local knowledge. A staggering '1,946 letters had been sent out, of which approximately 5½% were unanswered. In 77 cases the parson and the post-master were at variance as to the correct pronunciation. There were, however, 554 names about which parson and post-master were in agreement' (Minutes, 29 November 1928; R6 / 201 / 1).

As work continued, the Committee soon realized that the scope of the booklet had to be restricted to English place names (18 November 1928) and that an ad hoc sub-committee had to be set up 'to deal with the preparation of the pamphlet, and Professor Daniel Jones, Mr. Lloyd James and Mr. Stobart were appointed' (25 July 1929; R6 / 201 / 1).

But the place name consultation process undoubtedly reached its climax in 1929 with a full-page appeal in the *Radio Times* by Lloyd James. 'Listeners have already sent several hundreds [i.e.

place names with unfamiliar pronunciations]', he wrote, 'but more are required':

> Therefore, if any reader knows of a place name, be it a river, hamlet, lake or hill, the local pronunciation of which is not easily gathered from its spelling, he will be doing a service to the English language if he takes steps to have the local pronunciation permanently recorded. If he puts the name on a postcard, with as clear an indication of the local pronunciation as he can invent, and sends it to me at Savoy Hill, it will be included in the forthcoming booklet. (*Radio Times*, 3 May 1929, p. 219)

The reactions were overwhelming, and three weeks later, the *Radio Times* published the following statement:

> Pronunciations of Place Names.
> Mr. Lloyd James has received so many letters in reply to his request for place names of strange pronunciation that he is unable to reply to them all individually. He promises, however, to communicate in due course with those correspondents who raised special points. A listener has taken exception to our spelling the local pronunciation of 'Daventry' as 'Daintry'. This, she says, should be 'Dane-tree'. Daventry was the scene of the last stand of the Danes; and the town's crest is a 'Dane under a tree'. We thank her for this information, which was new to us. The next time we see a Dane under a tree anywhere, we shall think of Daventry. (Column, 'Both Sides of the Microphone'; *Radio Times*, 24 May 1929)

So should the location of the BBC station and transmitter be pronounced 'Daintree'—its historical local pronunciation—or 'Daventry', its current spelling pronunciation? The question had in fact already arisen more than four years earlier, and at the time Lloyd James had given a firm ruling: 'The B.B.C. has,

I think, sufficient authority to decide which pronunciation it will adopt. Let it be *Daventry*' (Lloyd James to Reith, 21 July 1925; quoted in Briggs 1995a: 222; see also Figure 3).

An undated report on the progress with respect to the Dictionary of Place Names (R6 / 196 / 1) states that 1,500 letters and postcards were received as a result of the appeal in the *Radio Times* and that an additional 1,778 new names had been added to the register,

> of which 1,400 appear to be suitable for inclusion in the pamphlet (the remainder being merely dialect pronunciations). This, with the 554 names already on the Register, makes a total of 1,954 names (England only) suitable for publication, if the replies from parsons and postmasters prove satisfactory.[9]

The highly opinionated Bridges, however, warned Lloyd James in a letter, dated 20 May 1929, that everyday common pronunciations of place names were utter nonsense. While according to Bridges Northern dialects were readily distinguishable, Southern dialects were not; for example, he singled out the dialect of Oxfordshire as particularly savage as locals dropped unstressed vowels at the beginning of words (R6 / 196 / 3). Attitudes like this show, of course, that the Advisory Committee's willingness to listen to the general public's views and take them on board was still rather limited; snobbery and upper-class values—at least for some members of the Committee—still prevailed unabated.

The minutes of the seventh meeting of the Advisory Committee, held on 25 July 1929, record that at least the 'question of alternative pronunciations was discussed', but that 'it was decided that one pronunciation only should be recommended for Announcers, but that accepted local pronunciations which

'DAVENTRY' OR 'DAINTRY.'

Despite the local variant of the name, the B.B.C. has kept to the phonetic pronunciation of Daventry in order not to confuse foreign listeners. In the accompanying article Mr. Lloyd James, secretary of the B.B.C. Committee on Spoken English, asks listeners to help him compile a list of place names the pronunciation of which presents difficulties to the uninitiated.

Figure 3 Facsimile of *Radio Times*, 3 May 1929, p. 219.

are still in general use should be given in a separate column'. It was further decided—and this is an innovation with linguistic consequences that will be discussed in Chapter 4—'that pronunciations should be given in phonetic script, but that a popular notation should also be given. It was suggested that the International Phonetic Script should be used' (R6 / 201 / 1).

On 11 June 1930, Lloyd James wrote to Daniel Jones enclosing 'the final proof of the place-name pamphlet which you were good enough to look through for me' (R6 / 196 / 4). The result was impressive; *Broadcast English II: Recommendations to Announcers Regarding the Pronunciation of Some English Place Names*, published by the BBC in 1930, contained 'some 1,500 English names, a few Manx names, and one or two Welsh names from border counties' (p. 5), as well as an Introduction outlining some general principles and explaining, in some detail, the 'International Phonetic Alphabet as adopted for the representation of English pronunciation' (p. 13).

Of course the main work was carried out by the Committee, particularly the three sub-committee members, but the input from listeners and the general public should not be underestimated. As for Daventry (Figure 4), both pronunciations were listed (phonetic script / modified spelling), first the current pronunciation recommended to announcers, *'dævəntri / dávventry*, followed by the historical and local pronunciation, *'deintri / dáyntry* (p. 36).

The second example of the 'listening BBC' relates to the pronunciation of the words 'ski' and 'margarine'. In the first (1928) edition of *Broadcast English I: Recommendations to Announcers Regarding Certain Words of Doubtful Pronunciation*, the pamphlet in which the Committee's decisions about words in general parlance were published, the word 'ski' does not figure; but the Norwegian and Swedish pronunciation, where <sk>

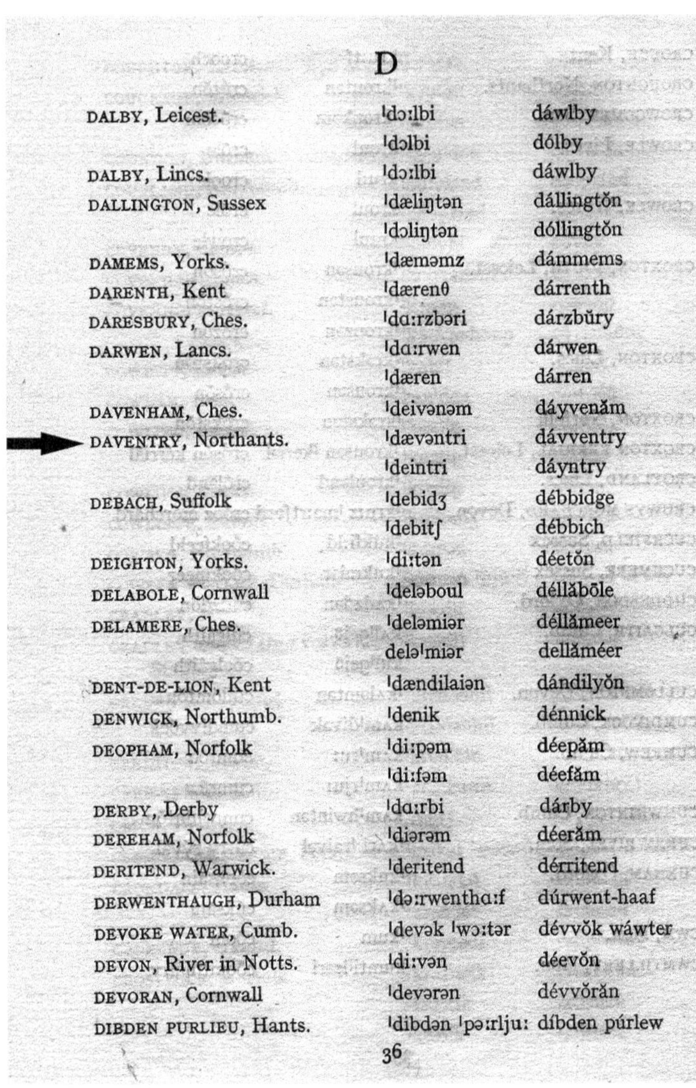

D

DALBY, Leicest.	ˈdɔːlbi	dáwlby
	ˈdɔlbi	dólby
DALBY, Lincs.	ˈdɔːlbi	dáwlby
DALLINGTON, Sussex	ˈdæliŋtən	dállingtŏn
	ˈdɔliŋtən	dóllingtŏn
DAMEMS, Yorks.	ˈdæməmz	dámmems
DARENTH, Kent	ˈdærenθ	dárrenth
DARESBURY, Ches.	ˈdɑːrzbəri	dárzbŭry
DARWEN, Lancs.	ˈdɑːrwen	dárwen
	ˈdæren	dárren
DAVENHAM, Ches.	ˈdeivənəm	dáyvenăm
DAVENTRY, Northants.	ˈdævəntri	dávventry
	ˈdeintri	dáyntry
DEBACH, Suffolk	ˈdebidʒ	débbidge
	ˈdebitʃ	débbich
DEIGHTON, Yorks.	ˈdiːtən	déetŏn
DELABOLE, Cornwall	ˈdeləboul	déllăbōle
DELAMERE, Ches.	ˈdeləmiər	déllămeer
	deləˈmiər	dellăméer
DENT-DE-LION, Kent	ˈdændilaiən	dándilyŏn
DENWICK, Northumb.	ˈdenik	dénnick
DEOPHAM, Norfolk	ˈdiːpəm	déepăm
	ˈdiːfəm	déefăm
DERBY, Derby	ˈdɑːrbi	dárby
DEREHAM, Norfolk	ˈdiərəm	déerăm
DERITEND, Warwick.	ˈderitend	dérritend
DERWENTHAUGH, Durham	ˈdəːrwenthɑːf	dúrwent-haaf
DEVOKE WATER, Cumb.	ˈdevək ˈwɔːtər	dévvŏk wáwter
DEVON, River in Notts.	ˈdiːvən	déevŏn
DEVORAN, Cornwall	ˈdevərən	dévvŏrăn
DIBDEN PURLIEU, Hants.	ˈdibdən ˈpəːrljuː	díbden púrlew

36

Figure 4 Facsimile of *Broadcast English II*, 1930, p. 36.

before palatal vowels (a vowel articulated high in the hard palate area, for example the [i:] in *ski*) is pronounced /ʃ/, was common in English at the time (see Jones 1924, 1937; Jones gives /ʃi:/ first in both editions, followed by the less common alternative /ski:/ in brackets). However, there was a constant stream of letters objecting to the pronunciation /ʃi:/. Here is one from 1927:

'Ski' or 'Shee?'

Dear Sir. Would it not be as well if the B.B.C. Advisory Committee on Spoken English gave attention to that vexed word 'ski'? When broadcasting some time ago from the Plymouth Station, I was informed by the Announcer that, so far as he was aware, the accepted pronunciation was 'shee'. If the Norwegian pronunciation be adopted, then presumably the Norwegian plural, without the final 's' should also be used: which I venture to think would ultimately lead to confusion. In any case, since the word is almost universally called 'ski' on the Continent, where the sport actually takes place, is it not somewhat absurd for us in England to adopt the sound by the minority in Scandinavia? . . . —F. McDermott, Tregoose, St Columb, Cornwall. (*Radio Times*, 16 September 1927)

The 'ski' question—the word was borrowed into English from Norwegian—is directly linked to the treatment of loan-words in English and, therefore, the question, as Lloyd James put it, of whether 'a foreign word has lived long enough among us to be given papers of naturalisation', i.e. to be 'Englished', a matter which he said was 'for the Committee to decide'. Of course there are no objective criteria of 'long' or even 'common use', the condition given in the 1926 general principles. According to the *Oxford English Dictionary* (*sub verbo*), there is an isolated early use in English dating from 1755, but all the other early attestations are late nineteenth and early twentieth century. But, after another three years of uncertainty, the Committee *did* come to a decision: on 17 January 1930 the pronunciation 'skee' was adopted (R6 / 199 / 2), and on 7 February 1930 the Advisory Committee's new ruling was published in the *Radio Times*. This, however, was not the end of it. The complaints continued, and so did the discussion. On 20 September 1934, the Consultant Members of the Advisory Committee suggested 'SHEE to replace SKI', that is, to 'de-naturalize' the loan-word again, so to speak—a suggestion that was adopted by the Full Committee on 20 September 1934 (R6 / 201 / 2).[10] The pronunciation 'shee' thus found its way into the second as well as third edition of *Broadcast English I*.

The letter 'g' in the word 'margarine' caused somewhat similar difficulties. Complaints ranged from letters in the *Radio Times* –

Half a Pound of 'Marge'!
The pronunciation of margarine, given in this week's *Radio Times* should not be 'marjareen', but with a hard 'g' margarine, as it derives from margaric acid, pronounced with the 'g' hard. Marjareen has resulted in the awful contraction 'Half-pound of Marje'.—Dr. C. Gordon, Jersey (*Radio Times*, 18 January 1929)

—to a letter from Unilever, the producers of Flora margarine, to the Committee giving various reasons why the word margarine should be pronounced with a hard 'g', and asking that the Committee should reconsider their previous recommendation 'marjareen':

The Secretary [Lloyd James] reported a letter received from Messrs. Unilever, Ltd., protesting against the Committee's recommendation that the 'g' in the word 'margarine' should be soft, and urging that the form with the hard 'g' was not only required by the derivation of the word, but was also in general use amongst educated speakers. After discussion the Committee decided that in view of the fact that the form MARJARINE was commonly used both by those who bought and those who sold the product [this] was not sufficient justification for reversing their previous recommendation. The Secretary was instructed to write to Messrs. Unilever to this effect. (Minutes, 7 December 1937; R6 / 201 / 2)

It is interesting to note, by the way, that the Consultant Members, who prepared the word lists before they reached the Full Committee, 'were unable to reach a decision on this point [i.e. hard vs. soft "g" in *margarine*] and agreed that it should be referred to the Committee' (R6 / 201 / 2). The colour-coded card index (see Appendix IV), which records the history of all the words discussed, lists *margarine* on a white card, used for 'ordinary words, included in 3rd edition of *Broadcast English I*', and gives the following chronology:

Date discussed	Comments
29. 11. 28	'márjăreen'
20. 9. 34	Altered to 'marjăre'en' [i.e. stress as in Jones 1924, 1937: s.v.; note, by the way, that in both editions Jones gives /dʒ/ as the preferred pronunciation, with /g/ in brackets as the less common alternative]
7. 12. 37	Word reconsidered at request of Unilever Ltd. (manufacturers of product), who suggested that g was required by derivation and usage. Committee did not feel justified in reversing previous recommendation. (R6 / 199 / 1)

The pronunciation of the word *margarine* illustrates particularly well the inability of the Committee to decide between a historically rooted, etymological approach and the common parlance version which was actually used. It should be added here that of course announcers, too, from time to time expressed their 'desire to have certain rulings reconsidered. It represents a very real difficulty in getting their tongues round unusual pronunciations which seem to go against the grain' (letter to Lloyd James, 29 August 1934, R6 / 196 / 6).

Although the consultation process was becoming more and more a two-way street, helped considerably, it has to be said, by the fact that the British public took an enormous interest in the BBC in general and issues of the English language in particular, the Committee was still reluctant to adopt the changes in pronunciation suggested by members of the public; time was to prove the Committee came down on the wrong side for *ski* and the right side for *margarine*. As was the case with the place names, however, the Committee was surprisingly open when it came to words being suggested to be ruled on; they received letters proposing everything from a list of correct pronunciations for plant and flower names, chemical elements, the names of famous scientists or politicians to words relating to the Mount Everest expedition of 1931—such as geographical and geological terms (20 November 1931; R6 / 201 / 1). More specifically, the Committee received twenty-seven letters relating to the pronunciation of the surname Joule, as in the scientist James Prescott Joule (19 January 1933). Other letters were concerned with the words *conduit* and *intuit*. In the light of such correspondence, the Committee decided (30 November 1933) on the pronunciations CÓNDEWIT, INTÉWIT and JOOL (Figure 5). And on 8 January 1936 it was agreed that 'the best method of obtaining opinions and suggestions from the general public would be to broadcast a

940 THE RADIO TIMES December 29, 1933

NEW YEAR RESOLUTIONS ON PRONUNCIATION

A. Lloyd James, Hon. Secretary to the B.B.C. Advisory Committee on Spoken English, discusses the latest pronunciation problems

THE fifteenth meeting of the B.B.C. Advisory Committee on Spoken English was held on Thursday, November 30. During the seven years of its existence this Committee has discussed some hundreds of words, and has produced some valuable booklets dealing with questions of pronunciation. At its last meeting the Committee passed the proofs of a booklet on the pronunciation of Welsh Place Names, which should go a long way towards the solution of one of the major native linguistic problems that the B.B.C. is called upon to handle. Nearly one thousand Welsh names are given, and their pronunciation is recorded, as in the other handbooks on place names, in two ways: one in a purely phonetic alphabet, the other in a modified spelling. In the first column will be found the purely Welsh pronunciation, and in the second an attempt is made to give the non-Welsh speaker something that he can manage that will be intelligible in Wales and not too wide of the mark. The preparation of this booklet has been interesting but difficult, for the ground has not been covered before, and numerous problems have arisen.

THIS IS AN ÁTTĔLLIAY

The Introduction ought to be interesting to all who have occasion to pronounce Welsh names.

Another matter of general interest is the advent of Empire broadcasting, for this in its turn raises language questions. A concrete example, which was discussed at this meeting, will illustrate the point. The island of Labuan is one that to most of us is nothing more than a name, and has usually been pronounced as 'Láb-you-án'. But suddenly the question is raised as to what is the 'correct' pronunciation of this name. If the 'correct' pronunciation is the one that is most current in this country, then 'Láb-you-án' stands; but if people in Labuan and Malaya, hearing this pronunciation broadcast on the short-wave, say that the English version is 'incorrect', who is to decide? If the island is usually called 'Lab-óo-ăn' by those most qualified to talk about it, then 'Lab-óo-ăn' it must be for Empire broadcasting purposes.

It is no longer possible to legislate for the English language as though the English language belonged to these islands alone; internationalism is as much to be desired in pronunciation as in other departments of life, and the Advisory Committee has just taken a step that may have important consequences in after years. It has decided to get into touch with authoritative opinion on language questions in the U.S.A. and in the Dominions. Here, again, a concrete example will best illustrate the point. There is a branch of medical science known as 'psychiatry', which has to do with the treatment of diseases of the mind. Now anybody who wants to amuse himself for a few minutes might try to count up the number of ways in which this word *might* be pronounced, and then reflect upon the possibilities of chaos. It does appear desirable that there should be some attempt at unifying the pronunciation of technical words throughout the English-speaking world. Science knows no frontiers; American, Canadian, Australian, South African scientists visit this country for study and research, just as our scientists travel abroad in the pursuit of knowledge, and if there is a standard pronunciation for the technical terms of their work, nothing is lost and something is possibly gained.

THE NEW LIST

Recommendations made by the B.B.C. Advisory Committee on Spoken English at its Fifteenth Meeting, November, 1933.

Word	*Recommendation*
Atelier	Áttĕlliay
Charlatan	Shárlătăn
Chimera,-aera	Kyméeră
Conduit (*tubing and London street*)	Cóndewit
Crystalline	Crístallyne
Disputants	*Stress on 2nd syllable*
Exigency	*Stress on 1st syllable*
Indict, Indictment	Indýte, Indýtemĕnt
Intuit	Intéwit
Psychiatry	Sykýătry
Swastika	Swóstikkă
Tribunal	Trybéwnăl, *but* Tribbewne
Venue	Vénnew
Worsted (*woollen yarn*)	Wóosted
Proper Names	
Joule	Jool
Labuan	Labbóoăn

At this meeting the Committee had before it the views of American experts upon the usage current in America with respect to this word, and to a few other words concerning which there is doubt. 'Psychiatry' is to be pronounced 'sye-kýe-ătry', but what is to be done about 'Röntgen'? American usage favours 'rént-gĕn', with the hard 'g' of 'get'; will readers of THE RADIO TIMES who have occasion to use this word help by telling the Committee what their usage is?

It will be seen that the small Committee which started work very tentatively seven years ago is likely to expand into a more international body, taking counsel together on wider lines than hitherto.

Of the words left over for discussion from the previous meeting, probably the most interesting is the word 'Joule', the name given to a unit of electrical energy, taken from the name of the scientist. The conflict of

THIS IS CÓNDEWIT STREET

evidence is remarkable, and shows only too well how difficult it is to arrive at the 'truth', if indeed there is such a thing as the 'truth' in a matter of this kind. In the end the Committee decided to recommend 'jool'.

Another word that is very troublesome is 'conduit', given in most of the dictionaries as 'cúndit', a pronunciation which appears, from the Committee's investigation, to be obsolescent, and which they abandon in favour of 'cóndewit'. Purists may say that this is a spelling pronunciation, but in an age when everybody can read and write, most probably it is the spelling pronunciation that will win.

And here are two more words about which the Committee would like information: 'coiffure' and 'parquet'. As a printed word 'coiffure' is common enough, but who uses this word regularly in the course of his daily work, as a spoken word; and how is it pronounced by those who use it? Everybody knows what 'parquet-flooring' is, and most people know that the word is not of English origin; but is it pronounced 'parky', 'parkay', or 'parket'?

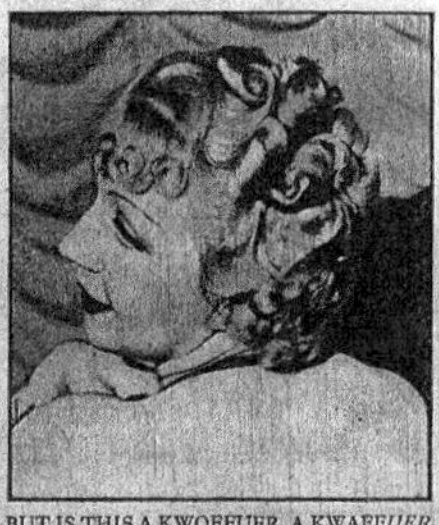

BUT IS THIS A KWOFFUER, A KWAFF*UER*, OR WHAT?

Figure 5 Facsimile of *Radio Times*, 29 December 1933, p. 940.

request for assistance in a series of talks dealing with different aspects of the spoken language' (R6 / 201 / 1; R6 / 201 / 2).

The fact that the Advisory Committee took such suggestions on board is thus also reflected in the contents of word-lists discussed during the first half of the 1930s and subsequently published.[11]

In spite of such apparent 'openness' to suggestions and 'pragmatism' in terms of decisions, the BBC still was, in many respects, a frightfully upper-class, public school, and Oxbridge organization where RP and no small degree of snobbery prevailed. In the letter pages of the *Radio Times* (12 February 1932, p. 371) a listener—the playwright and biographer St John Irvin—asked what the word *nesophile* meant which he had heard in a broadcast but could not find in any of the dictionaries. To which the 'Broadcasters who made use of the word in their account of Mr. Compton Mackenzie' replied, obviously tongue-in-cheek but nonetheless rather high-handedly:

> We apologize with horrid humility for having gone one better than the best dictionary. Our only excuse is a classical education. We derive the word, which means simply an 'island lover' from the Greek noun *nēsos* 'an island', and the verb *phileo* 'I love'. It is one which we have always used under the impression that it was supported by tradition.

In the actual reply, the Greek words were not transliterated but appeared in the Greek alphabet.

Excesses like these—patronizing though they were—should not, however, tarnish the larger picture, namely that from the late 1920s onwards the BBC had started to pay more and more attention to the public's suggestions for place name pronunciations and words to be discussed; in some cases (e.g. the original

1930 ruling on *ski*), they heeded the public's views on the pronunciation of individual words. It was also clear, however, that the Committee remained the final authority on pronunciation; to abandon that role would have meant depriving it of its *raison d'être*.

2.4 'A Public Service': Achievements

To recapitulate briefly: in its first dozen or so meetings, the BBC Advisory Committee on Spoken English achieved the following:

- it came up with general pronunciation guidelines for announcers and newsreaders;
- it drew up lists of words whose pronunciation were uncertain and made recommendations or suggestions for these;
- it compiled a card index for the pronunciation of place names;
- it decided to publish its findings and, if necessary, revise them.

The last two points—as we have already seen in the case of English place names and some words from general parlance—eventually led to the publication of a series of enormously popular pamphlets, called *Broadcast English.*[12]

Broadcast English pamphlets:

I: Recommendations to announcers regarding certain words of doubtful pronunciation (1st edn 1928; 2nd edn 1932; 3rd edn 1935; a fourth edition was planned for 1938 but never published (Minutes, 28 June 1938; R6 / 201 / 2).)[13]

II: Recommendations to announcers regarding the pronunciation of some English place names (1930)

III: Scottish place names (1932)

IV: Welsh place names (1934)
V: Northern Irish place names (1935)
VI: Foreign place names (1937)
VII: British family names and titles (1939)

An additional booklet on foreign personal names and titles, although extensively discussed and worked on over the course of 1938, never saw the light of publication; the main reason for its failure was the absence of sensible, consistent guiding principles for selecting names from around the world. Lloyd James explained that the words had been accumulated over 'a period of years from broadcast news bulletins and ordinary programmes' and had been dealt with by the Announcer on a case-by-case basis. However, the Committee should have adopted a 'definite principle' in selecting the names for publication (Minutes, 28 June 1938; R6 / 201 / 2). During the next meeting, the Chairman stated that

> the Corporation had not been able to accept the suggestion of the Committee that an expanded version of this pamphlet [Pronunciation of Foreign Personal Names] should be prepared for publication. The proof copies of the pamphlet in its original form were in the hands of the Announcers. (Minutes, 8 December 1938; R6 / 201 / 2)

Prior to that meeting, Lloyd James wrote to George Gordon, the then Chairman of the Committee, informing him of the decision, adding, as a sort of consolation, that 'the booklet, as it stands, is of considerable value to Announcers' (4 October 1938, R6 / 196 / 10). Tellingly, Lloyd James admitted in a memo to the Deputy Director General that he himself had 'never been completely satisfied with the booklet as it at present exists, owing to a combination of circumstances which were beyond my control at the time when it was compiled' (24 October 1938, R6 / 196 / 10).[14]

The pronunciations contained in the second edition of *Broadcast English I*, by the way, were recorded and published by the Linguaphone Institute.[15] The final paragraph to the preface in the first edition was omitted and replaced with the following sentence in the second: 'All the pronunciations contained in this booklet have been recorded on two ten-inch gramophone records which are published by the Linguaphone Institute' (Minutes, 26 March 1931; R6 / 201 / 1). Interestingly, as is evident in a letter by Lloyd James to George Bernard Shaw and the other members of the Committee, something similar had, at one time, been suggested for Bible readings:

> I suggested to Sir John Reith that the B.B.C. might make some gramophone records of passages from the Bible read by those people who had been found most generally acceptable and suitable to broadcast Bible readings. . . . Before they are published, however, I am anxious that members of the Spoken English Committee should have an opportunity of listening to these records and expressing their views as to the suitability for publication. (28 April 1932; R6 / 196 / 4)

I have found no further references to these Bible readings in the files of the BBC Advisory Committee on Spoken English, and we may therefore assume that this project, like the booklet on foreign personal names and titles, was abandoned and came to naught.

However, the work, time, and effort that went into the *Broadcast English* booklets—particularly those on place names—was very considerable and should not be underestimated, as we have already seen in connection with the wide-ranging consultation process for English place names. Staff members of the regional stations in particular contributed enormously, as did local academics and journalists, among others. With respect to, for example, the Northern Irish place names (*Broadcast English V*), a BBC memo from Lloyd James to Reith states that he, Lloyd James, had received from the Northern Ireland Regional Director, G. L. Marshall, 'a very remarkable piece of work on the pronunciation of about a thousand place names in Northern Ireland. There has evidently been at work a local committee, and they have carried out their task so extremely well that I feel it my duty to report the matter to you.' He concluded that 'the work is practically ready for publication as sent to me from Ireland' (27 December 1934, R6 / 196 / 6). Marshall of course 'was very pleased to hear that Lloyd James approved of the recent work on the pronunciation of place names in Northern Ireland'. In a letter to Reith, he explained that he had indeed formed 'a small Committee' which, besides himself, included Professor R. M. Henry of Queen's University, Belfast and Captain R. L. Henderson of *The Belfast News-Letter*. He continued:

> The first difficulty was to decide which place names to leave out, because Lloyd James only wanted a thousand or so, but that being settled, we soon got down to the business of pronunciation. Then, as with other Regions, we had to face the difficulty of deciding as between the local or rustic pronunciation of certain place names and the pronunciation of the educated man, at the same time always remembering that the names would be spoken before a microphone.

He went on to say that he expected that some of their decisions would be criticized, 'especially in a controversial place like this' (31 December 1934; R6 / 196 / 6). H. C. Wyld, by then a member as well as Specialist Consultant of the Advisory Committee, seemed slightly sceptical and, in a letter to Lloyd James, held forth that 'the first essential is, of course, to get the stress right', followed by other tricky questions, 'such as how far we should approximate to actual Irish pronunciation' (19 January 1935; R6 / 196 / 7). Lloyd James assured Wyld that 'we shall vet it [the manuscript prepared by the committee in Northern Ireland] before it is passed for publication' (22 January 1935; R6 / 196 / 7).[16] But Lloyd James's preface to *Broadcast English V* elaborates neither on the selection criteria nor on how far 'actual Irish pronunciation' had been approximated; it does state, however, that the transcription adopted is 'tentative' and, in the light of the adverse criticism expected by Mr Marshall, concludes: 'If it serves no other purpose than that of stimulating discussion or, indeed, than that of providing a starting-point for further research, it will be definitely useful' (1935: 3).

Other calls for cooperation and contributions included, in the case of British family names and titles, a circular issued by the Advisory Committee to all BBC staff in which Lloyd James asked for 'particulars of any names of members of the staff or their relatives, etc., the pronunciation of which might be likely to cause difficulty to Announcers'. The circular stated that it was 'essential that information should be in every case reliable, as it is not desired to add to the work of verification' (10 February 1938; R6 / 196 / 10). The latter remark was amply justified since a provisional pronunciation list for British family names, which was circulated in the summer of 1937, had to be recalled to incorporate corrections (Memo to Empire Announcers, 8 July 1937; R6 / 196 / 10). And the completion of the pamphlet was increasingly urgent as there were quite a few complaints, sometimes from the highest place; for instance, an internal memo to announcers on the subject of 'Lord HOME' states:

> Director General remarks that this name has recently been pronounced as in English, whereas the obligatory pronunciation of the Scottish title is "HEWM". The name is likely to occur in connection with the Glasgow Exhibition and it is very desirable to avoid repetition of the mistake. (9 May 1938; R6 / 196 / 10)

The pronunciation 'hju:m *(Earl of)* / hewm' is, of course, the one that also found its way into *Broadcast English VII* (1939: 52), which was the most extensive of the pamphlets, with over a hundred pages.

In those early years, the public tended to support the efforts of the BBC Advisory Committee on Spoken English, but isolated critical voices could also be heard. Here is one from 1929:

> Whenever I read of the activities of this body [the Advisory Committee on Spoken English] I am reminded of the proverb about straining at a gnat and swallowing a camel. For most of their findings are either disputable or unimportant—very often both. [Matthew Quinney in a Column in the *Radio Times*, 15 November 1929]

This foreshadows the dispute about alternative pronunciations and, ultimately, the fact that the Committee would run out of steam (see Chapter 5). Nonetheless, looking at these (often impressive) results of the Committee's work, particularly the seven *Broadcast English* pamphlets, one could be forgiven for assuming that the Committee ran smoothly during that period. Nothing could be further from the truth, however.

NOTES

1. For other, literary, examples of this generally well-meaning, albeit—from a present-day point of view—patronizing attitude in early twentieth-century Britain, see also John Carey, *The Intellectuals and the Masses* (1992).
2. 'In addition to the Central Advisory Committee, each station has its own Local Education Advisory Committee, and in this way we have been able to secure the co-operation and interest of Local Education Authorities throughout England, Scotland and Wales' (Reith 1924: 157).
3. William Le Queux (1864–1927) was a fairly well-known writer of thrillers and spy novels at the time, an 'avid self-publicist', according to the *Oxford Dictionary of National Biography* and the *Oxford Companion to English Literature*, who 'wrote his way from obscurity to celebrity' (*ODNB* 2004–13; Drabble 2000).
4. Jean Aitchison (1997: 9) quotes Norman (Lord) Tebbit, a former Tory government minister: 'If you allow standards to slip to the stage where good English is not better than bad English, where people turn up filthy . . . at school . . . all those things tend to cause people to have no standards at all, and once you lose standards then there's no imperative to stay out of crime.'
5. For a somewhat differing view, particularly with German media in mind, see Stuart-Smith 2007: 140–8, though she identifies a need for more research on the topic.
6. Thanks to Peter Trudgill and John Wells for their help on this point (private communication).
7. See Mugglestone 2003 on homophones (114–15), aspirated *h* /hw/ (186–8), vocalization of /r/ (86–9), and linking and intrusive /r/ (91–4). Linking /r/ refers to an /r/ that is pronounced in order to 'link' two words, such as *car engine,* in non-rhotic accents; and an intrusive /r/ also occurs in non-rhotic accents between vowels ending and starting consecutive words where there is no r in the orthography, for example in *Shah of Iran*, pronounced /ʃɑr ɒv ɪˈrɑːn/.
8. This symbol /ʍ/ represents the sound *wh* in those English dialects that distinguish *which* from *witch*, *whales* from *Wales*, etc. (Pullam and Ladusaw 1996: 193).
9. Note that the 'some nine hundred place names' on the 1927 card index were *not* restricted to England; so it seems that the number of 'the 554 names already on the Register' was arrived at by deducting all non-English place names from the 1927 index, i.e. from the original 900 and whatever had been added between 1927 and 1929.

10. The new two-tier system of Consultant or Specialist Members and Full Committee will be discussed in detail in Chapter 3.
11. Sometimes particular interests of individual Committee members were also reflected in the Committee's agenda. Daniel Jones, for example, was 'engaged upon transcribing phonetically the pronunciations contained in the new edition of Cassell's German–English Dictionary and…was unable to trace any recorded pronunciation of some 300 words' (Minutes, 20 November 1931; R6 / 201 / 1). Naturally he was keen to discuss 'a large number of doubtful words appearing in the forthcoming new edition'; this actually was included in the agenda for the meeting on 20 November 1931 (see letters sent to Committee members by the Assistant Secretary, 16 and 17 November 1931; R6 / 196 / 4), though in the end it was decided that 'as the majority of words were unusual or very rare the list was not suitable for discussion by the committee, but it was agreed that members should give Professor Jones what assistance they could in the case of any words with which they were familiar' (Minutes, 20 November 1931; R6 / 201 / 1).
12. The minutes from the meeting on 29 November 1928, i.e. immediately after the publication of *Broadcast English I*, record that 'the attitude of the Press was, on the whole, favourable, and that the pamphlet had aroused considerable interest throughout the country' (R6 / 201 / 1).
13. The third edition was accompanied by some external problems: a member of the Committee complained to the Assistant Secretary (16 January 1935) that he had received his copy of the latest edition of *Broadcast English I* 'a week after it was communicated to the press and announced as "now published" (see Times 10 Jan.)'. To which he received apologies on behalf of Lloyd James and the explanation that the 'delay was caused by a fire in our Publications Department, which complicated the work of distribution' (18 January 1935, R6 / 196 / 7).
14. Another idea that was never approved is Lloyd James's suggestion for a booklet dealing *exclusively* with American place names. The reason for the rejection of the project was, of course, that the booklet on foreign place names already included 'the names of such places in Canada and the United States as have caused difficulty' (BBC internal memos, 21 and 29 April 1936; R6 / 196 / 9).
15. See also the letter by Gladstone Murray, the BBC's Director of Publicity, to Lloyd James with respect to conditions of cooperation with the Linguaphone Institute, which included, among other things, 'that the words are given not as B.B.C. decisions, but as recommendations from the Committee', 'adequate financial remuneration by the Linguaphone

Institute', and 'no contract of permanent exclusivity with the Linguaphone Institute' (30 September 1929; R6 / 196 / 3).

16. Note, by the way, that 'it has been decided to omit place-names within the Irish Free State, as they may be dealt with in a separate publication at some future time' (Miss Simond to members of the Committee, 25 July 1935; a similar statement occurs in a BBC internal memo with the same date, R6 / 196 / 8).

Chapter 3
Crises and Reconstitution

On the surface, the Advisory Committee on Spoken English continued its work in a fashion broadly similar to that outlined in Chapter 2—that is, discussing lists of words of debatable pronunciation, and publishing and revising the *Broadcast English* series—until its suspension in 1939 at the beginning of the Second World War. The Committee still wanted to promulgate Received Pronunciation (RP), the non-regional, upper- and upper-middle-class accent of British English. But, even within RP, it was soon and painfully realized, some pronunciations of a word were solely a matter of preference.

Below the surface, however, there were various difficulties, conflicts, and crises; as a result of these, two important and wide-ranging sets of changes in policy and structure were implemented over the years.

First, there was a kind of opening-up process. The accession of new members to the Committee came in two waves, initially as the result of the Committee's first serious crisis in the autumn of 1929. The second, bigger wave of enlargement took place in 1934 and led to the creation of a Permanent Specialist Sub-Committee

Dictating to the Mob. First edition. Jürg R. Schwyter

whose members would make recommendations before the word-lists were put before the Full Committee.

The second set of changes was of a more linguistic nature: the International Phonetic Alphabet (IPA) started to be used by the BBC in 1934; and in 1937, the regular publication of the Committee's decisions, often reached by majority voting rather than unanimity since several alternative pronunciations were frequently found to be 'equally good', was now replaced by private instructions to BBC announcers about agreed pronunciations. These latter changes, together with the creation of a Sub-Committee for the Invention of New Words, will be discussed in more detail in Chapter 4.

3.1 The crisis of 1929

The Committee's first crisis was triggered by several factors personal and ideological as well as procedural. With respect to the personal dimension, there was increasing tension between Bridges and Lloyd James, that is, between the Committee's Chairman and its Honorary Secretary, with Reith somewhat caught in the middle. The matter was made worse by the fact that Lloyd James clearly was the driving force behind the Committee, its work and public visibility (with Reith's considerable support, it has to be admitted), whereas Bridges started to become dissatisfied with certain aspects of the Committee and thus attacked it in public, at least indirectly (Figures 6 and 7).

Ideologically, the diverging fundamental views within the Committee were increasingly difficult to reconcile. On the one hand, Bridges took a rather paternalistic, conservative, and prescriptive stance, much akin to a grammarian's prescriptive approach to written English. Lloyd James and Daniel Jones, on

384 WORDS OTHER THAN FRENCH

jealous, all absolutely repudiate any inclination to the *au* diphthong of *cow*; so here again there is nothing to overrule us in our decision.

Since common practice and phonetic propriety fail us, we may be allowed to consider the comparative agreeableness of the two sounds; that is, which of them makes the more pleasant word. Now those who have any feeling in this matter will all agree that *u* is a more pleasant sound than *au*: it is indeed the softest of all true Romance vowels and is preferable for its euphonic quality.

It was asserted in committee that scientists were almost all habituated to *coo*: on inquiry this turned out to be an exaggeration, because in Oxford and Cambridge, where Greek was still alive, both forms were in use among the scientists.

The O.E.D. puts *coo* in the first place and the American Webster and Century do the same. [B.B.C. approved.]

AERIAL. [B.B.C. noun *airial*; adjective *ay-ĕerial*.]

There are two objectors to the B.B.C. ruling, and both of them wish the two words to be pronounced alike; but one of them would have them one way, and the other, the other.

We will take the adjective first: it is a Latin word, very familiar to scholars and much used in poetry; though rarely, if ever, spoken; and from their familiarity with its place in Latin verse, I should have thought that the poets must have pronounced it with a short *ĕ—ey-ĕrrial*. I have always done so, and thus Gerard Hopkins rhymes it:

And flock-bells of the aerial
Down's forefalls beat to the burial.
Euryd. l. 8.

And this pronunciation seems necessary in Latin:

ipse locum, aeriae quo congessere palumbes.
Protenus aĕrii mellis caelestia dona.

But the O.E.D., though it recognizes this pronunciation, says the long *ē* is more common, and Webster knows only the long *ē*; and as none of our critics oppose it, we must conclude that this long *ē* [ī] is the usual pronunciation (compare *funereal*).

As for the noun, since our common pronunciation of the Latin *aer* is indistinguishable from our own *air*, we should expect that a word spelt *aerial* would, if offered to the

WORDS OTHER THAN FRENCH 385

public, be pronounced by them as we pronounce *Ariel*, and this appears to be what has happened in England since the 'wireless' inventions: there is no objection to it.

The deduction from these actual conditions seems to be that the adjective must henceforth have two forms: 1st, the old and longer 'Latin' form which has three full places in Shelley's syllabic verse, e.g.

Stand ever mantling with aĕreal dew.
Prom. III. iii. 143.

and 2nd, the new shorter form *airial* = 'wireless'. This being an adjective used for a noun is, and will be, as much one as the other. It will certainly be far more widely known than the old form and, unless it be differently spelt, will be misredd into the older poets: e.g. Shelley's line

Prone and | the' aĕ|real ice | clings o-|ver it
Prom. III. ii. 17.

will be redd

Prone and | the ai-|rial ice |

[B.B.C. approved.]

[M. BARNES.]

†ALLIES. [B.B.C. stress on 2nd syllable.] 3 objectors.

This and all the other words noted with the large dagger were selected for full treatment, but the scholar who had undertaken to deal with them was attacked by influenza and incapacitated for so long that we had to go to press without his contribution. I shall therefore only record here how the B.B.C.'s advice fared with our five critics. The words may be discussed later if the subject and our way of handling it prove acceptable to our readers.

†APPARENT. [B.B.C. *appárrent*.]
3 objectors.

†BADE. [B.B.C. *bad*.]
2 objectors—Lord Grey and Lord Balfour.

†BEDIZEN. [B.B.C. rhymes with horizon.]
2 objectors.

†COGNISANT. [B.B.C. *cógnizzant*.]
1 objector.

COMPARABLE. See *Disputable*.

Figure 6 Society for Pure English Tract, which attacked the committee indirectly and caused much controversy; Bridges also suggested alternative pronunciations to be given (Society for Pure English Tract No. 32, 1929, pp. 384–5).

410 WORDS OTHER THAN FRENCH

has been the avowed object of our Society. If it were possible to humiliate ignorant people many Englishmen would be humiliated to learn that true English tradition has often been more faithfully observed in America than in London, and that the outspoken contempt of all American speech which was fashionable in England 50 years ago was in this respect less justified than the reciprocal contempt which it provoked in America for our Southern English. In the few chance words which we have treated, there are some half a dozen examples.

This old mutual prejudice still rankles on both sides, but it has never found any echo in our Society, and we can now feel pretty sure that it is practically wiped out, though Americans who wish to be extra smart will still sometimes indulge in the old-fashioned raillery, and on our side we can occasionally hear something to match it.

What is needed in this conflict is what we have already got; that is, a good body of sane students on both sides who are practically agreed on all points and are working for the best unity of the language.

But other things are needed and first of all a hearty **co-operation of our Learned Societies** in a general movement, which it seems to us they would willingly give if they would fairly face the importance of it, and recognize the practical steps that can actually be taken to ensure results.

The first of these would be the **teaching of the vowels in the Board Schools.** I have rarely met any man outside phoneticians, teachers of elocution, and expert philologists who knew the scientific status of the vowels.

When I once said seriously that if I were to have my life again, with one common environment different, I should choose that my teachers should know the alphabet—when I said that, it had no meaning whatever to my hearers, because they all thought I was fooling, for my teachers of course knew the vowels and taught them: '*ay, ee, eye, owe, you, and sometimes double you and wai*'; but what they did not know was that the great standard vowels had been selected and isolated by human intuition and experience as distinct steps or stages in a scale of musical pitch (this being the simplest natural differentiations of tone and therefore the easiest trick for ensuring audibility), and that these whispered vowel-resonances were effected by certain definite positions of the mouth and tongue.

WORDS OTHER THAN FRENCH 411

We have had two tracts on this subject and our circulation ensures that a good many more people are now as well-informed on the nature of the vowels as Roger Bacon was, and perhaps better.

When I was at school, philology had not dawned in England: it was most graciously introduced from Germany by the popular lectures of Max Müller in Oxford some fifty years ago, and since it is now fully domesticated, we have no longer any excuse for not teaching the elements of speech scientifically.

The first step would be to instruct the true vocalization of the great vowels; and this should be practised in all our schools. There can hardly be two opinions about that. Wherever it is suggested the proposition is hailed with such enthusiasm that I suppose everybody recognizes what an overpowering effect it would have for good.

The difficulties, the great difficulties, which in the past may have justified inaction are now almost removed by the cheap multiplication of common machinery for reproducing vocal sounds, and it seems that it needs only a small committee of experts to draw up a scheme which, if it were adopted by the Board of Education, would in a few years bring the articulation and elocution of all our folk to as high a standard, and into as high respect with them as their own speech is with the French.

So long as we refuse to amend our disorderly practice we are under the shame of discourtesy to all who have to learn our tongue, and must bear the reproach that, in these matters, having of all nations the widest responsibility to the world, we are of all nations the worst offenders.

Figure 7 Society for Pure English Tract No. 32, 1929, pp. 410–11 © British Broadcasting Corporation.

the other hand, began to realize that a plurality of views regarding the pronunciation of spoken English reflected society more realistically. In fact, a secular linguistic approach to phonology based on empiricism became inevitable. Notions regarding 'correctness' and 'incorrectness' simply did not apply to spoken English and were becoming increasingly obsolete; matters of pronunciation required focus rather than fixity, as described in Section 1.2 (The problem of 'standard').

If the BBC files can be trusted with respect to their completeness, in late 1929 there also was less input into the Committee from George Bernard Shaw—and despite his interest in linguistics, also from Daniel Jones—than there had been in previous years;[1] and Forbes-Robertson and Pearsall Smith seem at times to have become almost semi-detached. So the procedural factor related first and foremost to the problem of irregular attendance by some Committee members and decisions taken by majority voting in a meeting where half of the members may have been absent.[2] A further procedural question was whether alternative pronunciations should be given and published, that is, whether the Committee should say that the first pronunciation given for a word was still the preferred one and therefore the one used by BBC announcers and newsreaders, but that one or more given alternatives were considered equally 'correct'. And finally, as the number of questions about the pronunciation of words coming from BBC announcers had decreased substantially since the publication of *Broadcast English I*, the Committee at times simply seemed to have not enough work.

A surprisingly honest and outspoken seven-page document (most probably drawn up by Lloyd James)[3] from the autumn of 1929, summarizing the purpose and work of the Committee after its first half-dozen meetings, shows that Forbes-Robertson attended only two meetings and Robert Bridges three, whereas Daniel Jones attended five and Lloyd James all six. The document then continues:

> There can be little doubt that the experiment [i.e. the Advisory Committee's work] is being watched with very considerable interest, and it would appear highly desirable that the Committee should continue its work. The standard of English speech set by the Corporation is slowly being accepted, and it is imperative that this standard should be a high one, and that the Corporation should have the best advice possible. (R6 / 196 / 3)

The report concludes by highlighting four principal issues which required urgent attention: (1) the Committee was evidently too small and poorly attended to provide a balanced view on pronunciation; (2) considering the potential impact of the Committee, words for discussion were to be actively sought rather than passively received from the BBC's announcers; (3) if the Committee's remit was to set a standard for Spoken English only for the BBC-internally, then communicating this advice to the public via the Press, especially the *Radio Times*, was not in line with the Committee's true function; and finally (4), the reputation of the Committee was exposed to risks which resulted from being overly academic and too peripheral.

With respect to the first issue, the document suggested that the 'responsibility of making decisions of this kind [i.e. on pronunciation] must not rest upon a small committee, some of whom are unable to attend'. The document suggests a possible expansion but not 'so large that it would develop into a Debating Society'. Importantly, new members were expected to have practical experience in answering questions regarding pronunciation rather than having 'idealistic views as to what should or should not be'. Hence, the document suggests the addition of the following as members: Lascelles Abercrombie, Granville Barker, Henry Cecil Kennedy Wyld, Walter Ripman, and Charles Talbut Onions—a mixture including a poet, a language scholar, and 'the great and the good' (R6 / 196 / 3).

As to the second issue, the Committee had noticed that as 'the number of words discussed increases, the number of queries from Announcers naturally diminishes'. This begged the question: should the Committee 'restrict itself to discussing words sent in by Announcers, or should it go further, and decide itself, as to what words it would discuss' (R6 / 196 / 3). In effect this would give the Committee the requisite licence to freely expand the scope of their work and regulate the pronunciation of any word.

Thirdly, intimately linked to this is the question regarding public outreach: decisions had been communicated to the Press, which was deemed to have 'worked well up to the present, and it might be as well to leave it as it stands'. The document claimed that '[n]evertheless the idea still persists that the B.B.C. is trying to "set a standard"'. With this in mind, the Committee wished their standardizing function to be publically recognized rather than remaining 'an accidental outcome' (R6 / 196 / 3). The Committee was thus expanding its function well beyond the BBC Charter to become something which could almost be seen as a precursor to a 'language academy'.

And lastly, given the composition of the original Committee and the breadth of its work, there was reasonable concern that the Committee had become 'unduly academic in its pronouncements, or insisted on maintaining a large proportion of foreign pronunciations' (R6 / 196 / 3).

The difficulties and contradictions in this document are rather striking. On the one hand 'the standard of English speech set by the Corporation is slowly being accepted', while on the other this standard 'is an accidental result of the Committee's work, rather than the Committee's function'; also, 'this standard should be a high one, and . . . the Corporation should have the best advice possible', but the Committee would lose the public's confidence if it 'became unduly academic in its pronouncements'; next, attendance figures by Committee members are poor, whereas the question is raised whether the Committee should 'decide itself, as to what words it would discuss' and therefore, presumably, increase substantially its workload. And then there is the proposal about enlargement. Would that *really* solve the problem of some members not attending, and therefore some decisions being taken by a minority of the full Committee (R6 / 196 / 3)?

Prior to that document, there was an almost frantic exchange of letters between Bridges and Reith, as well as between Reith and Lloyd James. The main issues raised in these letters were: whether the Committee should be enlarged and, if so, who the possible candidates should be; the problem of a decision-making process by simple majority; and whether the Committee should table the words to be discussed rather than solicit them from announcers. A letter from Bridges to Reith reports on a conversation between Bridges and Bernard Shaw about the work of the Committee. Bridges had made a number of recommendations, one of which had Bernard Shaw's strong support: Granville Barker and Lascelles Abercrombie should join the rather small and poorly attended Committee (1 October 1929; R6 / 196 / 3).

Harley Granville-Barker[4] (1877–1946) was a former actor, director, and producer, who had closely cooperated with G. B. Shaw and, from the late 1920s, became increasingly well known for his Prefaces to the new *Player's Shakespeare*; and Lascelles Abercrombie (1881–1938) was the famous poet and literary scholar, at the time Professor of English Language and Literature at Leeds (Drabble 2000: 427, 2; *ODNB* 2004–13). Reith replied less than a week later that he agreed 'it would be well that the Committee should be strengthened in numbers, and I think that the two men you suggest would be excellent for the purpose' (7 October 1929; R6 / 196 / 3). Lloyd James, too, supported Bridges' suggestion in principle, but pleaded in a letter to Reith for more linguistics experts, whose names eventually found their way into his Purpose and Work of the Committee document quoted above:

> I am all in favour of strengthening the Committee . . . after the last meeting I was afraid that the Committee was about to die, & this must not be. But we must have, in addition to the men you mention . . . , more language men e.g. Onions, Wyld & Ripman[5] (8 October 1929; R6 / 196 / 3)

To which he added in a later letter:

> I believe that if the Committee is expanded, and if the members attend, it can go on doing useful work without any radical change of procedure. Quite apart from actual work, it is an interesting institution—the first of its kind, I believe, in the history of the language. Its decisions are studied with interest abroad, where the study of English is increasing. (10 October 1929; R6 / 196 / 3)

In addition, another, rather unexpected problem started to cause Lloyd James increasing concern: there were too few questions on pronunciation coming from BBC announcers, and therefore a lack of work for the Committee. Lloyd James expressed his uncertainty about 'how far it [the Committee] can go, & how long it can continue to work' since 'the number of words that cause Announcers anxiety is decreasing, as our list of decisions mounts up. I have not had a query from the Announcers for months. I suggested the booklet on Place Names in order that we might have something to publish.' While the Committee's work was evidently important, the demand for judgements on pronunciation seemed to dry up. So much so, that Lloyd James asked, '[w]hat will be the position if there is no work? Is the Committee to find work for itself? Should the Committee take the initiative & determine what words it proposes to decide on? This, to me, appears of more importance than the question of procedure' (11 October 1929; R6 / 196 / 3).

To overcome this shortage of work for the Committee, a BBC internal memo was sent out a fortnight before the next meeting to all Head Office branch and section heads, and all regional and station directors and representatives, asking them to send to Miss Somerville, the Assistant Secretary, 'any words suitable for discussion' at the 17 January meeting of the Committee (2 January 1930; R6 / 196 / 4).

The search for additional members continued through the remaining months of 1929, and several other names were mentioned by various people. Among those suggested were: T. R. Hughes, KC 'a Cambridge man . . . , an excellent man of business and moreover a remarkably good speaker', who was treasurer of Lincoln's Inn (letter from F. Pellock to Bridges, 29 October 1929; R6 / 196 / 3); Sir Henry Hadow or Dr Percy Buck, representing the musical profession; and Roger Fry, representing the arts (letter from Bridges to Reith, 29 November 1929; R6 / 196 / 3).[6] Reith soon thereafter wrote to Bridges asking him whether he would agree to Granville-Barker and Dr Onions becoming full members, whereas the representatives of the various professions—Law, Music, Art, Science, and General Literature—would merely be 'corresponding members for reference in connection with any words within their specific domain', adding that 'Mr. Lloyd James is afraid that with the Committee enlarged by so many, it would be very difficult to get the work put through and decisions duly made' (9 December 1929; R6 / 196 / 3).

Bridges agreed to all of Reith's suggestions, as a committee enlarged by illustrious members was likely to meet the expectations of the public. The question of the national identities of Committee members continued to rear its head. According to Bridges, a committee comprising two Welshmen, one Irishman, and one American had always been subject to criticism, and the possible addition of C. T. Onions would tip the balance even more towards Wales. Bridges' view on procedure was different from Lloyd James's, who was afraid of having an unworkably large committee; Bridges thought that regular and full attendance at meetings was the bigger obstacle (11 December 1929; R6 / 196 / 3).

In the end, however, Onions and Abercrombie were invited; whether Granville-Barker was dropped or whether he had refused to join informally, that is before official invitations were sent out, is not clear from the BBC files. Abercrombie accepted his invitation to become a member 'with great pleasure' (letter to Reith, 1 January 1930; R6 / 196 / 4), as did C. T. Onions, who added that he had not attained professorial status (letter to Lloyd James, 7 January 1930; R6 / 196 / 4). Both confirmed that they would attend the Committee's next meeting on 17 January.

The eighth meeting of the Committee (17 January 1930) took up several of the crucial points discussed earlier, namely enlargement, the publication of decisions as provisional in the *Radio Times*, and the possibility of recommending more than one pronunciation. The minutes record that, of the two new members, only Onions was present: 'The Chairman [i.e. Shaw, in the absence of Bridges] welcomed Dr. Onions. Professor Abercrombie was unable to attend.' The minutes continue under the heading Procedure that it was unanimously agreed

> that Sir T. R. Hughes, Sir Henry Hadow, Mr. Roger Fry and Mr. J. B. S. Haldane, representing Law, Music, Art and Science respectively, be invited by the Committee to act as Honorary Advisers in order that reference might be made to them with respect to pronunciation of words coming particularly within that form of interest which they represented.

At this meeting, it was reiterated that 'the basis of decision should, in general, be the type of educated English that can be broadcast without arousing any considerable degree of criticism'; and, as we saw in Chapter 2, that 'decisions should be regarded as provisional and be published as such in "The Radio Times", being given as much publicity as possible', then 'reviewed at the following meeting, when they would be either confirmed as final, or altered in the light of criticism received'. Most importantly, however, the publication of alternative pronunciations was turned down, since 'no useful purpose would be served' (R6 / 201 / 1). All these decisions were eventually to have serious consequences, cause unease, and even trigger disputes amongst some members of the Committee—except one: the idea of inviting 'certain eminent scholars and artists' to become Honorary Advisors to the Committee came to nothing. As an enclosure to the minutes of 20 September 1934 points out, 'This suggestion was adopted, but never put into practice' (R6 / 201 / 2).

After the meeting, Lloyd James wrote to Onions informing him that 'our decisions will appear as provisional in "The Radio Times" within the course of the next week or two, and I hope the

Press will not come down too severely on us' (23 January 1930; R6 / 196 / 4). Maybe not so much the Press, but certainly Onions had strong opinions on a number of prior decisions. Owing to his perceived superior knowledge he wanted to re-open the debate on words such as *ski*, *acoustic*, and *imminent*, since the Committee's recommendation, he said, had brought ridicule from some academic quarters[7] (letter to Lloyd James, 15 February 1930; R6 / 196 / 4).

Lloyd James replied that he would be 'very glad if you would raise the question of revising earlier decisions at the next meeting of the Committee', as *Broadcast English I* would be reissued later on 'and we might make this an opportunity for revising some of our more doubtful recommendations'. As to the specific words mentioned by Onions, he added:

> I think you will find that the Committee will agree with you on 'acoustic' and more especially 'emanant' [i.e. pronunciation for *immanent*]. G.B.S. and the Poet Laureate, however, are adamant about the latter because it avoids homophony with 'imminent'. (R6 / 196 / 4)

When the proposals for the second edition of *Broadcast English I* were discussed in Committee, however, *immanent* was changed: 'IMMANENT: The committee substituted ÍMMANENT for their previous recommendation' (20 November 1930; R6 / 201 / 1). And the pronunciation of *ski*, as we saw in Chapter 2, was changed to /ʃiː/ in 1934.

In fact, the revision process for *Broadcast English I* started as part of the preparations for a meeting on 10 July 1930. Lloyd James wrote to all Committee members, explaining that the new edition of the booklet 'must be expanded to include words that have been discussed since its publication', and he asked for any suggestions to be brought forward at the meeting. A discussion of the final proofs of *Broadcast English II*, the pamphlet on English place names, was also scheduled for that meeting, so that it could be published after approval by the Committee (R6 / 196 / 4). However, a list of words suggested by Pearsall Smith—among them *citation*, *deprecatory*, *molecule*, and *simultaneous* (25 June 1930; R6 / 196 / 4)—was not tabled; Lloyd James explained: 'as you will see the Agenda is a very heavy one, and with your permission I think we had better defer discussion of your list till the next meeting' (R6 / 196 / 4).

The meeting on 10 July was indeed a heavy one—and a sad one: Robert Bridges had died on 21 April 1930, and George Bernard Shaw was elected Chairman. Although the proposals for the second edition of *Broadcast English I* were postponed, detailed discussion of some 1,500 place names did take place, and publication of the volume was authorized (R6 / 201 / 1). With respect to *Broadcast English I*, the Committee decided in its next meeting, on 20 November 1930, that it was time for a second edition of the booklet, which would include more than 200 new recommendations since the publication of the first edition in 1928, as well as more than a dozen emendations (R6 / 201 / 1).[8] As early as 13 March 1931, the proofs for the second edition of *Broadcast English I* were sent out to Committee members; this, together with the usual word-list, formed the main business of the Committee meeting on 26 March 1931, at which only two members were present, Lloyd James and C. T. Onions—which surely proves that adding two members had not really solved the problem of poor attendance.[9] Another seven emendations were made,[10] and a paragraph was added to Reith's Foreword outlining changes in the Committee's personnel; Lloyd James added to his Preface the information that, as we saw in Chapter 2, the pronunciations contained in the booklet had been recorded by the Linguaphone Institute (R6 / 196 / 4).

The search for 'doubtful words' for future meetings—and therefore work for the Committee—continued throughout the years 1930 and 1931. Lloyd James urged Daniel Jones to send him 'a select few of the five hundred doubtful words you have collected, so that I can include them in the agenda for next meeting' (23 October 1930; R6 / 196 / 4), to which Daniel Jones replied two days later:

> I had your note from the BBC, & send you a list of doubtful words and proper names. I think special investigations should be made of the following:
> **(1)** Proper names occurring in modern novels, etc.,
> **(2)** stars and constellations,
> **(3)** names of organ stops (bombardon, salicional, etc.),
> **(4)** Ordinary personal names.
> What say you? (R6 / 196 / 4)

Pearsall Smith also wrote to Mary Somerville suggesting a dozen words for consideration, among them *Pariah*, *endemic*, *liqueur*, *covert*, *epistle*, and *apostle* (6 December 1930; R6 / 196 / 4). To ensure that they continued to have work, the Committee members decided that 'at some time in the future a pamphlet should be published by the B.B.C. containing all the foreign names, foreign place names and English Christian and surnames which had already been discussed, together with such additions as the Secretary might think fit. It was recommended that the work of collecting such names should begin forthwith.' They agreed, however, that 'no general policy could be indicated in connection with the pronunciation of the names of stars and constellations and of organ stops'—one suspects this would have been too outlandish even for the Advisory Committee on Spoken English (20 November 1930; R6 / 201 / 1).

In October 1931, the process was repeated and, once again, Lloyd James wrote to the Committee members asking them for words and suggestions for the meeting on 20 November 1931. So while on the surface—and judging by the *Radio Times* articles—everything seemed to be going relatively smoothly, in fact, work had to be found and created in terms of revising *Broadcast English I* for a second edition and collecting foreign, personal, and place names, and so on; this puts the achievements discussed in Chapter 2 in a rather different light. After the autumn of 1929, the Committee was no longer primarily performing a service on demand for the public or the announcers; it was primarily concerned with keeping itself in existence.

And, even though the difficulties of 1929, which threatened the Committee's survival, seemed to have been surmounted by the enlargement and the members' pro-active stance about finding new topics to publish on, another crisis was already brewing which eventually led to Onions's resignation under rather acrimonious circumstances.

3.2 *L'affaire* Onions

Right from the start, the nomination of C. T. Onions to the Committee was ill fated. Onions was hesitant from the beginning and was never really committed to the work. And as early as 5 December 1931, he sent his first letter of resignation to Reith after having received the minutes of the Committee meeting. Onions had not even bothered to apologize for not attending the meeting. Reith wrote in blue pencil on Onions's note, forwarding it to Lloyd James: 'What is the matter? Is it work? . . . Seems a pity & it's the first time this has happened on a Cte.' (R6 / 196 / 4). This was the ominous beginning of a long, sometimes ill-tempered exchange of letters between Onions, Lloyd James, and Reith.

Five days after Onions's letter to Reith, Lloyd James replied. He proposed a meeting in Oxford to discuss the matter and urged Onions not to finalize his decision before they had seen each other, as 'the public announcement of your retirement would be used by certain sections of the Press to attack the Committee, its work, and possibly the B.B.C.' He added: 'This, of course, is only a personal appeal, but I am so interested in the work of the Committee that I would do anything to avoid the resignation of a member who carries such authority as you do in matters of language' (10 December 1931; R6 / 196 / 4). When Lloyd James had not heard from Onions for three weeks, he decided, on 1 January 1932, to send a second letter—this time not to Magdalen College, where he supposed the first letter had gone astray, but to the Old Ashmolean Museum on Broad Street. On 3 January, Onions finally had the courtesy to reply—and a stinging, at times patronizing and almost sarcastic, reply it was, questioning more or less everything about the Committee. He outlined his reasons for resigning, which were threefold. First, he had misgivings about the supposed remit of the Committee to advise the BBC on matters of doubtful pronunciation. In his opinion, the BBC appeared to have given itself a quasi-academy status in regulating spoken English. Secondly, considering its quasi-academy status, Onions found the Committee's processes not to be truly scientific owing to a lack of comprehensive and balanced assessments. Thirdly, in spite of the pleasantries of interacting socially with members of the Committee, he attacked its amateurish composition by making reference to his own academic background. He concluded emphatically that he wished to resign, albeit quietly (R6 / 196 / 4). Lloyd James was down with the flu at the time and thus only replied—coldly—a week later. He said that at the next meeting he would raise the question of procedure that Onions had criticized, but continued: 'inasmuch as Shaw is on his way round the world, I don't think we can do very much. Above all things, if you cannot come to the meeting, I should like you to send me your recommended pronunciations' (9 January 1932; R6 / 196 / 4).

There followed another long silence by Onions. Only on 28 February did he once more write to Lloyd James. In his letter he stated that he had thought about Lloyd James's appeal and sympathized with him and his role. However, Onions reiterated that the Committee's composition was fatally flawed from the very start. In his opinion, poor decision-making led to disastrous reversals later, which proved the uselessness of the Committee. He added a snide comment on the appointment of Abercrombie to whom he ironically attributed expert knowledge while others who knew even more were not present at various Committee meetings. Majority voting, however slim, might give rise to highly circumspect decisions. Finally, Onions offered to explain to Reith directly the reasons for his resignation and he also mentioned the lack of suitable remuneration for his professional services (R6 / 196 / 4).

Reith, upon learning this from Lloyd James, was flabbergasted. In a letter to Lloyd James about the Onions affair, he first remarked that the reasons Onions had given for his resignation 'do not seem to me to stand criticism' because the Preface to *Broadcast English I* and the minutes of the first meetings, which had been sent to Onions upon his appointment, outlined the general principles underpinning the Committee's work. Reith's understanding of how the Committee functions was in stark contrast to Onions's perception. Unlike Onions, Reith fully recognizes the tension of an expert being the arbiter in a field where, regarding the pronunciations of certain words, notions of 'correctness' and 'incorrectness' are futile. Yet, Reith comments on Onions's self-perception; despite 'the futility of making decisions that have to be reversed', he alludes to '"those who know", meaning, presumably, experts like himself'. He was bewildered, since Onions 'must realise the extent to which the experts disagree among themselves' and Reith asks the rhetorical question: '[w]hat need would there be for this Committee if we had a really authoritative pronouncing dictionary?' Reith continues describing his bafflement with Onions:

> I understood originally from Mr. Bridges that the whole trouble about English pronunciation was that there were no experts,—there were only 'users'; in fact that you could not possibly determine what was right or wrong according to any accepted system. A committee of experts would be quite as likely therefore to give birth to 'monstrosities' as any other body. That was, and is, the justification for a mixed committee including both experts and well-educated 'users'.
>
> It looks to me very much as if Onions had never faced up to the implications of that sentence of yours in the introduction to 'Broadcast English I', where you speak of the diversity of opinion among works of reference and the diversity of practice among educated speakers. (15 March 1932; R6 / 196 / 4)

Reith, of course, does not impose strict procedural rules but instead suggests that procedure is 'a matter open to constructive criticism for any member of the Committee. There is no reason why it should not be altered.' He asks Lloyd James to draft a letter to Onions 'stressing these various points, and inviting him to a conference on the future of the Committee'. Reith also expresses the wish 'to meet him myself and hear him defend his position in person' (15 March 1932; R6 / 196 / 4).

As becomes clear from a letter by the Assistant Secretary to Daniel Jones (6 June 1932), a meeting over lunch had in fact been set for 15 June to talk to Onions about his criticism of the Committee. Besides Onions and Jones, Reith and Lloyd James should have been present. But close to the meeting, Onions informed Lloyd James on 12 June 1932 that he was unavailable that day due to work and that he, in any way, could not foresee a change of his opinion regarding the Advisory Committee (R6 / 196 / 4).

It is difficult to reconstruct in detail what was discussed between Lloyd James, Daniel Jones, John Reith, and Mary Somerville over the summer of 1932; what is clear, however, is that for the first time the idea of a two-tier system of Specialists and a Full Committee must have been seriously contemplated. On the one hand, it is undoubtedly the case that these considerations were directly linked to Onions's scathing attacks on the 'amateur opinion' of some Committee members; on the other, it would be wrong to give him any credit for the 1934 reconstitution of the Committee (see Section 3.3). This reconstitution was to lead to yet more acrimonious exchanges between Onions and the BBC; but even among the other Committee members there was not, in 1932, a unanimous welcome for the procedural changes proposed by Lloyd James.

On 26 September 1932, Lloyd James wrote to Bernard Shaw (and a day later, sent a similar letter to Pearsall Smith, Jones, Abercrombie, Onions, and Forbes-Robertson), explaining that 'the work of the B.B.C. Advisory Committee on Spoken English is likely to diminish as time goes on, and it may be desirable to reconsider the method of procedure'. He envisaged as little as one Committee meeting per year and suggested that 'in future ad hoc recommendations be made by the Secretary, after correspondence with what might be called a technical sub-committee consisting of Professors Abercrombie, Jones and Dr. Onions. Their recommendations would remain provisional until the annual meeting of the full committee' (R6 / 196 / 4).

Daniel Jones found Lloyd James's proposal 'excellent' (27 September 1932); Forbes-Robertson also agreed with his recommendations (29 September 1932). Pearsall Smith (28 September 1932) also wrote to say that he approved; he then added, obviously looking for new areas of activity and thus continuing legitimacy of the Committee's existence: 'I have sometimes thought that the Committee might possibly increase its usefulness by making suggestions for the naming of new inventions, new processes & new ideas as they arise.' This is an interesting point, which, as we will see in Chapter 4 (Section 4.2), eventually led to the creation of the Sub-Committee for the Invention of New Words. Abercrombie also completely agreed and was 'willing and proud' to be on the proposed technical Sub-Committee. He suggested, however, that Lloyd James, Daniel Jones, and he should 'occasionally meet over a cup of tea, which might in some cases expedite matters..., having of course Onions's views before us, provided no doubt by letter, as he does not...come to London'. He concluded with the question: 'Do I gather from your letter that Onions has consented to remain on the Committee?'

Shaw, however, totally disagreed with the suggestion for a technical sub-committee and raised serious questions in his reply to Lloyd James (30 September 1932). He was concerned with 'provisional decisions' and observed that '[o]nce a pronunciation is let loose on the ether we cannot change it without making ourselves ridiculous, especially if we solemnly announce the change in print'. In his opinion the 'full committee is as necessary as it ever was. If it isn't, it should be abolished altogether.' Shaw emphasized the value of face-to-face meetings to discuss words, because when 'there are big lists of words to be considered the most expeditious and sensible way of dealing with them is in full meeting viva voce. No member could be expected to write his comments on a hundred words and send them by post.' Conversely, Shaw argued that 'at the other end of the scale no member can reasonably be asked to give up a whole afternoon to deal with half a dozen words which he could dispose of by postcard. Then why not hold a meeting when there are enough words to make it worth while, and take a postal vote when the business is small enough?' Shaw considered the Committee meetings as highly beneficial 'with its Irish, American and Scotch elements to balance the university dialects; and there would be no possibility of the full committee changing the directions by a sub-committee and already in operation' (R6 / 196 / 4).

Besides organizational and procedural apprehensions, Shaw expressed his doubts as to the value of the Committee's work. He continued:

> I am not very keen on keeping up the business at all, because the committee wobbles and will not take an authoritative position; so that it ends too often in our giving our hall mark to ugly and slovenly English simply because it is common, and paying no attention to all the beauty of sound and rhythmical value. We are admirable in our endeavours to find out how people with more than £300 a year actually do pronounce; but as to seizing our tremendous opportunity of familiarizing their ears with something better, we funk it objectively every time. We shall presently find ourselves instructing the announcers to pronounce 'later' as 'lay her' and 'modern' as 'mon'. I shall someday have to resign to save my own credit as a talk merchant.
>
> In short, I am for either dissolving the committee and leaving you and Jones to make the best decisions you can after consulting whom you please, or to go on as we are and take postal votes when the business is small

enough. I am against the sub-committee proposal. That's my opinion for what it is worth. (R6 / 196 / 4)

Shaw's letter of 30 September 1932 is the last document from that year in the Advisory Committee files; the first document relating to 1933 is a letter by the Assistant Secretary to Onions, dated 26 September 1933, in which she invites him to the Committee meeting on 30 November, whose main business was to be the proofs of the Welsh place names pamphlet (*Broadcast English IV*), as well as 'a certain number of words of doubtful pronunciation'. Similar letters were sent out to the other members of the Committee. What was new was the enclosure of a postcard on which the recipient could indicate whether or not he would be able to attend. Not surprisingly, the copy of the letter of invitation to Onions is marked by hand with the words 'no reply'. Instead, Onions wrote to Lloyd James—on 14 December 1933, a fortnight after the Committee meeting. He explained having been fully occupied by his dictionary work at Oxford. But, he continued, he had been informed of Shaw's misgivings about a Specialist Sub-Committee and that he, Onions, was not able to suggest any viable alternative (R6 / 196 / 4).

The 'Onions affair' simmered for almost another two years. Lloyd James informed him of the Committee's far-reaching changes in personnel as well as procedures—including a two-tier system of linguists as advisers and an enlarged Full Committee—that were pushed through in the first half of 1934 (see Section 3.3). Onions applauded the formation of the Specialist Sub-Committee and the reconstitution of the Advisory Committee conceding that—in his opinion—there were a few members who actually were sufficiently knowledgeable. Nonetheless, Onions's decision to resign was final, not least due to hurt feelings. Reminding Lloyd James that he had delivered some recommendations to the Committee, he could not get over the fact that Reith had failed to respond to him (Onions to Lloyd James, 15 June 1934; R6 / 196 / 5).

Lloyd James forwarded Onions's letter to Mary Somerville. 'I have accepted his resignation', he wrote on an accompanying note, 'and told him that the reason J. R. [John Reith] did not reply to his letter was that the matter was left to me' (24 June 1934; R6 / 196 / 5). And to Reith he wrote, 'Onions has resigned: I have handled the matter privately as tactfully as I could. It might perhaps be as well if you were to send him a line saying how sorry you were that his work prevents him from continuing with us' (1 July 1934; R6 / 196 / 6).

Reith remarked that some two years earlier, instead of replying to a letter from Onions, he had asked Lloyd James and Miss Somerville to talk to Onions on his behalf. Even so, Reith sent a letter of regret (2 July 1934; R6 / 196 / 6). This letter to Onions—cold in tone and factual in content—reads as follows:

I was sorry to hear from Professor Lloyd James that you have now definitely decided against membership of our Advisory Committee on Spoken English. When you wrote me some time ago with respect to resignation, Professor Lloyd James suggested that he should see you and discuss the matter fully with you on our behalf, rather than that I should endeavour to deal with it by correspondence. It was for this reason only that I did not reply to your letter, and I hope you did not feel it to be discourteous on my part.

With respect to the reconstitution of the Committee, the preliminary discussion which led up to the re-arrangement was handled by Professor Lloyd James and one or two of his colleagues on the Committee, the Corporation then approving the scheme as presented by them, and it was understood that, in view of your difficulty in attending meetings, it might be advisable to appoint another scholar to represent the philologist's point of view. [i.e. H. C. Wyld]

Professor Lloyd James now tells us that there is no possibility of your reconsidering your resignation, so we must perforce accept it; but it is a matter of great regret to us. (10 July 1934; R6 / 196 / 6)

On 8 October 1934, Onions officially resigned from the Committee for good due to 'pressure of other work', as the press was informed. But his true reasons, as we saw, were far more serious: Onions criticized not only the composition of the Committee, but perhaps even its whole existence; he was particularly annoyed at the lack of academic rigour of so many members, which was reflected in slapdash decision-making and successive revisions; this made it impossible for the decisions made by the Committee to acquire the necessary weight and prestige in accordance with a quasi-academy status. In short, Onions was unhappy with the broad consensus and public feedback that the BBC had been seeking since the late 1920s. In addition, he wanted a fee for his services—which he did not get (exchange of letters between Onions and Reith, 8 October and 9 October 1934; R6 / 196 / 6).

Onions was bitter until the very end, simply could not let the matter rest, and always found new grounds for going on the offensive. In his letter to Reith on 8 October 1934, for example, he not only complained that, in his opinion, the press had been misinformed about his reasons to resign, which the BBC had attributed to his workload. But Onions also felt that the new two-tier system as well as remunerating Specialist Sub-Committee members had been his idea, the benefits of which would not be accrued to him. He thus felt unjustly treated (R6 / 196 / 6).

On 26 November 1934, after seven weeks, Reith finally replied to Onions (the letter is marked Private), two days after Lloyd

James had felt that 'the time has come to take off one glove, so to speak' (R6 / 196 / 6). Reith first apologized for the delay in his reply, as he had been in South Africa, and then both gloves really came off as he rejected Onions's criticisms point by point, plainly and clearly. Reith's response addresses a number of topics related to the governance of the Advisory Committee. In Reith's opinion, Onions's resignation 'owning to pressure of work' gave an accurate and face-saving reason. Reith took offence at the fact that Onions 'disapproved of the Constitution of the Committee and perhaps also, in principle, of its existence', since in Onions's opinion 'decisions were acquiring a degree of prestige to which they were not entitled'. Reith continues:

> It was also known that you objected to the importance attaching to what I believe you referred to as the 'amateur opinion' of so many members. And although the Corporation does not feel that only the views of the academic professional linguist should be taken into account, it could quite see your point of view. It was understood also that you were unwilling to co-operate in this work without fee.

Interpreting Reith's words, the BBC's governance model was characterized by the BBC's view that its committees comprised 'eminent public men, who were not only prepared, but quite glad to give the benefit of their opinion [and] was better left unpaid'. He said that the BBC was not 'unwilling to spend the money', but that the BBC's experience has been that 'those whose advice we seek are glad to give it in view of the public importance'. Reith pointed out that the BBC derived absolutely no commercial benefit from its committees.

As a consequence of the reconstitution of the Advisory Committee, the BBC had decided to set up a Permanent Specialist

Sub-Committee whose members were being paid due to the high workload and its professional nature (see Section 3.4):

In this case the decision held until it was decided to re-constitute the Committee and an exception was made, because it was felt that the work devolving upon the consultant members had so increased; was different from that done by any of our other advisers or consultants; and that it was only right that they should be offered a fee.

While Reith gave Onions some credit for his role in the reconstitution—'You certainly had made a suggestion for reconstruction, but the changes that were brought about originated, I am told, elsewhere'—he immediately ruled out Onions's participation because

when the scheme was finally drawn up for submission to our Governors, it was felt that since you had expressed disapproval of the Committee, and had not attended its meetings or given the Corporation the benefit of your expert advice—that advice in fact which in your view was lacking—the only course open was to invite the co-operation of another specialist.

Reith was unable to resist taking a final swipe at Onions and his personal animosities towards (fellow Oxford academic and equally difficult) H. C. Wyld,

It was not thought that a retaining fee would in any way have removed your objection to the Committee, or induce you to take an active part in the work; and further, I understand that the specialist whom it was in mind to invite [H. C. Wyld], was one with whom you had expressed some reluctance to co-operate.

I am very sorry if you feel that you have been in any way unfairly or improperly treated—as sorry as I was that you did not feel able to participate in this interesting and important work from the start. (R6 / 196 / 6)

This finally *was* the end of *l'affaire* Onions—at least as far as it can be reconstructed on the basis of written documents. Some good did come from this: it was the trigger for a second, bigger wave of enlargement and, with it, the establishment of a two-tier system of Specialist Consultants and a Full Committee.

3.3 Reconstitution

As a result of the difficulties and discussions in 1932 and 1933, the Advisory Committee drafted a letter of invitation, dated January 1934, to be sent out to potential Specialist Members. It briefly recapitulates the history of the Committee, lists its membership, and defines its responsibility as 'making recommendations to the Corporation as to the pronunciation of debatable words, and of such words and names, both English and foreign, as are not to be found in the dictionaries'. It then continues:

During the past seven years, which have been in a way experimental, much valuable experience has been gained. But it is felt that the time has now come when in view of the increasingly specialised nature of the words to be discussed, and especially in view of the introduction of Empire Broadcasting,[11] the membership of the Committee should be increased so as to include a larger body of authoritative opinion. (R6 / 196 / 5)

This draft letter makes reference to Kenneth Clark, Director of the National Gallery; H. J. C. Grierson, Professor of Rhetoric and English Literature at Edinburgh University; F. L. Lucas, critic, poet, and fellow of King's College, Cambridge; P. H. B. Lyon,

Headmaster of Rugby; I. A. Richards, a fellow of Magdalene College, Cambridge, and co-founder of Basic English; Virginia Woolf; and H. C. K. Wyld, Merton Professor of English Language and Literature at Oxford. The minutes of the Committee's fifteenth meeting on 30 November 1933 had already recorded the decision that the 'personnel of the Committee should be strengthened by the addition of new members' and gave geographical and generational diversity as the reason:

> It was agreed that one or more [new members] should be drawn from the younger generation, so that the modern trend in pronunciation might be represented on the Committee, and that at least one of the new members should represent Northern England or Scotland. (R6 / 201 / 1)

Whether or not this represents a precursor of a departure from RP is questionable, but it suggests an emerging need for diversity of opinion, including geographically. However, as is evident from a letter by Lloyd James to Pearsall Smith, the continuation of the Committee was still in the balance in January 1934. 'Sir John Reith is considering the whole question of the future of the Committee', he writes, 'and I think he would like to have in his own mind a clear idea of the whole situation, before he invites the members that we have suggested. Our last decisions have not been very well received' (15 January 1934; R6 / 196 / 5).[12] Approximately three months later, as a memo by Mary Somerville makes clear, this led him to establish an Expert Committee in addition to the reconstituted and substantially enlarged Main Committee. The procedure envisaged would be that the BBC would submit its lists of words to the expanded Main Committee, accompanied by a report from the smaller Expert Committee. She not only mentioned the new scheme in the memo, but, in the light of the critical reform-or-die situation, insisted that the two committees should be set up at once in order to arrange a meeting early in June for the Expert Committee to edit *Broadcast English I* (the 3rd edition); the reconstituted Main Committee could then be convened at the end of July to approve this 3rd edition for publication (R6 / 196 / 5). However, the first meeting of the reconstituted Main Committee was postponed until 20 September 1934; 'it should be possible to get Broadcast English I into page proof', she wrote in a BBC memo, but 'we shall not be able to adhere to the original scheme of publication on October 1st' (R6 / 196 / 6).[13]

Later in the spring of 1934, Reith gave his consent to the new proposals, but it also became evident that, with a new Experts Committee ('a sub-committee in the ordinary sense of the term') in addition to an enlarged Main Committee, even more members had to be recruited. A letter by Mary Somerville to Pearsall Smith dated 7 May 1934 suggests the following names, in addition to the potential members already mentioned, and asks Pearsall Smith whether he would be prepared to approach them informally: Mr Kenneth Sisam, Lord David Cecil, Mr Maurice Baring, Lady Leconfield, Miss Rose Macaulay, Mr Edward Marsh, someone from *The Times* staff, Professor George Gordon, and Lady Cynthia Asquith 'in place of, or as well as, Lady Leconfield'. She added: 'It seems to me quite clear that we must offer some kind of fee to the "Professors"' (R6 / 196 / 5). The reason for this initially informal approach was to 'avoid refusals to a formal invitation'.

Pearsall Smith replied to Mary Somerville that 'perhaps it would be better to substitute Lady Cynthia Asquith for Lady Leconfield—I leave that to you. I don't know much about Lady Leconfield, except that she is interested in linguistic matters, & has sometimes written to me about them. I don't know Lady

Cynthia, so someone else had better find out if she will be willing to join' (9 May 1934; R6 / 196 / 5).

Pearsall Smith also mentioned that he would see Bruce Richmond, the editor of the *Times Literary Supplement*, and would ask his advice about who from *The Times* would be suitable. 'Perhaps he himself would be the best person' (9 May 1934; R6 / 196 / 5). On 15 May 1934, Pearsall Smith confirmed to Miss Somerville that he had spoken to Bruce Richmond and Eddie Marsh, both of whom would be glad to join the Committee. He told her that he would have to write to the others but insisted, no doubt in the light of the Onions affair, 'before doing that I want to be able to tell them exactly what will be expected of them; & I want to be sure that the plan is really going through, & that, if they are willing to join, they will receive official invitations' (R6 / 196 / 5).

Three days later, discussions about and selection of new members, as well as the exact composition of the new Specialist Sub-Committee, seemed to have advanced sufficiently for Mary Somerville to have sent a memo to John Reith with draft letters of invitation to join the Main Committee to Lady Cynthia Asquith, Mr Maurice Baring, Lord David Cecil, Mr Kenneth Clark, Professor George Gordon, Professor H. J. C. Grierson, Mr F. L. Lucas, Mr P. H. B. Lyon, Miss Rose Macaulay, Mr Edward Marsh, Mr I. A. Richards, Mr Bruce Richmond, Mr Kenneth Sisam, and Miss Virginia Woolf. The third paragraph of the draft letter then states:

> It is suggested that the procedure of the Committee shall be slightly modified. In future the B.B.C., in submitting to the Committee lists of words for discussion, will accompany each list with a report from a group of specialist consultants, consisting of Professor Wyld, Professor Jones, Mr.

H. Orton, and Professor Lloyd James. This report will contain such evidence as is available regarding modern practice, such evidence of traditional usage as will be of assistance, and finally, any special considerations arising from the peculiar requirements of broadcasting.

Attached to the memo are draft letters to Wyld and Orton, formally inviting them to join the Main Committee as well as becoming Consultant Members, along with Reith's instruction to have these letters typed (R6 / 196 / 5). On the same day, Pearsall Smith could confirm that 'Mr. Edward Marsh & Kenneth Clark have agreed to join the Committee', but 'Virginia Woolf has decided not to do so, & Mr. Bruce Richmond writes me that the authorities of the Times will not allow members of their staff to join any Committee of this kind'. He adds further that 'Miss Rose Macaulay will join &, I think, Maurice Baring, though he hasn't quite made up his mind. I should send him an invitation, if I were you.' But in a few instances the answer was negative or uncertain: 'Kenneth Sisam approves of the Committee, but is too busy to join. Kenneth Clark told me that he could join—he is abroad at present, & so is Lord David Cecil, so I haven't heard from him' (letter from Pearsall Smith to M. Somerville, 28 May 1934; R6 / 196 / 5).

Pearsall Smith jubilantly wrote again in early June (from the yacht *Ivernia*, RYS, Havre, France): 'I have just received a note from Maurice Baring saying that he will be glad to join the B.B.C. Committee, so an invitation should be sent to him. I am on a cruise down the French coast' (to M. Somerville, 2 June 1934; R6 / 196 / 5).

A second memo of 18 May 1934 from Mary Somerville to Reith contains a draft letter to Bernard Shaw, the Chairman, 'giving the substance of what must be said to Mr. Shaw as soon as possible'. It speaks of the decision that 'a very definite reconstitution is desirable if the work is to proceed smoothly and to obtain a greater measure of support from the public than in the past' and outlines the changes in procedure and personnel:

> (1) We have arranged that in future the lists of words which are submitted to the main body will be accompanied by a report from four experts—Professor H. C. K. Wyld, Professor Daniel Jones, Mr. H. Orton (of Newcastle), and Professor Lloyd James. These experts, when it is possible, will report jointly on the words, but will have the right to represent their individual views if they disagree amongst themselves.
>
> Each expert will be paid a consultant's fee by the B.B.C., but will also serve on a voluntary basis as a member of the main Committee.
>
> (2) The main Committee itself will be very considerably expanded in personnel. . . . (R6 / 196 / 5)

On 24 May, the official letters of invitation from Reith went out to the prospective Specialist Members Wyld and Orton—after, of course, they had informally agreed to join;[14] a day later Reith wrote to Daniel Jones thanking him for his willingness to serve, in addition to being on the Main Committee, also as a Consultant Member, 'and at the same time would ask you to accept a fee of fifty guineas per annum in respect of this work'.[15] In a similar letter, also dated 24 May 1934, Reith offered one hundred guineas to Lloyd James, adding: 'This remuneration would not, of course, cover any specially commissioned report or article which it might be in our interest to ask you to prepare from time to time, and for which we would offer you a separate fee' (R6 / 196 / 5).[16]

The wheels were put in motion immediately. A meeting of the Consultant Members was scheduled for 22 June—the main business of which would be preparation of the third edition of

Broadcast English I, including 'a further list containing all the more recent recommendations'—to be followed by a meeting of the reconstituted Main Committee (letter from the Assistant Secretary to Consultant Members, 29 May 1934; R6 / 196 / 5). Wyld was very enthusiastic: 'I have already been through No 1 [*Broadcast English*], and have made a preliminary list of words the pronunciation of which should, I think, be discussed afresh.... Dr. Onions would be valuable if you can get him back.' He went on to express his great appreciation of the allowance, emphasizing that 'it would be especially convenient if you could send me a cheque early next week [his emphasis]' (30 May 1934; R6 / 196 / 5). Mary Somerville replied to Wyld that 'the Chief Accountant is away at the moment and I am not sure whether the cheques will be paid before his return or not'. She then took up his suggestion with respect to Onions: 'I think myself that it would be better not to re-open the Onions question as yet' (31 May 1934; R6 / 196 / 5).

A few days later, Wyld sent the BBC a list of words for the small committee to discuss at its next meeting. It consisted of the following (those already in the first edition of *Broadcast English I* are in italics):

Acoustic, *Aerated*, *Amateur*, *Apparent*, *Commandant*, *Contumely*, *Courtesy*, Desiccate, *Dilemma*, Dirigible, *Discern*, *Disputable*, *Divan*, *Eleemosynary*, *Ensemble*, *Ephemeral*, *Equerry*, Expiration, Fanfare, *Fantasia*, *Fecund*, Fracas, *Geyser*, Ghoul, *Hallucination*, *Homogeneous*, *Humour*, *Ideal*, *Importune*, *Issue*, Livelong, *Lucubration*, *Metallurgy*, *Miniature*, *Ordeal*, Paraffin, *Premature*, Profile, Projectile, *Rotatory*, Ski, Sough, Tenable, *Trait*, *Unprecedented*, *Untoward*, *Vehement*, *Wesleyan*. (2 June 1934; R6 / 196 / 5)

On 7 June 1934, finally, the formal letters of invitation to join the Main Committee went out to the other proposed members. On the same day, similar letters were sent to the British Academy, the Royal Society of Literature, and the English Association, inviting them to nominate a representative to serve on the Committee (R6 / 196 / 5).[17] In addition, Shaw was keen to have S. K. Ratcliffe join the Committee, a man who he said

> is well known at Broadcasting House. He is very sensitive to shades of pronunciation, and as he does a lot of lecturing in America and comes up against all the differences between spoken English and spoken American, he will be very useful. We badly want some public speakers on the Committee to balance our academic gentlemen. Will you put him on the list of invitees? (19 June 1934; R6 / 196 / 5)

This was done, and John Reith formally invited him on 26 June 1934 (R6 / 196 / 5).

As could be expected, since all the potential new members had been approached informally beforehand and their willingness to serve secured, the formal letters of acceptance came flooding in over the next few days; some of them expressed enthusiasm, while others warned that they might not be able to attend meetings as regularly as might be desired.[18] As for the various associations and societies contacted, the English Association nominated the Revd H. Costley-White, Headmaster of Westminster School, to serve on the committee, the British Academy Dr W. W. Greg, and the Royal Society of Literature W. W. B. Maxwell. The Secretary of the Royal Society of Literature, J. L. Rudston Brown, wrote to Reith about the Society accepting the invitation to George Gordon (16 June 1934; R6 / 196 / 5).

On 14 June 1934, Lloyd James wrote to the new members, thanking them for accepting and enclosing the minutes of the previous meeting and copies of *Broadcast English II*, *III*, and *IV*.

> 'Recommendations to Announcers Regarding Certain Words of Doubtful Pronunciation' [i.e. *Broadcast English I*] is now out of print... but a third edition is in preparation. I am sending you a rough proof of the Introduction to this booklet... It is proposed to hold a meeting of the reconstituted Committee about the middle of July to discuss the proofs of Broadcast English I, which in its new form will contain recommendations for some 800 words. (R6 / 196 / 5)

Superficially, the newly structured and re-established Full Committee and Permanent Specialist Sub-Committee now seemed re-energized and fit for purpose from the viewpoint of form and content. At the core, however, the fundamental issue of prescription versus description remained.

3.4 New committee—problems new and old

By the summer of 1934, the newly reconstituted and enlarged Main Committee together with the Specialist Consultants Sub-Committee were in place and ready to start work (Figure 8), though the Full Committee did not actually meet until September of that year (for a summary of biographical data on the members of the two committees, see Appendix I).

At the same time, this reconstitution was the beginning of a set of problems that were to cause periodic friction throughout the remaining five years of the Advisory Committee's work.

The first issue was money. As was already clear with Onions, fees had the potential of becoming a source of conflict. In the case of Wyld, the problem was that he was desperately short of money and therefore constantly needed advances. On 14 June 1934, Wyld wrote to Mary Somerville, asking her again whether she 'could arrange for me to have my cheque... at the end of this

ENCLOSURE B.

THE BRITISH BROADCASTING CORPORATION

REPORT OF CONSULTANT MEMBERS OF ADVISORY COMMITTEE ON SPOKEN ENGLISH UPON (i) BROADCAST ENGLISH I (SECOND EDITION) AND (ii) LIST OF WORDS TO BE CONSIDERED ON SEPTEMBER 20th, 1934.

The consultant members met at Broadcasting House on June 22nd, 1934, and at Merton College, Oxford, on July 6th. They considered, in the first instance, the Second Edition of Broadcast English I, and reviewed, in addition, the decisions taken since the publication of that edition. They make the following recommendations:-

1. That the pronunciation of the following words, as previously recommended, should be submitted to the committee for reconsideration:-

APPARENT	CHIROPODY	CONDUIT	COURTEOUS	COURTESY
PROFILE	RESTAURANT	TRAIT	WESLEYAN	

2. That the following words should be referred to the Committee for reconsideration after more evidence had been collected as to their pronunciation in modern usage:-

ACOUSTIC	AMATEUR	DECOROUS	DISPUTABLE	DISPUTANT
EQUERRY	FUSELAGE	GARAGE	HUMOUR	ROUTE (MARCH)
PROPHECY				

3. That the pronunciations originally recommended for the following words should be withdrawn and replaced by the variants indicated:-

AERATED	ÁIRAYTĔD	to replace	ÁY-ERAYTĔD
ALLIES	ÁLLIES	" "	ĂLLÍES
BUFFET	BÓOFFAY	" "	(b) As in French
CAISSON	CÁYSSŎN	" "	CĂSSÓON
CONTUMELY	CÓNTEWMLY	" "	CŎNTÉWMLY
CORONACH	CÓRRŎNĂCH	" "	CÓRRONACH; ('a' as in 'man')
CURVET (n.)	CURVÉT	" "	CÚRVĔT
EQUIPAGE	ÉCKWIPĂGE	" "	ÉCKWIPAYGE
HOMOGENEOUS	HOMMOJÉENIŬS	" "	HOMMOJÉNNIŬS
MINIATURE	MÍNNICHER	" "	MÍNNIĂTŬRE

(BBC ACSE, Minutes, Enclosure B; 20 September 1934; R6 / 201 / 2)

Figure 8 Facsimile of Consultant Members' 'pre-treatment' of words from *Broadcast English I* before they reached the Main Committee for discussion (BBC Advisory Committee on Spoken English Minutes, enclosure B: 20 September 1934; R6/201/2).

week' (R6 / 196 / 5). The BBC files record that on 15 June 1934 a letter and cheque from the Programme Services Executive were sent to: Daniel Jones: 50 Guineas; H. Orton: 50 Guineas; H. C. K. Wyld: 100 Guineas; and Lloyd James: 100 Guineas (R6 / 196 / 5). The Expert Members could now claim expenses on top of their regular fee; for example, after the first Experts' Meeting at Merton College, Orton sent an expenses sheet to Mary Somerville for his stay at an Oxford hotel (13 July 1934), and Wyld wasn't quite sure 'whether it is allowed to claim for wine' (14 July 1934).[19] In the same vein, on 23 March 1935—five days before a Full Committee meeting—Wyld wanted to ascertain 'whether the Chief Accountant would allow me to charge the cost of a car hire from Oxford to Alvescot', which was granted (R6 / 196 / 7). The introduction of paid expenses goes back to an exchange of letters between Reith and Shaw, in which the latter suggested that

> in the case of members domiciled at universities outside London, we ought to pay railway fares. A first class return ticket and afternoon tea, in addition to our most distinguished consideration, might prevent them from following the example of Onions and asking why the B.B.C., wallowing in millions (as they all believe), should not pay them a thousand a year apiece for teaching us how to speak with an Oxford accent. (22 June 1934; R6 / 196 / 5)

Wyld's requests for advances continued over the next years. A BBC internal memo dated 17 April 1935 states that 'we ought to meet the request of Professor Wyld... for an advance payment of £50. He is evidently in need of the money before Easter, otherwise he would be willing to wait for the full fee of 100 guineas which he knows to be due within a few weeks' (R6 / 196 / 7). On 18 March 1936, Wyld again wrote to the Chief Accountant asking for a £50 advance on his fee (due on 1 June) as a member of the Expert Committee. The Chief Accountant agreed to this in a letter sent on 25 March but then, ironically, forgot to actually enclose the cheque with his reply—Wyld of course duly complained, and this was put right a day later (R6 / 196 / 9). The Chief Accountant was polite enough, however, not to mention to Wyld a single word of the following BBC internal correspondence: 'As discussed. I recommend the advance payment this year as he got it last but you may think it advisable to warn him now that we cannot continue the practice' (20 March 1936). But on 2 January 1937, Wyld wrote to the Chief Accountant yet again—note that Wyld's requests for advances were made earlier every year—asking for the usual £50 advance, to which the Chief Accountant replied:

> As requested I enclose a cheque for £50, being an advance for your fee as adviser to the Committee of Spoken English for the year ending 31st May, 1938.
>
> I am afraid that our auditors are liable to object to this system of making payments in advance of the year to which they refer as there can be no proper authorisation of the fee under the terms of the arrangement with you until the year has actually begun. I should be glad, therefore, if in future the original arrangement of payment of fees at the beginning of the Committee's year, 1st June, could be adhered to. (12 January 1937; R6 / 196 / 10)

The suspension of the committee after the outbreak of war in 1939 was to prove very difficult financially for Wyld, and he lobbied for continuation of his advisory role to the BBC; but this was not to be granted (see Chapter 5).

Interestingly, Daniel Jones's Consultant Member fee eventually went up to 100 guineas as well; according to a confidential BBC memo on 27 June 1937, Lloyd James 'regards Jones' services as at least as valuable as those of Wyld' and said that Jones 'is constantly being called upon for advice owning not only to his knowledge but to his accessibility'. Lloyd James remarked that 'Orton, on the other hand, is not accessible and is much younger and needs not, therefore, be considered for the higher fee on these grounds' (R6 / 196 / 10).

The second problem was that, with an enlarged Main Committee and a Sub-Committee of Specialist Consultants, the difficulty of getting all the members together for all the meetings simply increased—and this was true both for the Specialists[20] and, especially, for the members of the Main Committee. This became apparent right from the start of the new system, so that even the *first* full meeting had to be postponed by two months, finally being held on 20 September 1934.[21] Records show that the following new members were absent at this first meeting: Cynthia Asquith, Maurice Baring, and F. L. Lucas; of the old members, Forbes-Robertson and Pearsall Smith had sent in apologies (R6 / 201 / 2). And as early as 8 October 1934, Maurice Baring wrote to Lloyd James asking him to take his name off the Committee members' list as he would very seldom be able to attend meetings (R6 / 196 / 6).

Even more than a year after reconstitution, letters like the following, with reference to a Full Committee meeting on 28 November 1935, abound: the Private Secretary of Magdalen College, Oxford, wrote to Miss Simond, the Committee's new Assistant, informing her that 'the President of Magdalen is at present abroad and will not return to England until 10th January of next year' (26 October 1935; R6 / 196 / 8); and the Accountant of the Zoological Society notified Miss Simond on Huxley's behalf that he 'is abroad on leave and will not be returning until about the 18th November. Your letter, however, will be laid before him immediately upon his return' (28 October 1935; R6 / 196 / 8).

A third issue was that the Full Committee meetings were simply too long. After the first meeting of the reconstituted committee, Ratcliffe complained to Lloyd James that 'the September meeting lasted almost two and three-quarter hours. Towards the end of so long a sitting unsatisfactory discussions become unavoidable, for always in such circumstances the later discussion over difficult words is hurried up.' He therefore suggested

> that the list coming before the general Committee should be in two parts, Part I consisting of words that have received the unanimous vote of the Sub-Committee. This list would be the longer of the two, and it might be submitted for acceptance by the Committee, with the minimum discussion, or none. The general Committee would then have a manageable list of disputed pronunciations to deal with at each meeting. (29 November 1934; R6 / 196 / 6)

As the minutes of the next meeting make clear, Ratcliffe's suggestion was accepted as a way of curtailing discussion and speeding up decisions; for that meeting, Consultant Members had submitted their report, divided into two sections: '(a) Words upon which they were unanimously agreed. (b) Words upon which there had been a difference of opinion.' The minutes go on: 'The Committee agreed that the recommendations in Section (a) should be accepted with the minimum of discussion, and that the words in Section (b) should receive more detailed consideration' (28 March 1935; R6 / 201 / 2).

The fourth problem was that, with the increase in the number of people involved in the committees, there were more and more suggestions for words to be discussed. As we shall see, the problem now was no longer lack of work, as in 1929, but an ever-increasing number of 'old words' whose recommended pronunciations were questioned again and again, and of new words sent in by various Committee members which they thought merited consideration. For example, after a Consultants' meeting on 9 January 1935, and thus during the preparations for the Full Committee meeting, Lloyd James wrote to Wyld, Jones, and Orton explaining that, 'In view of the fact that there are already over seventy words for consideration . . . I think the additional words we suggested had better form the nucleus of the list for the next meeting' (29 January 1935; R6 / 196 / 7). Similarly, a letter by Miss Simond to Orton before the Consultants' meeting of 23 July 1936 stated: 'We have a very big agenda so would you hold over your list of additional words until the next meeting? There are about seventy words to discuss besides the proofs of the Foreign Place Name Pamphlet' (R6 / 196 / 9). The question of revisions and, therefore, alternative pronunciations will be looked at in more detail in Chapter 4.

A final matter, though one which was relatively easy to resolve, was Bernard Shaw's chairmanship of the Main Committee. In a letter to Mary Somerville, he emphasized that, since the reconstituted Main Committee 'will practically be a new Committee, it must elect its own chairman'. Although he was willing to stand for re-election, he wanted to 'have a mandate from the new people' and therefore suggested that

> if we get the new members I shall resign the chair so that the first business of the new Committee will be to elect a chairman, who may be Wyld or me or anyone else who can secure a fairly unanimous vote. If we have any standing orders, or if we adopt any, we should make a rule that the chair should go to election after twelve meetings. Please break this to Ll.J. and to Sir John, as soon as you think they can bear it. (9 June 1934; R6 / 196 / 5)

Reith replied to Shaw ten days later 'to assure you that the enlarged Spoken English Committee are certainly expecting you to continue as Chairman'. He went on to say that members 'have one and all accepted our invitation to serve and in that invitation they were asked to join the existing Committee, not to serve as members of a brand new body'. Reith himself was to pave the way for Shaw's continued chairmanship: 'I think it would be a great pity if you were to resign except on the understanding that you would present yourself for re-election. Would it suit you if I were to open the next meeting myself, welcoming the new members on behalf of the Corporation, stating the terms of reference and so on, and finally explaining your position and inviting them to re-elect you or to elect another as they chose?' Also, Lloyd James prepared a memorandum outlining the Committee's previous findings and the new working procedures, which he was to share with Shaw prior to circulation among the members of the enlarged Committee (19 June 1934; R6 / 196 / 5).

Shaw replied to Reith on 22 June 1934, confirming that he was happy for the first meeting of the reconstituted Committee to be arranged as suggested by Reith, as it would be 'essential that the newcomers should be received and the new phase inaugurated' by Reith himself. Shaw continued:

> My main difficulty as chairman—the one which will make me eventually impossible in this capacity—is that I am beginning to forget people's names quite ridiculously. At Emerson's funeral, Longfellow, who was overwhelmed with grief, said to the man next to him: 'Sir: will you be so good as to remind me of the name of that dear friend of ours whose loss we are now lamenting'. It will come to that with me presently.
>
> When the Irish Academy of Letters was founded I managed to get a rule registered that the average age of the Committee of Management should

not be allowed to exceed—I think it was 65; but at any rate it was a means of shoving off the octogenerians who persist in 'lagging superfluous'. Lloyd James might keep this admirable precedent at the back of his mind when he drafts the standing orders. (R6 / 196 / 5)

The minutes of the first meeting of the reconstituted Advisory Committee on Spoken English, held on 20 September 1934, not only list the old and new members of the Committee, but they open with a statement by Colonel Alan Dawnay, the Controller (Programmes)—'speaking on behalf of the Director-General, who was out of the country'—welcoming the new members, outlining the reasons for the changes undertaken, and explaining the working mechanisms of the new two-tier system. One of his remarks is particularly interesting: that the Consultant Members would prepare a report for the Full Committee, 'having in mind the relevant considerations concerning past and *present* usage, making recommendations as to pronunciations to be adopted for the purposes of broadcasting' (R6 / 201 / 2; my emphasis). This is a clear departure from the initially strict emphasis on 'traditional usage' and the aim of creating something like a spoken standard (see Section 2.2). The BBC now formally recognized that then present-day pronunciations were equally worthy of consideration, leading to recommendations based on current usage. Dawnay concluded his statement with the following:

Mr. Bernard Shaw had felt it his duty, upon the reconstruction of the committee, to offer to resign from the Chair . . . Mr. Shaw said that he was prepared to continue in office provided that the committee would agree to the inclusion in the standing orders of a provision that the chair should go to election after four meetings, the retiring Chairman being eligible for re-election only once. (R6 / 201 /2)

The minutes state that 'after modification', the standing orders were accepted, that is, Shaw was duly re-elected as Chairman. (The standing orders are reprinted in Appendix II.)

3.5 Later changes to the Main Committee

The reconstituted Main Committee was now ready to begin its work. Although the constitution and procedures of the Advisory Committee on Spoken English remained largely unchanged until its next crisis in early 1937,[22] some new members were invited to join and some old ones dropped out. On 27 September 1934, shortly after the first meeting, the Royal Academy of Dramatic Art was invited to nominate a representative to the Committee; they put forward Kenneth R. Barnes (R 6 / 196 / 6).

The minutes of the second meeting of the reconstituted Committee not only record the accession to the committee of Dr Costley-White (representing the English Association), Dr Greg (representing the British Academy), and Mr Maxwell (representing the Royal Society of Literature), as well as the 'recommendation of the Consultant Members that in view of the increasing number of scientific terms submitted for discussion, a scientist should be elected to serve on the Committee', but also the first resignation, that of Maurice Baring (28 March 1935; R6 / 201 / 2). In a letter to Reith, Lloyd James explained that '[t]he experts suggested the inclusion of a scientist on the general committee to advise upon scientific vocabulary: I have to submit to you the names of Sir Richard Gregory (the editor of Nature), Sir Richard Paget, and [Professor] Julian Huxley for the Corporation to choose one. I think Huxley would be the best.' He then continued:

> Lastly, a private suggestion of my own. Mr Alistair Cooke, your new Film Critic is a very brilliant man who did English at Cambridge, got a

> Commonwealth Fellowship and did work on Dramatic Criticism for three years at Harvard and Yale. He is an excellent phonetician, and very familiar with modern educated American usage. His talk last week on speech was so good that I immediately got in touch with him on these matters. He might very well come on to the Committee in place of Maurice Baring, who has resigned. (31 March 1935; R6 / 196 / 7)

A day later Reith replied, accepting Lloyd James's suggestions, adding that invitations would be sent out to Huxley as well as Cooke; their official invitations went out on 11 April 1935. Huxley accepted a day later and Cooke wrote to Reith on 20 May 1935, apologizing for the delay and explaining that his first reply must have gone astray. He then explained:

> I should feel more nervous of accepting your invitation on more general grounds but I believe that I might be of some real help on American usage . . . American friends often remark with sad amusement—to give one example—on the lack of uniformity the B.B.C. announcers have shown in the pronunciation of American place-names. If I might be of any help in this field—(I am in touch always—directly—with Professor Hanley, of Wisconsin, the editors of American Speech, and Mr. H. L. Mencken; indirectly with Dr. Hans Kurath, the leading American phonetician)—I shall be only too eager and delighted to accept your invitation. (R6 / 196 / 7)

Lloyd James did indeed have great plans for utilizing Alistair Cooke's talents. He sent an internal memo to Reith, quoting a suggestion by Cooke himself for the *Broadcast English* series to include a pamphlet on the pronunciation of American place names; he envisaged that the booklet would deal with about 4,000 names, and Cooke himself would be the man to undertake the research for a fee of between £300 and £400. Alas, nothing would ever come of it, as the reply to James's memorandum makes abundantly clear: 'While we all of us feel that the suggestion is interesting, we do not think that the matter is of sufficient immediate importance to justify commissioning Mr. Alistair Cooke and paying him a fee of three to four hundred pounds' (21 April 1936, 29 April 1936; R6 / 196 / 9).

Cooke's eventual move to America meant that he could no longer attend meetings. Lloyd James thus wrote to Cooke suggesting that he 'remain a member of the Committee, even though domiciled in America, acting as it were as a sort of "corresponding" member, to whom I could refer such problems as may fall within your sphere of specialised knowledge' (17 October 1938; R6 / 196 / 10). Cooke replied that Lloyd James's suggestion was exactly what he had in mind. He added that 'there were several things that struck me during the summer which showed there would be no harm in having an American reference'. One of them was that 'place names should be specified more accurately. The habit is that of naming the State immediately after practically all town or city names'—something which 'comes as second nature to the natives' (25 October 1938; R6 / 196 / 10).

There were other small changes to the Committee in terms of its members as well as their functions. In the fourth meeting of the reconstituted Committee on 29 January 1937, Shaw 'reminded the Committee that in accordance with the Standing Orders, the Chair must go to election after four meetings' and added that he would not stand for re-election. The Committee elected George Gordon as its new Chairman (R6 / 201 / 2). However, the election of Gordon was not a straightforward affair at all. According to the minutes, at the meeting Shaw put forth the suggestion 'to invite the Poet Laureate, Mr. John Masefield, to join the Committee as Chairman'. After some discussion, 'it was decided that it was desirable for the new Chairman to be familiar with the working of the Committee, and that an already existing member should therefore be elected. In the view of the Corporation it was undesirable that the Chair should be occupied by a Consultant Member.' It was only then that 'Professor Wyld moved: that Professor George Gordon be invited to take the Chair. Professor Gordon accepted the invitation' (R6 / 201 / 2). But the minutes offer only a very small portion of the story. Discussing potential candidates in January 1937 before the meeting, Shaw wrote to Reith that 'Wyld is such a stupendous swell academically on our subject that if he will accept we have really no choice in the matter', adding that 'if he unexpectedly refuses or dies of influenza, the only way to avoid invidiousness between the other professors will be to nominate Rose Macaulay!' In his reply, Reith made it clear that, in the BBC's view, the appointment of Wyld, one of the paid Consultant Members, would be difficult anyway, as 'in our view, a paid consultant should not occupy the chair of the larger Committee'; instead, he suggested Logan Pearsall Smith. Shaw was furious: 'Damn it all, Logan's an American!' he exclaimed, adding that the papers would be scathing with headlines of 'another BBC Scandal'; he was no less severe on Wyld: 'I did not know that Wyld was paid for his perfectly useless consultant job.' A BBC memo records that 'the objections to Logan Pearsall Smith are on the score of his nationality—though he graduated at Balliol in 1893 and has apparently had a purely English connection since then—and that he is deaf and would be a bad Chairman. On the other hand, in previous discussions with Shaw and the original members of the Committee, he was always regarded as the natural successor to Shaw, being the senior member of the old Committee' (24, 26, 27, and 28 January 1937; R6 / 196 / 10). This definitely seems to have been the case BBC-internally; at least, a memo from Wellington to Graves dated 7 January 1936 shows that Logan Pearsall Smith was under consideration to succeed Shaw as Chairman even then. However, with Pearsall Smith rejected on the basis of his nationality—and perhaps also, at least in part, because of his rather misguided overenthusiasm for the disastrous Sub-Committee for the Invention of New Words (see Section 4.2)—the only other member of the old Committee not on the payroll as a Consultant was Lascelles Abercrombie. Whether Abercrombie rejected an offer of becoming Chairman or was objected to by the BBC, Lloyd James, or Shaw cannot be reconstructed from the Advisory Committee files. One can imagine, however, the many phone calls on the evening of 28 January and the morning of 29 January 1937. In the end, the BBC stuck with its decision not to have a paid Consultant in the chair, but it abandoned its wish for the Chairman to be a member of the original 1926 Committee. Professor George Gordon, then, was the compromise candidate—and he was a language specialist.

Prior to that fourth meeting and the debates raging around George Gordon, the third meeting on 28 November 1935 saw the official welcome of Julian Huxley and Alistair Cooke and the resignation of Johnston Forbes-Robertson (R6 / 201 / 2).[23] Forbes-Robertson had been ill for some time. His daughter Diane wrote to Lloyd James in the summer of the same year, saying that, because of his poor health, her father regrettably would not be able to attend and actively contribute to meetings, and therefore had to step down from the Committee (30 July 1935; R6 / 196 / 8). According to Miss Simond's records, however, Forbes-Robertson 'has never attended any of the meetings beyond the first, as far as I can make out', adding the question: 'Will D.-G. wish to write to

Sir Johnston F.-R.?' (1 August 1935; R6 / 196 / 8). In the end, Lloyd James wrote to him, expressing his and the Committee's great regret, adding, 'Sir John Reith particularly asked me to say how sorry he is that you are unable to continue as a member of the Committee' (2 August 1935; R6 / 196 / 8).

The minutes of the sixth meeting of the reconstituted Committee, which was held on 28 June 1938, not only record Sir John Reith's departure from the Corporation, to which the Committee expressed their 'unanimous regret', but also the retirement of Miss Simond and Miss Henderson, the two Assistant Secretaries, along with the Committee's thanks 'for their loyal cooperation'. At the next meeting, the new Chairman, George Gordon, announced the deaths of two members, Mr Maxwell and Dr Abercrombie. The minutes record that 'The Royal Society of Literature had written to express the wish that Sir Edward Marsh should succeed Mr. Maxwell as their representative member on the Committee' (8 December 1938; R6 / 201 / 2). Marsh had, of course, been asked to give his consent prior to this. A letter from the Secretary of the Royal Society of Literature confirmed the role of Sir Edward Marsh as their representative and hoped this to be acceptable to the BBC (28 October 1938; R6 / 196 / 10).

Although Marsh had replaced Maxwell, the committee continued to experience problems with the membership. Abercrombie's replacement, N. B. Jopson, Professor of Comparative Philology at Cambridge, had been agreed upon, but he never took up his post (9 November 1938; R6 / 196 / 10). There were also two near resignations, by Hugh Lyon and Frank Laurence Lucas. However, they were persuaded by Lloyd James to remain on the Committee (19, 24, and 26 October 1938; R6 / 196 / 10).

Thus, by the winter of 1938, which also witnessed the Committee's last official meeting, the composition of the reconstituted

Advisory Committee on Spoken English, i.e. the Main Committee, was as follows (for a summary of biographical data on these members, see Appendix I):

> Professor George Gordon (Chairman)
> The Lady Cynthia Asquith
> The Lord David Cecil
> Sir Kenneth Clark
> Alistair Cooke
> Professor Julian S. Huxley
> Professor Daniel Jones
> Professor A. Lloyd James (Hon. Secretary)
> F. L. Lucas
> P. H. B. Lyon
> Miss Rose Macaulay
> Sir Edward Marsh (Representing Royal Society of Literature)
> Harold Orton
> Emeritus Professor Sir H. J. C. Grierson
> George Bernard Shaw
> Logan Pearsall Smith
> S. Ratcliffe
> Dr. I. A. Richards
> Professor H. C. K. Wyld
> Dr. W. W. Greg (Representing British Academy)
> The Rev. Canon H. Costley-White (Representing English Association)
> Sir Kenneth R. Barnes (Representing Royal Academy of Dramatic Art)
> (Memo, 31 October 1938; R6 / 196 / 19)

It was also part of the Committee's opening-up process to initiate cooperation with 'authorities on pronunciation' in America. The Advisory Committee minutes for 30 November 1933 report an exchange of letters between Lloyd James and Professor Krapp of Columbia University in New York. Professor Krapp approved of Lloyd James's suggestion 'that an American Advisory Committee on Pronunciation might be formed to act in conjunction with the B.B.C. Committee, so that one Committee might co-operate with the other in ascertaining general usage in debatable cases'. The BBC were keen to have a Canadian representative on the American Committee, so that 'Canadian usage might also be consulted'. At the same meeting, it was further suggested that 'in view of the introduction of Empire Broadcasting steps should be taken to obtain the co-operation of authorities on pronunciation in Australia, New Zealand, South Africa, and Canada (if not already represented on the American Committee)'. The thinking behind this suggestion was that

> an Advisory Committee on Pronunciation might be formed in each of the above-mentioned dominions, in order that the English Committee might ascertain the views of authoritative English-speaking persons throughout the Empire before making recommendations in the case of debatable words. (R6 / 201 / 1)

A statement by Lloyd James at the first meeting of the reconstituted Committee confirms that 'in 1933 tentative steps were taken to set up co-operation with the U.S.A. and correspondence with two American Scholars has taken place'. But as far as the Dominions were concerned, 'no action has been taken' (20 September 1934; R6 / 201 / 2).

It is therefore impossible to say whether a list of two dozen American place names with recommended pronunciations which was found in the Advisory Committee files from April 1935 is the result of these 'tentative steps' towards cooperation, or of queries by announcers, complaints by listeners, or Alistair Cooke's first input. The list included the following US states (with 'chief stress on syllable underlined; secondary stress accented; syllable in brackets hardly sounded'):

ALABAMA	Al-a-bah-ma
ARKANSAS	Ark'n-saw
CONNECTICUT	Cun-net-ti-cut
DETROIT	D'-troit (rhymes with quoit)
MASSACHUSETTS	Máss(a)-choo-sets
MICHIGAN	Mishy-gun (last syllable hardly stressed)
(R6 / 196 / 7)	

Whatever their origin, two years later most of these pronunciations had found their way into *Broadcast English VI.*

Although, judging from the BBC files, cooperation with language specialists from other English-speaking countries did not materialize, the creation of the two-tier system in 1934, consisting of a substantially enlarged Main Committee and a new Sub-Committee of Specialist Consultants, had far-reaching effects on the decision-making process, as we just saw. It also resulted in some important linguistic changes: the introduction of the International Phonetic Alphabet, the formation of the Sub-Committee for the Invention of New Words, and the consultation of experts in other languages and foreign embassies.

NOTES

1. It should be added, however, that Shaw—although abroad for some considerable time later in 1934—always made an effort to attend meetings. In a letter to Miss Somerville, for example, he explained that he was busy

with the production of two plays ('I must work hard at the rehearsals'), but at the same time said that he could attend the meeting in question if necessary: 'if it must be it must' (29 June 1934; R6 / 196 / 5).

2. At the Committee meeting held on 25 July 1929, for example, only two members, G. Bernard Shaw and A. Lloyd James, were present (Minutes; R6 / 201 / 1).
3. See Lloyd James's letter to Reith, dated 24 October 1929, which refers to an enclosure that is 'imperfect & possibly lacking in detail'. In the BBC file, the seven-page summary of the Committee's work precedes this letter by Lloyd James and is interrupted only by a brief letter from Reith to Lloyd James about rescheduling a meeting (16 October 1929) and a postcard by George Bernard Shaw to Lloyd James (23 October 1929). Reith replied to Lloyd James one day later and calls 'what you have sent along... an excellent basis for discussion' (R6 / 196 / 3).
4. He started to hyphenate his name after the Great War (Drabble 2000: 427).
5. Charles Talbut Onions (1873–1965) was the Oxford grammarian, lexicographer, and co-editor of the *Oxford English Dictionary*, and Henry Cecil Kennedy Wyld (1870–1945) was the then Merton Professor of English at Oxford, well known for his use of the terms 'Public School English' and 'Received Standard' in his publications on modern colloquial English (McArthur 1992: 726–7, 1135; Drabble 2000: 743; *ODNB* 2004–13). Walter Ripman (1869–1947) was a member of the Simplified Spelling Society and author of the 1912 pamphlet in which he put forward proposals for a spelling reform (*The Spectator*, 12 March 1988: 19; *ODNB* 2004–13).
6. Sir Henry Hadow (1859–1937) was a well-known musician and educationist, and Dr Percy Buck was an organist. Roger Fry (1866–1934) was a painter and art critic (Drabble 2000: 386; *ODNB* 2004–13).
7. *Broadcast English I* (1st edn, 1928: 21, 27) has 'ACOUSTIC: acóostic' and 'IMMANENT: immáynent, to avoid confusion with *imminent*'. Regarding the protracted discussions of *ski*, see Section 2.3.
8. The pronunciation of the following words was changed or clarified: *apothegm, basalt, cinema, decadence, fertile, fragile, garage, hors de combat, hors d'oeuvre, idyll, immanent, iodine, kursaal, luxury, machination, memoir.*
9. Three weeks earlier Lloyd James wrote to Bernard Shaw, who would be abroad during the March meeting, asking him for comments or modifications on the proofs. Shaw's secretary replied: 'Do not bother to send the proofs to Mr. Shaw. He is going abroad on the 3rd March, and could not

possibly find the time to comment on them before leaving London.' Shaw was not the only Committee member unable to attend the 26 March meeting; Abercrombie was scheduled to be in Paris that day—but at least he had offered some comments on the proofs (R6 / 196 / 4).

10. *Apothegm, bulletin, dirigible, project (noun), resolution, sacrosanct,* and *sarcophagi.*
11. Reith had been looking into the various possibilities of Empire Broadcasting by the BBC long before the first regular transmissions started on 19 December 1932. For details, see Section 6.2, and Briggs (1995b: 342–80).
12. When Lloyd James contacted Wyld to arrange for a preliminary meeting in Oxford, he was equally explicit about the necessity 'either to reorganize on a different basis or to abandon the whole project' as 'we, that is, the Corporation, are not satisfied with recent developments' (7 May 1934; R6 / 196 / 5).
13. When Mary Somerville wrote to Shaw, informing him that the first meeting of the reconstituted Committee had to be postponed to 20 September, Shaw wrote with red ink in the bottom right corner: 'Reserved accordingly. I'm 78 today. Pity me' (26 July 1934; R6 / 196 / 6). She of course sent similar letters to all the other members of the reconstituted Committee.
14. Orton wrote to Reith, on 24 May 1934, expressing a very keen interest in the problems the Advisory Committee assessed and wholeheartedly accepting the invitation to serve on it. Wyld also accepted (22 May 1934; R6 / 196 / 5).
15. Daniel Jones replied that he was 'very willing to act as a consultant' and 'appreciate[s] very much your kind proposal as to remuneration' (28 May 1934; R6 / 196 / 5).
16. A BBC internal memo, dated 29 May 1934, lists the fees for the Specialist Consultants as follows: Wyld and Lloyd James 100 guineas each, Daniel Jones and Harold Orton 50 guineas each (R6 / 196 / 5).
17. It should be added that the possibility of inviting a representative of the English Association came up as early as 1930, but it was decided that 'no useful purpose would be served by such representation, and that it was inadvisable to add to the Committee at present' (Minutes, 20 November 1930; R6 / 201 / 1).
18. Edward Marsh, Rose Macaulay, Kenneth Clark, Hugh Lyon, Cynthia Asquith, H. J. C. Grierson, I. A. Richards, and Samuel Ratcliffe all expressed that they felt honoured, and they accepted with pleasure (letters of 8, 9, 10, 12 and 28 June 1934). George Gordon and Frank

Laurence Lucas, although they said they were generally elated with the invitation, expressed some minor concerns about holidaying abroad and the number of meetings, which Reith, however, seems to have threatened very few of (letters from George Gordon and Frank Laurence Lucas to Reith dated 8 and 11 June 1934; R6 / 196 / 5).

19. In the end, Orton was paid £5.6.8 and Wyld £1.16.3 (R6 / 196 / 6).

20. Wyld, for example, wrote in to say that the 22 June meeting of the Consultants would be difficult for him because he had to correct university exam papers (30 May 1934), though he did make it in the end—after having clarified that '14.30 means 2.30 p.m.' (31 May 1934; R6 / 196 / 5).

21. Lady Asquith, for example, informed Lloyd James that she would be abroad until 20 July 1934, so that she regretfully was not able to attend (14 June 1934). Lyon was equally unsure whether he would be able to attend the July full meeting owing to his already full calendar (15 June 1934). Similarly, I. A. Richards wrote to Lloyd James, thanking him for the letter and papers, adding: 'Unfortunately I shall not be in England again until the autumn and will therefore have to miss the first meeting' (20 June 1934). Lucas told Lloyd James that he would be in Iceland from 10 July to about 13 August 1934 (23 June 1934; R6 / 196 / 5).

22. See Section 4.2, for the Sub-Committee for the Invention of New Words, and Section 5.1, for the suspension of routine publication.

23. Shaw, as Chairman, apparently forgot 'to ask for a formal resolution of regret on the resignation of Forbes-Robertson' and subsequently wrote to him 'in the proper manner'. On 6 December 1935, Shaw wrote to Lloyd James, asking him to make sure 'to get this on the minutes . . . the next agenda should start with "The Chairman has written to Sir Johnston Forbes-Robertson expressing the regret of the Committee at the resignation of so distinguished a member." Somebody can move that the committee approves, and this will dispose of the matter' (R6 / 196 / 8).

Chapter 4
Some Linguistic Changes

The great changes in personnel and procedure outlined in Chapter 3 were followed by changes of a more linguistic nature. They include the (partial) introduction of the use of the International Phonetic Alphabet (IPA), the formation of a Sub-Committee for the Invention of New Words, and the involvement of scholars of other languages as well as foreign embassies to advise on the 'correct' pronunciation of foreign words and names. The final retreat from the public eye (i.e. from the routine publication in the *Radio Times* of decisions on pronunciation and 'new words', and therefore of the Committee's prescriptive approach) and a re-focusing on BBC-internal recommendations will be treated in Chapter 5.

4.1 The International Phonetic Alphabet (IPA)

The first Experts' (or the Permanent Specialist Sub-Committee) Meeting was held on 22 June 1934 and, apparently, went quite well. This was unexpected, since Wyld was known for his strongly elitist approach to Received Pronunciation, having stated that 'it is spoken by those often very properly called "the best people"'

(McArthur 1998: 125); unsurprisingly, he was also perceived as having a difficult personality. Lloyd James informed Reith that

> Wyld was exceedingly in favour of listening in affable [manner], but naturally firm in his views. He was much less intransigent than Bridges & Onions had us suppose he would be. He disagrees with the early principles laid down by Bridges, as Jones and I do, and we all knew Wyld would. (1 July 1934; R6 / 196 / 6)

On 17 September 1934, Lloyd James sent out the invitations and papers for the first full meeting of the reconstituted Committee, including 'the list of doubtful words with pronunciations recorded in various standard dictionaries'.[1] In the invitation letter to Shaw he added an extra paragraph, outlining how 'extremely gratifying' the first meeting of the Consultants constituting the Permanent Specialist Sub-Committee had been. 'I cannot help feeling that we have made a step in the right direction.... The accession of Professor Wyld is a great asset and our co-operation with him so far has been cordial in the extreme' (R6 / 196 / 6).

Although not explicitly mentioned in any BBC document, it is quite reasonable to assume that the introduction of a Sub-Committee of language experts was responsible for the wider use of the IPA. As Lloyd James pointed out in the first meeting of the reconstituted Full Committee on 20 September 1934, '[t]he early recommendation to record pronunciations only in the modified spelling system proved unsatisfactory, and a strictly phonetic pronunciation (using the International Phonetic Alphabet) was adopted in addition. This was first used in Broadcast English II' (R6 / 201 / 2).

In the Introduction to *Broadcast English II*, the pamphlet on English place names, Lloyd James wrote, 'Speech cannot be written perfectly, but it can be written better in a phonetic alphabet than in another.' He then continued:

In this booklet we have tried the experiment of representing pronunciation in two ways:—
(1) by means of the International Phonetic Alphabet, in the form used for what is known as 'broad transcription';
(2) by means of modified spelling with diacritical marks. (1930: 11)

Lloyd James's Introduction is followed by three pages of symbols and examples, neatly divided into vowels, diphthongs, semi-vowels, and consonants, so as to familiarize the reader with the IPA (see section in the preliminary matter). Typical place name entries read:

WOUGHTON, Bucks.	'wuftən	wóoftŏn
WOULDHAM, Kent	'wuldəm	wóoldăm
WRANGATON, Devon.	'ræŋətən	rángătŏn
WREA GREEN, Lancas.	'rei 'gri:n	ráy gréen
WREAY, Cumb.	riə	reeă

(1930: 82)

This system of giving pronunciations in the IPA followed by modified spelling was also used in the remaining *Broadcast English* pamphlets (*III* to *VII*). Strangely enough, though, if the files of the minutes can be trusted as being complete, the IPA was considered to be of reasonable use for the general public but not for the Committee members: the minutes make only occasional use of the IPA in connection with the words discussed and laid before the Full Committee (for example, one of the Consultant Members' recommendations with respect to the Irish place name booklet states that 'the vowel sound contained in words like burn, fir, earn, etc.' should be 'represented in the phonetic spelling by the symbols [ə:r] in place of [ər]' (28 November 1935; R6 / 201 / 2). Otherwise, modified spelling was used throughout, even though this frequently necessitated additional comments, for example:

RÖNTGEN	RÚNTGEN ('g' as in 'get')
BOWER (Bow Anchor)	BÓWER (-ow as in 'now')
COLCHICUM	CÓLCHICUM ('ch' as in 'church')
HALLIARD	HÁLYĂRD (first 'a' as in 'man')
PHTHISIS	THÍSSIS ('th' as in 'thin')

(Report of Consultant Members, 20 September 1934; R6 / 201 / 2)

It should be added, however, that discussion on whether or not to use the IPA started as early as 1928; the minutes of the sixth meeting record a motion by J. C. Stobart, one of the BBC representatives on the Committee, that

> pronunciation recommendations should be given in two forms, (i) a simple notation, interfering as little as possible with the original spelling (such as that used in 'Broadcast English I'), and (ii) a phonetic script. Professor Jones proposed the adoption of a script based on South-Western English, which would retain the letter 'r'. The Chairman [Pearsall Smith, in the absence of Bridges] suggested that Mr. Bridges should be consulted before any decision was made in this matter. (R6 / 201 / 1)

The rhotic accents of South-Western English as spoken in Cornwall, Devon, Dorset, Somerset, Gloucestershire, and Wiltshire are 'closer to script', with the *r* being pronounced everywhere, as was intended by the BBC in the early days (see Section 2.2). As we saw, it took another two years for the IPA to find its way into the *Broadcast English* pamphlets (starting with *Broadcast English II* in 1930); and as far as the Advisory Committee itself is concerned, it never really took hold—except to clarify modified spelling, which was often open to differing interpretations.

Sometimes, however, the use of phonetic script did not solve all the problems either. On 17 March 1937, Lloyd James wrote to the Consultant Members Orton, Jones, and Wyld, explaining that 'one of the chief problems encountered during the compilation of "Broadcast English VI" [foreign place names] was the treatment of the vowel [y] in the English versions'. Although, he continues, 'most educated speakers now-a-days can and do make some attempt at reproducing this vowel when they meet it in foreign or partially naturalised words', the objective of the pamphlet would be to give 'anglicised versions made up of purely English sounds as far as possible'. Consequently, [y] was 'variously anglicised as [u], [u:], or [uə] according to its surroundings'. Now that the Advisory Committee was engaged in the compilation of a booklet on foreign personal names, the question was even more acute, 'as there are very few "accepted anglicisms" to help us out, and experience in the Corporation has shown that in the public estimation a fairly close approximation to the native forms is required of Announcers, especially in the names of those still living'. He then gives the treatment of [y] in the four leading dictionaries—the *Shorter Oxford*, Daniel Jones, Wyld, and Fowler's *Modern English Usage*—and concludes:

It looks as though the Englishman's fronted u-sound will have to be represented either by [ü] in both the phonetic and modified spelling versions of the English pronunciation, or by [y] in the former, and by [ü] in the latter only. (R6 / 196 / 10)

Jones suggested 'that y be used in the phonetic and ü in the modified spelling in all cases where an attempt is made by announcers to use the French (German) sound' (19 March 1937); Orton stated that he also preferred [y] in the phonetic spelling and *ü* in the modified spelling (22 March). Miss Henderson replied to Orton on Lloyd James's behalf:

Professor Lloyd James agrees with you that the best solution of our problem is to introduce the symbol [y] into the phonetic rendering of the English versions, and to use ü for the modified spelling. In the rare cases where complete anglicisation has taken place, as in the name Victor Hugo, we shall of course stick to the principle adopted in the Place Name pamphlet of recommending that anglicised version. (7 April 1937; R6 / 196 / 10)

Unfortunately, as we saw in Chapter 2, the pamphlet on foreign personal names was never completed. In *Broadcast English VI* (Figure 9), however, *ü* was not used in the modified spelling entries; instead we find the nearest phonetic equivalent in English, a process called phoneme substitution. As a consequence, and in order to avoid too large a gap between the IPA and modified spelling pronunciations, the pamphlet on foreign place names introduced three pronunciation columns after the headword:

The native pronunciation appears in the first column after the name itself, and is represented in the alphabet of the International Phonetic Association. Then follows either the traditional English pronunciation or, when such tradition is lacking, as near an approximation to the native version as it is

DIREDAWA, Abyssinia	di:re:dəwa:	diriˈdauwɔ	dirridów-wă
DJIBOUTI, French Somaliland	ʤabu:ti	ʤiˈbu:ti	jiboóti
DNIESTER (riv.), Russia	ˈdn̥ɛstər	ˈ(d)ni:stər	(d)neéstĕr
DODECANESE, Greek isls. in Ægean	ðoðeˈkanisos	doudekəˈni:z	dōdeckăneéz
DOLORES, Col., U.S.A.	dəˈlɔ:rəs	dəˈlɔ:rəs	dŏlórĕss
DOMINICA, British W. Indies	dɔmiˈni:kə	dɔmiˈni:kɔ	dommineékă
DOMINICAN REPUBLIC, Central America	[repuβliˈkana ðominiˈkana]	douˈminikən riˈpʌblik	dōmínnicăn rĕpúblic
DOMO, Cameroons	domo	ˈdoumou	dṓmō
DOMODOSSOLA, Italy	domoˈdɔssola	doumouˈdɔsələ	dōmōdóssŏlă
DOORN, Holland	do:rn	duərn	dŏŏrn
DORTMUND, Germany	ˈdɔrtmunt	ˈdɔ:rtmund	dórtmŏŏnd
DOULLENS-SUR-SOMME, France	duˈlɑ̃:s syr ˈsɔm	du:ˈlɔ̃s suər ˈsɔm	dooló(ng)ss-sŏŏr-sóm
DRAMA, Greece	ˈðrama	ˈdrɑ:mə	draámă
DUALA (plain), Cameroons	duˈala	duˈɑ:lə	dŏŏaálă
DUISBURG, Germany	ˈdy:sburk	ˈdju:zbə:rg	déwzburg
DUM DUM, India	dɔm dɔm—*Ben.*	ˈdʌmdʌm	dúmdum
DUNEDIN, New Zealand	dəˈni:din	dəˈni:din	dŭneédin
DURANGO, Col., U.S.A.	duˈræŋgou	duˈræŋgou	dŏŏráng-gō
DURAZZO (= DURRËS), Albania	duˈrattso	duˈrætsou	dŏŏrátsō
DÜREN, Germany	ˈdy:rən	ˈdjuərən	déwrĕn
DURRËS, Albania	ˈdurrəs	ˈdurəs	dŏŏrĕss
DÜSSELDORF, Germany	ˈdysəldɔrf	ˈdusəldɔ:rf	dŏŏssĕldorf

E

ECUADOR, S. America	ɛkwaˈðɔr	ekwəˈdɔ:r	ekwădór
EGER, Hungary	ˈɛgɛr	ˈægɛər	ággair
EIFFEL TOWER, France	[tur ɛˈfɛl]	ˈaifəl ˈtauər	íffĕl tówer
ELANDSFONTEIN, S. Africa	ˈʔe:lãtsfɔnˈtein —*Afr.* ˈi:ləndzfənˈtein—*Eng.*	ˈi:ləndzfənˈtein	eélăndzfŏntáyn
ELEUTHERA, Bahamas	eˈlju:θərə	eˈlju:θərə	elléwthĕră
EL GORO (well), Italian Somaliland	el qoro	el gɔˈrou	el gorrṓ
EL MEKHERIF, Sudan	il meˈxe(i)rif	el meˈkeirif	el mekkáyrif

32

Figure 9 Facsimile of *Broadcast English VI*, 1937, p. 32.

possible to perform when using speech-sounds that are purely English. Exception has to be made in the case of some foreign sounds that appear to be now within the capacity of the average educated speaker of English, viz., nasalized vowels, not necessarily French in quality, and the *ch* sound as in 'loch'. The sound of French *u* in *tu* and of German *für* has been variously rendered by [ju], [u:], or [u] according to its position in the word and the surrounding sounds. The sounds of French *eu*, as in *peu* and as in *peur*, corresponding to those in German *schön* and *Götter*, have been represented in the English versions by [ə:], or in the unstressed position by [ə]. . . . The fourth column in the book is merely an attempt to represent the recommended pronunciation in modified spelling, as has been done in all the other handbooks of the series. (1937: 11)

The use of the IPA undoubtedly increased the scholarly value of the *Broadcast English* booklets *II* to *VII* and helped to disambiguate the recommended pronunciations in modified spelling. What is more surprising is that it was only after the Committee's reconstitution that the inadequacy of solely using a modified spelling system was officially admitted; and even then, modified spelling remained the tool of preference, at least for the Full Committee.

4.2 The Sub-Committee for the Invention of New Words

In spite of eminently sensible measures like the use of the IPA in the later *Broadcast English* booklets, there were lapses back to the old days of active language engineering, for example introducing 'made-up' words for new concepts. In 1935 another sub-committee was set up, this one to deal with the invention of new words—eventually simply named The Sub-Committee on Words (Figure 10), so as to make it 'sufficiently elastic' to deal with everything from 'suggesting new words to fill the ever-increasing number of gaps in the language' to making 'recommendations to the Main Committee on any aspect of spoken language' (Sub-Committee on Words, minutes 8 January 1936; R6 / 201 / 2).[2]

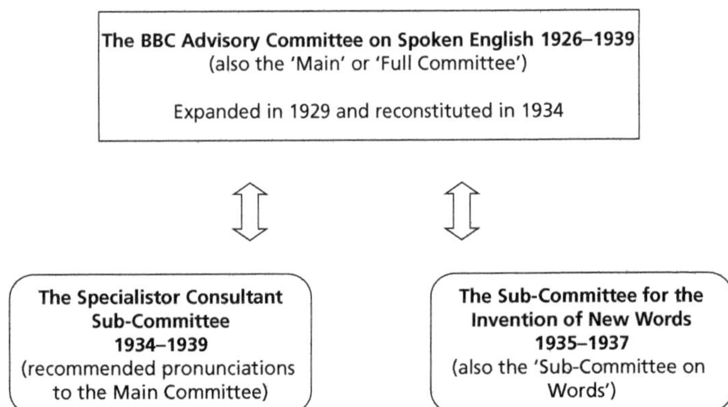

Figure 10 The BBC Advisory Committee on Spoken English and its sub-committees.

It consisted of the following ten members: Logan Pearsall Smith (Chairman), Lord David Cecil, Kenneth Clark, Rose Macaulay, Edward Marsh, and Professors Abercrombie, Grierson, Jones, Lloyd James, and Wyld (see Appendix I for biographical data of these members).

The creation of the Sub-Committee on Words was pressing, since 'the progress of television had made it necessary that a suitable word should be found to describe users of television apparatus'. In the meantime, the Main Committee had provisionally 'approved the use of the word "televiewer" pending the invention of a more suitable word, but expressed a preference for the shortened form "viewer"' (28 March 1935; R6 / 201 / 2). This decision was immediately communicated to the Controller of Programmes, adding that the Committee also recommended that 'we might have a short chatty talk introducing the word some time' (29 March 1935; R6 / 196 / 7), and that 'criticisms and suggestions in connection with the word "televiewer" should be submitted to the sub-committee as soon as possible' (R6 / 201 / 2).

To be fair to the BBC, judging from the remarks in a letter by Lloyd James to Reith dated 31 March 1935, this new Sub-Committee and its proposed work on the vocabulary of television was never taken seriously by the people in charge of the Main Advisory Committee on Spoken English. Lloyd James wrote:

I think all is well . . . but Logan Pearsall Smith, who has great ideas on new words, did, I think, feel that the Committee should have been given the chance. At first they all resented 'televiewer', but had no idea of anything better; I said that most of the suggestions that had come to me had been much worse, and they accepted it under protest. No harm has been done. (R6 / 196 / 7)

At least, not yet.

Logan Pearsall Smith was indeed enthusiastic and, as we shall see later, had plenty of ideas for new words. Three days after the Main Committee's meeting and provisional decision on *(tele) viewer* (the idea was for the new Sub-Committee on Words eventually to evaluate and recommend alternatives) he wrote to R. C. Norman, the Vice-Chairman and later Chairman of Governors of the BBC, and explained that he could not find an alternative preferable to *televiewer*, and informally *viewer*, adding, however, that he was attracted by the word *gazer*. He further expressed his regret that the BBC seemed to object to the phrase *to look in*,[3] as

[all] such new expressions would seem objectionable at first; but if they prove useful and fill a real need, this sense of awkwardness due to their novelty soon wears off—especially if the innovation is the product of those processes which have governed the development of our language in the

past. One of the oldest & most advantageous of these linguistic processes is the formation of what we call 'phrasal verbs'—verbs followed by an adverb or preposition.

He then went on to elaborate that such expressions 'have from the earliest times added to our English speech a flexibility and expressiveness which renders it comparable to the Greek language, and superior in this aspect to French and Italian, in which idioms of this kind are scarcely found' (31 March 1935; R6 / 196 / 7). We will see below that the apparent necessity of exploiting the 'native resources' in order to expand the English lexicon is one of the recurring themes in Pearsall Smith's approach to language change. Norman found Pearsall Smith's comments 'most interesting and entertaining' and stated how glad he was that both Pearsall Smith and the Committee favoured *viewer*; with respect to the question of phrasal verbs he added:

I am sorry if I gave the impression that the Board objected to the phrase to 'look in' on principle. I don't think they ever considered that aspect of the matter. But, forced to find immediately a word, they shied off the noun 'looker-in', and still more 'tele-looker', on the ground of cacophony, and also because to 'look in' has already a defined meaning unrelated to television. (3 April 1935; R6 / 196 / 7)

The idea that 'Professor Lloyd James should broadcast a request after the News for suggestions for a word to describe users of television apparatus... has now been rejected' (14 April 1935; R6 / 196 / 7), though not without BBC-internal controversy;[4] it was instead decided to use the written channel for an appeal to the public, and the following article by Lloyd James was published in the *Radio Times* on 19 April 1935:

The problem of finding a suitable name for the person who receives a broadcast television programme is one that has given the daily Press much exercise; the coining of new words does not strictly come under the jurisdiction of the Spoken English Committee, but in this case the Corporation has asked the Committee for its blessing upon the suggested word 'televiewer', which is hoped will rapidly learn to disguise its mongrel origin by shedding the prefix and showing itself to the world as 'viewer'. Some name has to be found, and 'viewer' will serve for the present. It is not unlikely, however, that the man-in-the-street, with his customary genius for the *mot juste*, will hit upon the word that will finally be accepted into the language. Here is a good chance for the Reading Listener and the Listening Reader to help us decide what name shall be given to those who look as well as listen. (*Radio Times*, 19 April 1935, p. 6)

A BBC memo criticizes as 'very poor' the many suggestions for alternatives to *televiewer* received from the public (27 May 1935; R6 / 196 / 7). Unfortunately, the full list of these words is not in the BBC files, but we can reasonably assume that it was not dramatically different from the list sent by Lloyd James to Rose Macaulay and all the other members of the Sub-Committee on Words about a week later, which contained the following suggestions received from a variety of sources:

auralooker, glancer, looker, looker-in, optavuist, optovisor, seer, sighter, teleseer, teleserver, televist, teleobservist, televor, viewer-in, visionnaire, visionist, visor, vizior, vizzior, witnesser.

Lloyd James commented dryly that in his opinion 'none of them deserves serious consideration and I hardly think it worth while summoning the Sub-Committee to discuss them at this stage' (5 June 1935; R6 / 196 / 7). Rose Macaulay replied that she herself preferred *looker-in* but did not think it warranted a meeting; Abercrombie was of the same mind about not calling a meeting on this and, surprisingly, also agreed that 'the word which will win in the long run' was *looker-in* (5 June 1935, 7 June 1935; R6 / 196 / 7).

The agenda for a meeting of the Main Advisory Committee, scheduled for 28 November 1935, contains, besides the usual report of the Specialist Members and list of pronunciations for discussion, an item entitled: 'Paper by Mr. Logan Pearsall Smith: Suggestions for the B.B.C. Advisory Committee on Spoken English' (R6 / 196 / 8). This fourteen-page paper, whose main purpose was to create a mission for the Sub-Committee on Words, is a very remarkable and revealing document, as it illustrates the prescriptive, often pompous and judgemental linguistic instincts prevalent among (at least some of) the people who advised the BBC on language matters at the time. First, Pearsall Smith explained that 'the linguistic problems by which the English-speaking public are faced today are by no means confined to the pronunciation of words', thus setting the agenda to broaden the Main Committee's brief and to generate work and a purpose for the Sub-Committee on Words beyond the *televiewer*/*looking-in* question. 'New inventions are made', he stated, 'and all these need their names and their respective vocabularies', so that 'we must ask ourselves whether our language is responding with all its old efficiency and vigour to the demands which are now being made upon it. These demands are urgent', he continued, because 'if happy words are not found, ugly and awkward ones will take their place' (R6 / 196 / 8).

The paper then gives a brief account of the various possibilities for expanding English vocabulary—such as 'borrowing boldly from other languages', 'creating words out of its own materials', 'the revival of old words', and 'the perpetual drifting into standard English of words and idioms from dialects and popular or local forms of speech'—before sliding into value judgements again. 'All these [word formation] processes', Pearsall Smith went on, 'have been greatly aided in the past by our English writers, who have enriched our language with an immense number of useful and often beautiful words.' But unfortunately, according to him, things have worsened considerably since Shakespeare, Dryden, and 'our romantic writers', as 'on examining the more recent additions to our vocabulary, as recorded in the supplement to the Oxford Dictionary, we notice . . . a certain deterioration in their quality'. He speaks of 'false fashions of taste which prevail at present', the worst of which in his eyes is to keep 'unassimilated aliens in our language':

> A word, for instance, like aviator was readily accepted, while airman was intensely disliked at first and only succeeded in establishing itself owing to the persistent usage in The Times. . . . when the word handbook made its modest appearance as an English competitor with the Greek enchiridion and the Latin manual, it was received with loud abuse. (R6 / 196 / 8)[5]

What could be done to 'remedy' the situation? In a section of his paper that is almost reminiscent of Richard Verstegan's 1605 *Restitution of Decayed Intelligence*, Pearsall Smith asserted that 'it must be a matter of concern for us all' that new words 'should be vivid and expressive words, English in shape and sound, formed according to the traditions of our language, and capable of being incorporated in our speech and made available for the common use. Each individual can do something in the matter', he suggested, by giving 'his preference, when a choice is possible, to vivid, concise, designatory words, rather than to cumbrous and multisyllabic definitions', adding:

If, then, each individual can do something, how much greater would be the efficiency of a committee like ours, working as it does with the immense sounding-board of the B.B.C. behind it! We have already acquired some experience in our attempts at linguistic reform; why should we not extend the scope of our activities a little further, and take into our consideration not only the pronunciation, but the choice and the formation of words? (R6 / 196 / 8)

Somewhat surprisingly, though, Pearsall Smith claimed that he was not proposing 'a mint for making new words' or 'to pass off our coinages to the public', as this would lead to even greater outcries of protest than their attempt to regulate pronunciation ('A mob of linguistic die-hards would storm this modern building, and our committee would be dissolved in lynchings, blood and slaughter'); instead he said he advocated a 'tentative, experimental' approach, 'devoid of any assumption of superior guidance'—something which, according to him, the Committee had in fact already done by expressing a preference for *airplane* to replace *aeroplane* (R6 / 196 / 8).[6]

Pearsall Smith was clearly treading a thin line in his paper. On the one hand, he had to be careful not to appear too prescriptive, too adventurous, and not to propose to turn the BBC into a kind of national language academy in charge of corpus planning, an activity that certainly was never envisaged in the BBC Charter, nor would it have found the support of most senior BBC staff. On the other hand, his instinct was clearly going in precisely that direction: his Sub-Committee on Words was nowhere near representative of the speech community at large, but consisted of (mostly elderly) members of the British cultural elite; their linguistic judgements were conservative, even backward-looking, and based on notions of purity by eradicating foreignisms and on notions of a kind of golden-age literary and stylistic beauty—all elements traditionally associated with the conscious standardization efforts undertaken by European language academies from about the sixteenth century onwards (Wright 2004: 54–5).

This strongly prescriptive, puristic, and value-laden agenda is most clearly visible in Pearsall Smith's vision for the mission of the new Sub-Committee on Words. He felt that its major focus of activity should be to assimilate or, if that proved difficult, to translate words of foreign origin. Here are a few examples Pearsall Smith gives from German:

> German words are, as a rule, impossible to naturalize (Kindergarten, meeschaum [*sic*], poodle, waltz are exceptions). We must, if we need them, translate them if we can. Time-spirit for Zeitgeist we owe to Carlyle, World-outlook for Weltanschanung [*sic*] to Henry James, and superman for Übermensch to our present Chairman [George Bernard Shaw]. No equivalents have been found, however, for those useful words, Sehnsucht, Schwärmerei, or for the Blüthenzeit [*sic*] for an artist's career. Carlyle's suggestion of mischief-joy for Schadenfreude has not found acceptance. (R6 / 196 / 8)

Another vital task would be filling 'serious gaps in our language'. For example, 'the names doctor and physician do not include surgeons, and the old word leech has fallen out of use. Nor have we any inclusive appellation, like the French combatants [*sic*], the Italian combattente, for members of the defensive forces of the Crown—for sailors, soldiers and airmen' (R6 / 196 / 8).

He further suggested that the Sub-Committee should concern itself with 'the revival of fine old words which have perished, or which are in danger of perishing from the language'—the examples Pearsall Smith provides are: 'thole and nesh and lew and *fash* and *douce*, which have never found their way into the standard language, or have long since faded from it'—and with 'giving deliberate help to . . . the process of Differentiation . . . as that between *defective* and *deficient*'. All this would 'awaken in the public an intelligent interest in the great inheritance of our speech and provide us with an ideal of convinced and not merely habitual usage' (R6 / 196 / 8).[7]

The minutes of the actual meeting somewhat dryly record that the Main Advisory Committee 'considered a paper by Mr. Logan Pearsall Smith' and that

> after some discussion, it was agreed that the Paper should be submitted for more detailed consideration to the newly-appointed Sub-committee created with the question of the invention of new words. It was proposed that the Sub-committee should present concrete proposals to the Corporation suggesting that the general public might be invited to co-operate with the Committee by sending in suggestions for new words, stating cases where new words were urgently needed, etc. (28 November 1935; R6 / 201 / 2)

In other words, Pearsall Smith succeeded; the Sub-Committee on Words seems to have been given a brief that went much beyond what was originally envisaged in connection with the advent of television. Pearsall Smith was given the green light by the Main Committee—though clearly not by all members thereof, since the phrase 'after some discussion' is usually BBC code for disagreement—not only to define the fields of activity of the Sub-Committee on Words but also to enlist the public's support in this language engineering exercise.

In its first—and, as we shall see, only—official meeting on 8 January 1936, Pearsall Smith, in the chair, defined the Sub-

Committee's tasks more systematically than he had done in his initial proposal; in particular, he identified three areas in which the Sub-Committee might intervene.

First, the Sub-Committee should 'recommend one name or term where two were struggling for survival'. This would be the case for words that had two plural forms, one English and one classical (e.g. *cactuses—cacti*; *hippopotamuses—hippopotami*; *terminuses—termini*; *sanatoriums—sanatoria*; *formulas—formulae*). There were also 'words and terms which were duplicates in sense' (e.g. *traffic lights—stop-and-goes*; *gyratory circuses—roundabouts*; *zoological gardens—zoo*; *aeroplane—airplane*; *ultra-violet rays—ultra rays*, etc.). For the former category, the Sub-Committee recommended that 'as a general principle, where two plural forms of a word existed, the English form should prevail'.[8] As for the latter type, 'the simpler (and usually the more graphic) form should prevail' (R6 / 201 / 2). This meant *stop-and-goes*, *roundabouts*, *zoo*, *airplane*, and *ultra rays*.

Secondly, 'the Sub-committee might perform a useful service in suggesting new words in place of existing ones which were, for one reason or another, undesirable'. Examples of such 'undesirables' were: *anticyclone*, to be replaced by *halcyon* or *halcyon weather*; and *television set*, to be replaced by *view-box*, though in the latter case 'other more suitable suggestions might be obtained from listeners' (R6 / 201 / 2).

Thirdly, the Sub-Committee should discuss 'deficiencies in the language' and, if possible, close these gaps. For example, it provisionally suggested *art-researcher* as a fitting equivalent to the German *Kunstforscher*, though the Sub-Committee thought that 'other more suitable words might be obtained by listeners, etc., and particularly from persons engaged in such research'. Other recommendations for the Main Committee were the term *serviceman* as 'an inclusive term to describe persons belonging to the Navy, Army or Air Force', equivalent to the French *combattant*; and *novelet* (from French *nouvelle*) for a very short novel or long short story. As for 'the feeling now described in English by the French word "Malaise"', it was agreed that 'the old word *malease*, which was used by Malory and Wyclif' should be recommended for revival. And finally,

> Two other words invented by members of the [Sub-]Committee, Miss Macaulay's YULERY for Christmas festivities, and Mr. Edward Marsh's 'portmanteau' word INFLEX for 'Inferiority complex', were also recommended by the Chairman [Pearsall Smith]. It was agreed that these words should be forwarded for consideration to the main Committee. (R6 / 201 / 2)

All these issues are not just prescriptive and value-laden in nature (e.g. the idea of 'undesirable' words in the language), but some of the recommendations seem not particularly well thought-out either. What, for example, should the verb collocating with *view box* be—*to watch the view box*? Or the agentive noun for that matter—*view-box viewer* or, following Pearsall Smith's preference, *view-box gazer*? While *servicemen* (and today of course *-women*) is admittedly widely used, creations such as *ultra rays*, *halcyon weather*, or *inflex* have never become popular outside the Sub-Committee and met a quiet death. As for *art-researcher*, a loan-translation from German, we would probably use *art-historian* or even *art-critic* today.[9]

A final point in the Sub-Committee minutes relates to yet another request for programme time as 'the best method of obtaining opinions and suggestions from the general public would be to broadcast a request for assistance in a series of talks dealing with different aspects of the spoken language'. In the end the Talks Director made space available for two twenty-minute talks, the first of which would focus on 'general remarks on the subject of the increasing number of gaps in the language' and list 'words suggested for popularization . . . e.g. HALCYON, SERVICEMAN.' The second talk would solicit suggestions for 'new words in particular cases . . . e.g. a word in place of "Television Set", a word to indicate an "Art-Researcher", etc.' (R6 / 201 / 2).[10]

The memo of a meeting in June 1936 between Lloyd James, Lindsay Wellington (the Director of Programme Planning), and Miss Simond (Assistant Secretary to the Committee) makes clear that the work of the Sub-Committee on Words did not go down well amongst some of the BBC's senior people. Wellington, for example,

> felt that having read the Minutes of the Sub-Committee's first meeting, at which all kinds of suggestions had been made with regard to new words, some sort of restraint should be placed upon this Sub-Committee. It was not the Corporation's policy to initiate proposals of this kind, which were rather the function of some outside body. In any case, in his opinion some of the suggestions—e.g. 'halcyon' in place of 'anti-cyclone' or 'view Box' for television set—were so ludicrous that irreparable harm to the main Committee's prestige might be done should any of these suggestions be broadcast. (28 June 1936; R6 / 196 / 9)

'Considerable discussion' (BBC code for *serious* disagreement) ensued, which resulted in the decisions that Reith should make a statement to the Main Committee in order to 'explain why the Corporation was not at present in a position to accept the Sub-Committee's proposals' and that 'the suggestion might be made that the Sub-Committee should function in an advisory capacity only' (28 June 1936; R6 / 196 / 9).

In the end, the statement was made not by Reith but by R. C. Norman, the Chairman of Governors, during the Main Committee's meeting on 29 January 1937; its terms are even more restrictive than what was originally proposed. 'The Corporation', it says,

> has read with interest the minutes of the Sub-Committee appointed to make recommendations as to the framing of new words. It feels that it must define more closely the extent to which it can accept the advice of the Sub-Committee. Such advice will be sought by the Corporation when new words have to be found for its own purpose—as in the creation of vocabulary of television terms. The Sub-Committee, however, has recommended the introduction to the public of new words for general use (e.g. 'halcyon', 'stop-go'). This responsibility for modifying the English vocabulary is one which the Corporation feels it cannot accept. (R6 / 201 / 2)

This, not surprisingly, was the end of the Sub-Committee on Words, and one can imagine Pearsall Smith's regret, although, according to the minutes, he was not present at the meeting.[11] Even the small consolation with respect to 'the creation of vocabulary for television terms' is little more than a mirage: a memo by Wellington from October of the previous year states he understood 'that a glossary of television terms is being compiled at Alexandra Palace'[12]—and not by the members of the Sub-Committee on Words (15 October 1936; R6 / 196 / 9). At the same time, Norman's statement is part of a BBC 'back to basics' trend of the late 1930s, in the sense that what was really needed by the Corporation was concrete and specific advice for its announcers and not groups of scholars and well-meaning laypeople interfering with the language at large. This, as we shall see, also affected the Committee's publication activities (Section 5.1).

The sudden termination of the Sub-Committee on Words had two immediate effects. The first was that, BBC-internally, explanations of what had gone wrong were sought. While Lloyd James put it all down to a 'misunderstanding of the body', which was only to 'adjudicate on suggested words which the Corporation itself required to use, and not to supply words to fill lacunae in the language other than those connected with broadcasting' (11 February 1937; R6 / 196 / 10), Mary Somerville, Director of School Broadcasting, who also attended the meetings of the Main Committee, blamed Shaw's inadequate chairmanship. Her memo to Reith is very plain on this point:

> I remember that Shaw was even more muddled than usual at the meeting at which the Sub-Committee on Words was set up. There was a discussion as to the Spoken English Committee's right to extend its terms of reference to include the invention of new words, and Professor Lloyd James tried in vain to keep Shaw in order. I remember a kind of duet—
>
> Shaw—'our duty to the public . . . '
>
> Lloyd James—'no, to the B.B.C . . . .'
>
> Shaw—'our duty to the public . . . '
>
> Lloyd James (sotto voce, and in despair)—'to the B.B.C . . . .'
>
> A non-committal minute was drafted. But at the next meeting there was a proposal that 'The Sub-committee should present concrete proposals to the B.B.C. suggesting that the general public might be invited to co-operate with the Committee by sending in suggestions for new words, stating cases where new words were urgently needed, etc.' Someone . . . ought at that point have jumped up and said 'Don't be so silly!' But no one did. (4 February 1937; R6 / 196 / 10)

The second immediate consequence was that not all members of the Sub-Committee on Words accepted the BBC's decision without protest. Kenneth Clark, for example, wrote to none less than the BBC's Director General to express his 'disquiet' about Norman's statement. In his reply, Reith reminded Clark that the Sub-Committee on Words was founded only with the intent 'to settle the term which should be used for the Television service, analogous to "listener" in the sound service'—and not to expand the general vocabulary of English, an activity that lay well outside the BBC's responsibilities as defined by its Charter; consequently, when 'the Sub-Committee suggested new words with which broadcasting was not specifically concerned, the Corporation although much interested was a little alarmed' (10 February 1937; R6 / 196 / 10).

A few days later, Clark wrote to Reith again. He objected to the procedural fact that Norman's statement was not circulated before the meeting; after all, it involved 'the whole future of the Committee', so his protest was understandable. But Clark also took a very strong prescriptive approach—to the work of the Main Committee as well as that of the Sub-Committee on Words—and insisted that 'the public felt the need of some responsible guidance, and that the Corporation was the only body from which this guidance could possibly come'. He expanded on this: 'Words tend to become degraded, vowel sounds to lose their sonority and variety and this is what is rightly known as the decadence of the language.' Clark thus not only felt it necessary that the Advisory Committee on Spoken English should 'prevent homonyms arising from degraded sounds' (the example he gives is *fissure* / *fisher*), but added with respect to the Sub-Committee for the Invention of New Words:

I fully understand that the Corporation would not wish to undertake any extravagant new usages, but it often happens that for a new phenomenon alternative names arise, one being much better than the other: such for example were the names for crossings on the new roads. I believe that it was proposed to call these 'gyratory circuses', and that the [Sub-] Committee recommended that they should be referred to as 'roundabouts'. Surely there is something to be said for a body which can prevent such a cumbrous and pedantic usage as the former from becoming current. (15 February 1937; R6 / 196 / 10)

This is very much the regulatory tone that we first encountered in 1926: the BBC as a guiding authority that prevents 'degraded sounds' and 'cumbrous and pedantic usage'. Reith accepted that it would have been better if the BBC had circulated Norman's statement before the meeting, but otherwise was non-committal with respect to the language issues. He placated Clark by asking him whether he was not perhaps interpreting 'the caveats of the memorandum [as] going further than intended' and that he, Reith, believed that '[your] fears can be made to prove unfounded' (18 February 1937; R6 / 196 / 10).[13]

As for the Sub-Committee on Words, however, Norman's statement and the follow-up correspondence, some of which I have quoted above, mark its definite end. Neither the BBC files nor the Main Advisory Committee minutes—there were to be only three more full meetings before formal suspension at the outbreak of the Second World War—make any more mention of it, except for a short, undated paper slip among various documents from July 1940 stating that 'this sub-committee died a natural death and did not accomplish much. (A lot of the records dealing with this period have been lost in the blitz [1940–1])' (R6 / 196 / 11).

It is obvious, based on the evidence presented in this chapter, that the BBC Sub-Committee for the Invention of New Words was a complete failure. But why should a body that represented Britain's only broadcaster at the time, and whose members included some leading linguists, have been so spectacularly unsuccessful in achieving their stated mission? The answer, I believe, lies in a combination of institutional and, above all, linguistic reasons.

First, the Sub-Committee's exact mission was never explicitly defined by the BBC. While the advent of television may have made it desirable for broadcasters if not to invent then at least to agree on a set of lexemes that could be used consistently in front of the microphone, the Sub-Committee immediately took it upon itself to reform and regulate the English lexicon as a whole. Linguistic legislation and actual language practice are two quite different things; the former has an impact on the latter only in very restricted, often state-controlled areas (such as the civil service or education), so that the Sub-Committee's attempt at large-scale linguistic reform through 'the immense sounding-board of the B.B.C.' was doomed to fail from the start.

And secondly, the composition of the Sub-Committee meant that tensions were inevitable between the linguists on the one hand, chiefly Lloyd James and Daniel Jones, and some of the very prescriptive and purist members on the other, such as Kenneth Clark and particularly of course Logan Pearsall Smith. Initially, the latter seem to have had the upper hand, and thus so did the idea that the English lexicon somehow had to be fixed—ranging from filling 'serious gaps in the language' to eliminating 'undesirable' words. A recurring puristic theme was that lexical expansion should come through 'exploiting native resources' rather than through borrowing foreign words. Such a view of language was clearly very far removed from linguistic reality and went directly against the approach being taken more frequently not only by the linguists on both Committees but also by the BBC as a whole.

In other words, at the beginning of 1937 the BBC *did* cry 'Don't be so silly!'; equally, Kenneth Clark was right in his interpretation of R. C. Norman's statement—it signalled the end of the Sub-Committee for the Invention of New Words.

4.3 Experts in other languages and foreign embassies

The idea of obtaining the services of experts in foreign languages for the BBC originally came not from within the BBC, but from Bernard Pares of the School of Slavonic and East European Studies at the University of London, who was instructed by the Annual Conference of University Teachers of Russian and other Slavonic Languages to contact Reith by letter 'in case we can be of any service to you in regularising of spelling and pronunciation of Russian names':

> As to spelling, a regular and pretty consistent scheme was adopted after the war [First World War] and is in line with the practice recommended by the British Academy. It aims as far as possible at (i) fidelity to the original so that each name can be read back into Russian letters, (ii) simplifying pronunciation so that it should be as far as possible the same as in Russian.... As to pronunciation, the Conference is glad to place at your disposal any help that you might think desirable by its principal expert in this subject, Mr N. B. Jopson, who is Reader in Comparative Slavonic Philology in the University of London. (20 July 1934; R6 / 196 / 6)

Reith and Lloyd James thanked Pares, the latter adding that he 'shall be happy to discuss with Mr. Jopson, whom I know quite well, any problems that will arise in future' (25 July 1934, 31 July 1934; R6 / 196 / 6). Indeed, a letter from the Programme Contracts Department to Jopsen dated 3 December 1935 states that he, Jopsen, had 'kindly consented to advise us on the pronunciation of about 107 Slavonic names' for which he would be offered a fee of 5 guineas—which of course he accepted (R6 / 196 / 8). And in the following year, Professor S. Boyanus was commissioned to advise the BBC on 'the pronunciation of about 110 Russian names', for which a fee of 5 guineas was suggested (6 May 1936; R6 / 196 / 9).

A three-page BBC internal memo, dated 16 July 1934, from Lloyd James to the Controller of Programmes states that 'the time has come for a comprehensive and scientific treatment of the countless problems of pronunciation that arise every day in the course of broadcasting'. It goes on that 'the only department of this work that has been adequately dealt with has been the pronunciation of English words, and English, Scottish, Welsh and Northern Irish place names'. As these matters were 'well in hand', the memo goes on, it was now time to address 'the important question of the pronunciation of the foreign word', a problem of 'considerable magnitude'. After discussion with the four expert members, Lloyd James suggested producing a book along the lines of the *Broadcast English* pamphlets, but substantially larger; this would include, amongst others, such words as:

(i) Foreign place names;
(ii) Foreign authors, composers, politicians, etc.;
(iii) Titles of operas;
(iv) Names of foreign newspapers;
(v) Musical expressions; etc.

Pronunciation information would be given under three headings:

(a) Exact native pronunciation in International Phonetic Alphabet;
(b) Recommended English pronunciation in International Phonetic Alphabet;
(c) Recommended English pronunciation in modified spelling.

The memo continues with the remark that the work would 'have to be divided out among a number of specialists, and it may be advisable to appoint a small Advisory Committee of Oriental and African specialists to act on the lines of the Spoken English Committee'. It was envisaged that, in addition to Miss Simond, the Assistant Secretary, there would be another trained phonetician employed on a half-time basis; and the information gathered in the form of a reference library should be made available 'to all Home and Empire Broadcasting and News services' (R6 / 196 / 8).

This led to the appointment of Miss Henderson as the new phonetician, but questions about such things as 'facilities for enabling announcers to get authoritative pronunciations immediately before broadcasting' remained unanswered for a while. As a pragmatic measure, it was decided that the News Librarian, Mr Bachelor, should keep a card index containing 'all words from the five "Broadcast English" publications, foreign place names supplied by the new phonetician, Miss Henderson, and other words for which an emergency pronunciation has had to be obtained'. This would be a convenient place of reference as announcers 'habitually study the News in the News Librarian's room immediately prior to broadcasting' (BBC internal circulating memos, 26 September 1935, 8 October 1935; R6 / 196 / 8). At the same time, the News Librarian started 'to compile a list giving pronunciations of doubtful words, proper names, and place names, that have not yet been discussed by the Advisory Committee'; this list would then 'periodically be passed to Miss Simond for consideration by the Committee, and revised where necessary' (20 May 1935; R6 / 196 / 7). We can see that the BBC itself was in the process of setting up an internal, professionally organized and run service for its pronunciation purposes. This eventually diminished the role of the Full Advisory Committee on Spoken English, albeit not that of the Specialist Sub-Committee.

By the autumn of 1935, the process of getting advice on native pronunciations of foreign (place) names and words had come into its own. According to a memo from the Controller of Administration to the Director of Programme Administration, the services of approximately ten experts were secured to advise on lists of foreign place names, each list including 'from about twenty to one hundred' names. It was decided that 'a fee of about two guineas would be fair for the minor experts and those getting few names, and up to about five guineas for the hundred-name ones' (23 October 1935; R6 / 196 / 8). The range of languages is impressive (*Broadcast English VI* makes reference to over two dozen languages, from Afrikaans and Arabic to Yoruba and Zulu), as is the number and variety of experts consulted:

- **Italian.** A Mrs Hicks came to the BBC 'to help announcers with Italian names'. The copy of a letter to Mrs Hicks states that the BBC are glad 'to know that we may ring you up in the evening if occasion arises to seek further advice' (25 July 1935; R6 / 196 / 8).
- **Spanish.** The News Librarian thanked Kenneth Everill of the Latin-American Press Bureau Service 'very warmly for your kind and valuable help with Spanish pronunciations' (23 and 24 July 1936; R6 / 196 / 9).

- **African.** Mr Butlin advised 'on the pronunciation of a list of about 210 place names (mostly African)' for which he received a fee of 10 guineas (14 November 1935; R6 / 196 / 8).[14]
- **American.** The Programme Contracts Executive wrote to Alistair Cooke about his assistance 'with regard to the pronunciation of 100 American place names' and his 'very helpful suggestions and additions', for which he would be paid a fee of 5 guineas (29 May 1936; R6 / 196 / 9).
- **Malayan and Philippino.** A similar letter from the Programme Contracts Executive to Dr C. Blagden refers to the latter's advice on 'about 24 Malayan names and also one or two names from the Philippine Islands' (26 May 1936; R6 / 196 / 9).
- **Chinese.** There is a similar set of correspondence, letters, and memos relating to the work by a Dr D. E. Edwards, who advised on 'about 170 Chinese place-names' for which he received a fee of 7 guineas (6–10 February 1936; R6 / 196 / 9).
- **Japanese.** A letter from the Programme Contracts Executive to S. Yoshitake of the School of Oriental Studies offers him a fee of 2 guineas for advice on the pronunciation of 40 Japanese names (10 March 1936; R6 / 196 / 9).
- **Indian.** Dr Grahame Bailey, 'an expert on Indian languages', was offered a fee of 2 guineas for his consultancy work on 42 Indian names. After a fortnight, Bailey 'sent back the Indian cards; all completed except two, which he is keeping a little longer in order to verify pronunciations'. As a result, payment of £ 2.2s was made. Two months later, Bailey received another 3 guineas for 'a further list of Indian names, including the names of the seventeen Indian cricketers who are coming over here this summer'; the new list included a total of 70 more names. Additionally, W. Sutton Page, Professor of Bengali at the School of Oriental and African Studies, was offered a fee of 2 guineas for his consultancy work on 45 Indian

> names. This work was completed in February 1936 and the payment made. Interestingly, the Indian cricket team seems to have caused some difficulty for BBC announcers. A memo from Miss Henderson of the Advisory Committee on Spoken English to the Announcers' Executive makes reference to Bailey with respect to the pronunciation of the names of two Indian cricket players that were mispronounced on air the night before:
>
> "Kumar" was heard as KÓOMAAR, instead of KŎOMÁAR
> "Vizianagram" " VIZZIĂNÁAGRĂM, " VIZZIĂNÚGGRĂM
> (UG as in jug)
>
> And she reminded announcers to check 'if necessary the News Library, before to-night's broadcast' (6 January 1936, 20 January 1936, 12 February 1936, 16 March 1936, 22 April 1936; R6 / 196 / 9).

Reviewing the BBC files on the consultancy work of scholars of foreign languages, three interesting observations can be made. First, in spite of the above-mentioned expert advice, it was impossible for every announcer to have the 'correct' pronunciation of every foreign word or name at his fingertips. So there was, according to a BBC memo, 'always rather a risk that speakers [at the microphone] may drop an occasional brick. Such bricks may pass unnoticed by listeners at home but may create a most unfortunate effect overseas.' Consequently, there had been complaints 'from listeners overseas about Empire names and the like being wrongly pronounced at the microphone'. Going back to the Indian cricket team, the Chief News Editor recorded a complaint by Lady Grigg, the wife of the Finance Member in India, who apparently had listened to the eye-witness account in a bulletin about the cricket match:

In the first place, the speaker referred to a ball having struck an Indian player's 'dusky anatomy'. On this, Lady Grigg remarked that such a phrase would not be felt to be tactful by any Indian listeners who might hear it.

The second point was that the last part of the Indian captain's name was pronounced just like the English word 'anagram', and here again she thought that perhaps a greater effort might have been made to cater for Indian susceptibilities. (13 July 1936, 2 July 1936; R6 / 196 / 9)

Lady Grigg obviously had a point, but sometimes the complaints were simply the result of listeners not being familiar with the BBC policy that 'foreign words in common use should be Englished' (see Section 2.2). Professor E. Allison Peers of Liverpool University, for example, complained about BBC announcers inaccurately stressing Spanish place names, such as Alcazar, Santander, San Sebastian, Aragon, and Cadiz. He was told that BBC announcers and the Committee alike were aware of the position of the native stress, but deliberately followed traditional, Englished forms in announcements (R6 / 196 / 9).

However, in order to minimize the possibility of real 'bricks', Lindsay Wellington, the Director of Programme Planning, appealed to announcers and newsreaders, similarly to Miss Henderson, to

redouble your efforts to verify the pronunciation of the proper names and words which confront you in News Bulletins. It seems that there has been a little bunch of mispronunciations recently which has drawn attention to human fallibility of announcers, e.g. Theiler, Eberle, Tollemache, Malaga, etc. I don't expect you automatically to know the pronunciation of every word you come across, but I do expect you to be sceptical of your own knowledge and to consult News Librarian or his card index in every case in which you are in any doubt at all. (31 July 1936; R6 / 196 / 9)

The second observation is that tendering out this consultancy work on foreign words and names attracted other experts and scholars who, neither contacted nor asked by the BBC, also wanted a piece of the cake. E. M. Gull of the China Association, for example, wrote to Stuart Hibbert on 11 June 1936 offering his services, having spent twenty years in China and speaking 'Northern Chinese', i.e. Mandarin. Gull was prompted to do so after having read 'a paragraph in the "Manchester Guardian" of the 10th that "A Chinese War is dreaded in the Announcement Department because of the peculiar names likely to be encountered"'. This offer was accepted by the News Librarian, who would draw up a list of the most important names that would be submitted to Gull as soon as possible (11 and 12 June 1936; R6 / 196 / 9).

Others, however, were not as lucky or successful as Gull. A letter from the Eastern Trading Co. to E. J. King-Bull, the Programme Presentation Expert, opens with the statement that 'since the B.B.C. has standardised the pronunciation of the English Language', its next achievement should be 'the correct pronunciation of Oriental Names, and Towns etc. (specially in the "News")'. The letter continues with the statement that the Eastern Trading Co. has at its 'service, an efficient Staff of Oriental University Graduates and our field of Service covers Indian, Persian and other Far Eastern languages.... we can always supply a native all-round expert on the spot, for a reasonable charge'. It then concludes: '[i]f you feel, we can render our humble service, we shall feel honoured to enter into further communication, in Person, or by post' (23 July 1936; R6 / 196 / 9). They were given short shrift: 'During the past few months we have been going into this question, in collaboration with the staff of the School of Oriental Studies', the reply says, 'which has been able to provide us with native forms, from which we derive anglicised forms suitable for use by Announcers' (31 July 1936; R6 / 196 / 9).

Similarly, a memo dated 17 October 1939 states that Sir Denison Ross, who 'is out of a job and has been trying to get one', had wanted to speak to the Director General, but was actually seen by the Deputy Director General. It turned out that Ross speculated about liaising 'between the Government and ourselves on the question of the correct pronunciation of the various place names and personal names that were cropping up in the news in connection with Turkey, Russia, etc.' Ross's offer was turned down politely. The memo then continues with the statement that, nevertheless, 'there is something, isn't there, in the point that Turkish residents in this country, for example, might get a little peeved if they heard us consistently pronouncing wrongly the name of one of their leading men?' (R6 / 196 / 11).

A third point is that, of course, the consultancy work was not limited to foreign place names only, although in the end it was just the foreign place names that found their way into *Broadcast English VI*. So, for example, a Miss Stanfield of Augener Ltd & Robert Cocks & Co. Music Publishers was contacted by Lloyd James 'in connection with a list of musicians whose nationalities you so kindly promised to try and discover for me a week or two ago'. Naturally this was in connection with the pronunciation of their names; their nationalities had to be established, so that 'correct' pronunciation could be recommended to BBC staff. 'If you are finding it difficult to track down some of them', Lloyd James wrote, 'please don't bother any further, as they are probably not very important, and the pronunciation could, in most cases, be ascertained by the announcers from the musicians themselves as the necessity arose.' Miss Stanfield replied that some of the names given to her by Lloyd James had indeed 'been difficult to trace, and some are a little dubious as not enough means of identification are given'. In spite of this, she hoped to have completed the majority by the next afternoon. Unfortunately, the actual list of names is not in the BBC files, but a BBC memo at least gives us an idea of the number of names involved: 'The list contained about 400 names', it records, 'and her job has been to ascertain from Augener's own records and from personal friends connected with the musical world, the nationality, and where possible, the usual pronunciation of the different names' (17 January 1936, 22 January 1936; R6 / 196 / 9).

Apart from regular and anticipated consultancy work, events of the day influenced the BBC's work on pronunciation. Besides the Mount Everest expedition and, connected to that, geographical and geological names (see Section 2.3), sporting events provide such an example. In June 1936, the News Librarian wrote to the Secretary of the Lawn Tennis Association to thank him for the help he gave 'with the pronunciation of foreign lawn tennis players last week', adding: 'If later on you are able to let us have the full list of Wimbledon players with the pronunciation approved by your friend at the Czechoslovak legation, we should be extremely grateful' (3 June 1936; R6 / 196 / 9). Interestingly, the 2002 football World Cup caused the BBC somewhat similar problems to those they faced in 1936 for the visiting Indian cricket team and the Czechoslovak tennis players. The BBC set up a special World Cup Pronunciation Unit to help football and sports commentators get the pronunciation right—not only for the names of players from around the world, but also for the place names of the various venues in Japan and South Korea (*The Times*, 14 January 2002; *Write-On*, BBC World Service, 17 February 2003, 18.45 GMT).

The evolution of a catalogue of words of doubtful pronunciation continued to shift away from words of common parlance towards foreign proper and place names. In addition, the services were targeted primarily at BBC announcers and newsreaders, and hence the role of the Advisory Committee on Spoken English continued to be marginalized.

NOTES

1. As a BBC internal memo records: 'There is a meeting of the Advisory Committee on Spoken English on Thursday next, September 20th, and Mr. Lloyd James has asked that the latest edition of Wyld's "History of Modern Colloquial English" should be available, and also Jespersen's "Essentials of English Grammar"' (14 September 1934; R6 / 196 / 6).
2. The name seems to have been agreed between Pearsall Smith and Rose Macaulay as 'the most convenient and non-committal' (letter Pearsall Smith to Miss Simond, 13 December 1935; R 6 / 196 / 8).
3. Although the letter and its enclosure erroneously talk about 'to listen in', the matter that caused concern in 1935 clearly was the parallel construction of the phrasal verb 'to listen in' for the activity of watching TV, namely 'to look in'. 'Listen in' and 'listener in' stirred some considerable debate in the 1920s (see Briggs 1995a: 222). Here is a letter from 1924 in favour of 'listener-in':

   > 'Listener' and 'Listener-in'.
   >
   > Dear Sir,—For some obscure reason the B.B.C. has taken a violent dislike to the term 'listener-in', although many of their own artists and quite 90 per cent. of wireless enthusiasts make use of it. To my mind, it expresses concisely what it is intended to convey. If one says, 'Did you "listen" last night?' in nine times out of ten the reply would be, 'To what?' But 'Did you "listen-in" last night' immediately suggests wireless. Yours faithfully, L.A.L.H., London N. (*Radio Times*, 20 June 1924)

   and another one, from 1927, that claims the correct term is in fact 'listener':

   > 'Listener' Has Come to Stay.
   >
   > Dear Sir,—The term 'listener-in' is undoubtedly an awkward one, and seems, as far as my observation goes, largely to have been

> dropped in favour of the fairly adequate word 'Listener'. In any case there is the great reluctance of the average person to use a coined word, unless it be of American origin.—J. H. Johnson, Bramhall, Cheshire (*Radio Times*, 16 September 1927)

4. Mary Somerville, by now the Director of School Broadcasting, followed up this decision with a memo to the Controller of Programmes: 'I should be grateful if we might know on what grounds you have rejected the proposal', she requested and then explained the reason why the broadcast appeal had been considered a sensible one:

   > The idea was that the first meeting of this sub-committee should discuss the words received as the result of the broadcast. The main Committee had in mind that a broadcast appeal of this kind might produce material otherwise inaccessible, such as a half-forgotten dialect term for 'looking at' or 'watching' a performance. It would inevitably produce a lot of nonsense, but in view of the unanimous feeling on the Committee that the B.B.C. was in a unique position to stimulate interest in the creation of the new words necessary for modern developments in Science, I personally would have been glad to see the experiment tried. (2 May 1935; R6 / 196 / 7)

   The handwritten reply by the Controller of Programmes at the bottom of the memo puts it all down to 'some misunderstanding'.
5. In another paragraph, Pearsall Smith not only claims that 'this exasperated dislike for new words of native origin is undoubtedly tending to weaken the creative powers of the language' but he also seems to know where to put the blame for some of the more recent loan-words in English: 'Such words, coming to us, as many of them come, from the gutter and the gutter-press, are tainted with the vulgarity of their origin; fastidious people dislike them because they dislike the people who use them; while the fact that so many have drifted across the Atlantic makes them offensive to the ears of linguistic patriots' (R6 / 196 / 8).
6. Interestingly, Lloyd James used the word *aeroplane* in an article which he published in 1936 in *The Magazine of the English Association* (p. 59; R6 / 196 / 9).
7. Although it is not always clear which meaning (or part of speech) Pearsall Smith had in mind for the 'fine old words' he wanted to revive, the following definitions from the *OED* (*sub verbo*) seem most likely to me: *thole*, n. (*obs. rare*): patience, forbearance, endurance; *thole*, v. (*north. dial.* or *arch.*): to be subjected or exposed to (something evil); to be afflicted with; to have to bear, suffer, undure [*sic*], undergo; *nesh*, a., n., and adv.

(now *regional*): soft in texture or consistency; in later use chiefly tender, succulent, juicy; in extended use: soft, not harsh or violent; lacking courage, spirit, or energy; timid, faint-hearted; lazy, negligent (now *Eng. regional*, chiefly *north. rare*); *nesh*, v. (*now regional*): to become soft; to make soft; to turn faint-hearted; to draw back; to back out; to lose one's nerve; *lew*, a. and n. (*now dial.*): warm, lukewarm tepid; sheltered from the sun; warmth, heat (*obs.* exc. *Sc.*); *lew*, v. (*obs.* exc. *dial.*): to make warm or tepid; to become warm; to shelter; *fash*, n. (*Sc.* and *north. dial.*): trouble, vexation; bother, inconvenience; also, something that gives trouble; *fash*, v. (chiefly *Sc.* and *north. dial.*): to afflict, annoy, trouble, vex; also, to give trouble to, bother, weary; to bother or trouble oneself; to take trouble; *douce*, a.: sweet, pleasant (a well-known epithet of France, from *Chanson de Roland* onwards); quiet, sober, steady, gently sedate; not light, flighty, or frivolous (*Sc.* and *north. dial.*); *douce*, v. (*obs. rare*): to sweeten; to soften, mollify, soothe.

8. Upon receiving the draft minutes of the Sub-Committee's meeting, Daniel Jones remarked: 'I am doubtful if recommendation (a) about Latin plurals was unanimous.... Personally I am not at all sure that formulas is an improvement on formulae' (1 March 1936; R6 / 196 / 9).
9. The *OED* (*sub verbo*) does list *novelet* and its variant forms ('now rare'), as well as *inflex*, though in the sense of a particle prefixed to a root to form a noun in the Bantu languages rather than as a blend of *inferiority complex*, but the Sub-Committee inventions *halcyon weather*, *ultra rays*, and *art-researcher* are absent. (Though of course there are *OED* entries for *halcyon* (noun and adjective) and a sub-entry for *halcyon days* (obs.); for *ultra-* (prefix), *ultra*, and *ultraviolet* (both: adjective and noun); and of course for *researcher* and *art*.) The combinations listed in the *OED* that come closest to the Sub-Committee's suggestion for an English equivalent of *Kunstforscher* are *art-critic* and *art-historian* (s.v. *art*, V.18). As for the German *Kunstforscher* itself, a Google search (27 April 2013) produced 592,000 hits, but the lexeme is listed neither in the *Duden* (2006) nor in the *Variantenwörterbuch des Deutschen* (2004), which suggests relatively low-frequency usage.
10. A letter from the Advisory Committee's Assistant Secretary, Miss Simond, to Pearsall Smith, dated 20 January 1936, asking him for his approval of a draft of the Sub-Committee minutes, contains an interesting remark: 'I should be grateful if you would make any corrections you think necessary. I am sure you will disagree with some of my definitions of non-existing words. I am afraid that in one or two cases I had not a very clear idea of what they meant myself' (R6 / 196 / 9).

11. As George Gordon, member of both the Main and Specialist Committees, observed after the meeting, Pearsall Smith would be deeply dissatisfied but had to be reined in (George Gordon to Lloyd James, 1 February 1937; R6 / 196 / 10).
12. Alexandra Palace was the location of the BBC's first television centre.
13. A draft version of Reith's letter has an interesting paragraph that was omitted in the actual letter as sent to Clark: 'With regard to both committees [i.e. the Main Advisory Committee on Spoken English and the Sub-Committee for the Invention of New Words], I wondered years ago whether it would not be better for it (or them) to establish themselves independently of the B.B.C., on the clear understanding, of course, that the B.B.C. would be likely to accept their guidelines' (16 February 1937; R6 / 196 / 10). Independent of the BBC, these bodies then would have been able to be much more prescriptive and definitive than was possible for the actual committees under the BBC Charter.
14. When Mr Butlin had 'returned the African cards with the pronunciation filled in', a memo states that 'his fee is now due'. But BBC internal communications did not always work smoothly, as an exchange between Programme Finance and the News Executive shows: 'Can you tell me what the ten guineas paid to R. Butlin is. I have absolutely no knowledge of the man or the occasion.' 'There are a few of these chaps being engaged to advise on pronunciation of foreign names...They appear to be charges closely connected with news' (BBC internal circulating memos, 31 January 1936, 26 and 28 February 1936; R6 / 196 / 9).

Chapter 5
The End

During the lifetime of the Advisory Committee on Spoken English and its Permanent Specialist Sub-Committee from 1926 to 1939, it became increasingly clear that standardizing spoken English is impossible. Owing to the Committee's composition and self-imposed role as the guardian of 'properly' spoken English, in effect Received Pronunciation (RP), from the outset it tried to reach far beyond its remit of advising and guiding BBC announcers. This was particularly so when it came to equally valid pronunciations, which effectively had to be outlawed in order not to put at risk the *raison d'être* of the Committee. While the BBC fuelled and took credit for the publicity about their recommended pronunciations published in the *Radio Times*, it became apparent that prescriptive notions were incompatible with the BBC's charter. Thus, routine publication of their recommendations was suspended and the Committee was disbanded at the outbreak of the Second World War. Its legacy with regard to the pronunciation of proper and geographical names, however, lives on and will be dealt with in Chapter 6.

Dictating to the Mob. First edition. Jürg R. Schwyter

5.1 Majority voting, 'alternative pronunciations', and the end of routine publication in the *Radio Times*

Shaw was first to express dissatisfaction with the routine publication of the Committee's findings in the *Radio Times*. A day after the third meeting of the reconstituted Full Committee on 28 November 1935—a meeting which must have been little less than disastrous—Shaw wrote to Reith as a matter of urgency:

> After yesterday's meeting of the new Committee, which was an aggravated repetition of the previous one, I must advise the Corporation to reconsider its practice of publishing lists of pronunciations certified as standard on the strength of majority decision by the Committee.
>
> Here we have 20 persons chosen as representative presentable speakers to determine polite usage. Obviously only decisions either unanimous or very nearly so could justify the Corporation in declaring that one single usage is standard.
>
> Well, yesterday, decision after decision was carried by 8 to 7, 9 to 8, 10 to 9, and in three cases by the casting vote of the chairman, a superannuated Irishman in his eightieth year. No unqualified instruction to an announcer, much less to the public at large, could properly be based on such divided voting. The utmost that could be done would be to give two (sometimes three) pronunciations as equally passable.
>
> I suggest that when the Corporation discusses this result of the new Committee's experience . . . the publication of the lists is quite uncalled for. It always has been uncalled for; but it was a talking point of some interest in the infancy of the B.B.C., whereas now it is only a laughing matter with the laugh against the Corporation. (R6 / 196 / 8)

The old problems of alternative pronunciations, even within RP, and majority voting simply could not be solved; and public consultation and publication had become little more than sources of ridicule and embarrassment for the BBC.[1] Such criticism coming from the Committee's Chairman had to be taken seriously; it was, and this consequently caused a flurry of frantic activity within the BBC.

First, Reith immediately replied to Shaw, acknowledging that 'there is a good deal' in what he had said, but Reith also wanted to discuss the issue with a few other people before giving Shaw a final reply. He agreed, however, that 'in the meantime we will hold up the publication of the list of words agreed at the last meeting'. Shaw restated his previous arguments in a follow-up letter, and he also added yet another deficiency of the reconstituted Committee—its composition in terms of age and class:

> The new Committee, so far, is a ghastly failure. It should be reconstituted with an age limit of 30, and a few taxi drivers on it. The young people just WON'T pronounce like the old dons; and Jones and James, who are in touch with the coming race, are distracted by the conflict.
>
> And then, are we to dictate to the mob, or allow the mob to dictate to us?

Shaw ended his letter to Reith with a postscript: 'You must be present next time' (2 and 3 December 1935; R6 / 196 / 8).

In a way, Shaw's second letter is even more damaging than his first, as it questions the Committee's stated purpose 'to lay the foundations of a standard pronunciation which would eventually be common to most educated persons'. Not surprisingly, it was the author of *Pygmalion* who had a sense of linguistic reality—that there is class and age variation in the spoken language; that therefore pronunciation would be difficult to fix; and finally, that actually very few people spoke RP or even wanted to speak RP.[2] Shaw, it seems to me, therefore recognized that anything beyond advising announcers on 'place names and the like' was doomed to fail.

What actually happened at that ominous meeting on 28 November becomes a bit clearer in a memo written by Lindsay Wellington, the Director of Programme Planning, to the Controller of Programmes, a memo marked Private And Confidential. He wrote:

> The quarrels of experts in an atmosphere which often approached pandemonium, the way in which the Committee brushed on one side the preliminary investigations of Lloyd James and the Sub-committee, the unscientific way in which the personal prejudices of people like Dr. Costley-White were put forward by him as principles, and the assumption of the Chairman that in matters of pronunciation the Committee was the B.B.C., all struck me as an unfortunate example of the workings of Brain Trusts.

He then continued his memo with four questions and suggestions, all of which were, from the Committee's point of view, quite devastating. First, the original remit of the Committee to advise announcers on pronunciation was clearly not being met. In fact, he legitimately asks whether it would make sense for him 'to attend these meetings in future?' since they are an 'irksome waste of time'. Second, Wellington criticizes the composition of the Committee as the 'oddest mixture of experts and members of a more general public which evaded close definition'. He even questions whether members of the upper class such as Rose Macaulay, Lady Cynthia Asquith, and Lord David Cecil can 'give us the view of the normal educated person living in the 20th century'. Here we encounter the conflict of paternalistic and conservative 'amateur opinions' with those of twentieth-century pronunciations as described by linguists such as Daniel Jones and

Lloyd James, and by G. Bernard Shaw, who was able to capture the zeitgeist. Third, Wellington wanted the Committee to provide alternative pronunciations when desired: 'On Thursday, for instance, they agreed that the word "towards" could equally properly be pronounced "to-wards" or "tords", but they forced a decision that "to-wards" should be accepted, simply because they do not recommend alternative pronunciation. This seems to me the sort of ridiculous decision which makes an announcer's life difficult.' And fourth, Wellington insisted that the Committee recommends rather than prescribes. For example, 'findings such as "Armāda" do suggest that a commonsense judgment by the people [i.e. announcers] who have got to take responsibility for using these pronunciations in public might not come amiss' (3 December 1935; R6 / 196 / 8).

Note that in the minutes of this meeting it is laconically stated that the Committee upheld a number of their previous decisions, among them 'that ARMADA should be pronounced ARMÁYDĂ' (R6 / 201 / 2). This, however, glosses over the actual controversies that become apparent in the card index of words discussed, where *armada* is recorded on a yellow card, indicating words dealt with since the third edition of *Broadcast English I* (see Appendix IV):

ARMADA	armáydă
Date discussed	*Comments*
9.1.35	Deferred by Consultants for further inquiries
28.3.35	See results of same, all in favour of 'arma'adă'
28.11.35	Committee confirmed 'armáydă', in spite of criticism received (R6 / 199 / 1)

It is interesting that Shaw's recollection of the decision with respect to *towards* seems to differ from Wellington's. Shaw, writing to Lloyd James, said that 'the worst decision was twards for towards. It is not only customary but correct in point of emphasizing the significant syllable to say inwards, outwards, towards and forwards (this last has been bowled out by contrairy)' (6 December 1935; R6 / 196 / 8). The minutes of the 28 November meeting as well as the Consultants' report record *towards* under the (a) heading, signalling agreement was reached, and give TŌŌWÁRDS as 'recommended pronunciation' (R6 / 201 / 2). The card index also records the discussion of *toward*, albeit only for 9 June 1927 (on a blue card, used for deferred words or those not for publication) and recommends 'tŏwárd', adding the comments 'two syllables' and 'not for publication' (R6 / 199 / 2). Modified spelling, again, makes it difficult to reconstruct what precisely was discussed and decided. On the basis of Wellington's memo, the minutes, and the card index, it seems to me that the actual recommendation for the pronunciation of *toward* was as two syllables with the main stress on the second /tə'wɔːdz/, rather than the monosyllable /'tɔːdz/ (see section in preliminary matter for the phonetic alphabet). Shaw seems to have preferred the stress on the first syllable, as in the archaic predicative use of the adjective *toward* (see *OED* s.v.). One may wonder why no distinction was made between *toward* as a preposition and an adjective in the Advisory Committee's records.

Be that as it may, the mere fact that Shaw's and Wellington's reports seem to differ is indication enough of 'an atmosphere which often approached pandemonium', not to mention Wellington's claim that BBC staff on the Committee were not being listened to and that announcers' requirements with respect to pronunciation were not being met. The Committee was simply too upper-class, old-fashioned, out of touch, and unworldly. A BBC internal memo thus records 'that we should cease publication of lists', adding that 'concrete proposals with regard to the way in which the Committee should work in future' should be discussed with Lloyd James and Shaw, the Chairman (5 December 1935; R6 / 196 / 8).

Lloyd James's thoughts on the subject are best revealed in a long, six-page letter to Cecil Graves, the Controller of Programmes. Lloyd James also had strong words for the 28 November meeting, referring to it as 'rather a sorry affair . . . personally I could not help feeling somewhat ashamed, and found it difficult to persuade myself that I was entirely guiltless'. He said that, after giving the subject a great deal of thought, he had the following observation: 'I feel that the Committee fails. It fails not because it is wrongly constituted, but because it is called to perform a task for which it has no qualification:—to function in a department of knowledge in which it is largely incompetent, namely the spoken word' (9 December 1935; R6 / 196 / 8).

He attributed this failure to the fact that 'education has concerned itself mainly with the written word and with the literary language' so that, as a result, 'the level of knowledge, and consequently of relevant criticism, in all that pertains to speech is lamentably low'. So in his view, opinion on speech and pronunciation mainly 'rests upon prejudice'.[3] After a side-swipe at historical and comparative philology and the teaching of elocution and diction, he seemed to advocate a more sociolinguistic approach, as we would call it today:

It has always appeared to me that the requirements of the B.B.C. are best met by an inquiry into the present state of our spoken language—an inquiry that is long overdue.... But finding out the present state of our spoken language is not an easy matter, and the investigator who so far forgets the function of speech as to overlook its social implications is not likely to meet with much success: the proper study of the Spoken Word must wait until we have trained a generation of researchers, all equipped with the relevant physical, sociological, psychological and linguistic knowledge. In any event the B.B.C. is in a unique position to carry out the inquiry, and its responsibility to our spoken language makes it incumbent upon the Corporation to continue its labours. (9 December 1935; R6 / 196 /8)

Lloyd James recognized having been overtaken by sociolinguistic reality. It is most remarkable how much the above passage differs from the Advisory Committee's initial mission statements, where all emphasis was put on 'traditional usage' and 'stemming modern tendencies'. Lloyd James suggested a dramatic change of direction as the only way to ensure the Committee's survival, but had to admit that the composition of the present Committee would make that impossible. However, he added that he was 'so firmly persuaded of the fundamental rightness of our attitude to the subject, that I shall continue in it. I shall continue to carry out investigation and research into the present state of English speech so long as it pleases the Corporation to allow me to do so' (9 December 1935; R6 / 196 /8).

While the shift from traditional and upper-class RP pronunciations to 'the present state of our spoken language' was a necessary correction, Lloyd James recognized that the thorny issue of alternative pronunciations, as raised again in the Wellington memo, if accepted, would basically deprive the Committee of its *raison d'être*. He consequently refused to give any ground on that front, reminding Graves that 'the B.B.C. constituted the Committee expressly for the purpose of recommending one and only one pronunciation. The variants are known, as a rule, and to publish them would merely duplicate work already done in the reputable dictionaries' (9 December 1935; R6 / 196 / 8).

Wellington, however, who had a meeting with Lloyd James sometime in December or early January, had a slightly different agenda, as becomes apparent in his memo of 7 January 1936 to Graves. After asking 'whether the main Committee should be disbanded' and immediately rejecting the suggestion as 'inopportune', since 'the enlarged Committee has only existed for eighteen months or so, and . . . we ought probably make a determined effort to make it work properly before we write it down a failure', he proposed shifting the balance of power away from the Main Committee to the Specialist Consultants and the BBC:

> The procedure suggested is that the Specialist Committee should prepare a statement of reputable pronunciations of a given word, arranged in order of preference. The main Committee should be asked to comment on that order and suggest its revision if thought desirable. The final suggestion should be passed on to the B.B.C. which would, if it wishes, use the power of veto implicit in the fact that the Committees are asked to make 'recommendations to announcers regarding certain words of doubtful pronunciation'. This veto would mean in practice reference back to the Specialist Committee or to the B.B.C.'s adviser, Professor Lloyd James. The final recommendations could then be published showing alternative, reputable pronunciations, it being understood that announcers would adopt the first preference. (R6 / 196 / 9)

The memo was forwarded to Reith. Two days later he wrote a letter to Shaw which employed delaying tactics, explaining that 'there have been discussions amongst some of our senior people here with Lloyd James', but that no recommendations could be drawn up before the latter returned in April from his three-month lecturing tour in America.[4]

Reith and Lloyd James saw each other on 7 April, and a follow-up letter by Graves dated 14 April 1936 indicates the urgent need 'to discuss outstanding matters with regard to the Spoken English Committee'. But it was not until a meeting between Lloyd James, Miss Simond, and Wellington towards the end of June 1936 that, apparently, a compromise decision was reached with respect to the problem of alternative pronunciations and the Committee's publication activity. On the one hand, as we have already seen, the latest list of recommendations had not been published in the aftermath of Shaw's letter to Reith, in which, among other things, he recommended giving alternative pronunciations, particularly in cases where the voting had been close. The memo of the meeting states that Wellington 'strongly supported this suggestion and also urged that Announcers might be allowed to use whichever alternative they preferred'. On the other hand, Lloyd James realized that 'such a policy would in fact do away with the necessity for a Committee, since one of its chief aims had been to achieve some sort of uniformity in the pronunciation of Announcers'. He fully recognized that 'Mr. Shaw's suggestion was in direct contradiction to one of the oldest principles, that alternative pronunciations should not be recommended'.

Lloyd James then suggested a compromise, namely 'to publish alternative pronunciations but in a certain order of preference, the first recommended pronunciation being that which should be adopted by Announcers'. After some discussion, which is BBC speak for disagreement and, eventually, a lukewarm compromise, the Director of Programme Planning agreed with the proviso that 'more care should be exercised in choosing the list of words upon which the Committee should adjudicate', but he still felt very strongly that 'an Announcer should not be obliged to say "tŏwárds", for example, if his usual practice were to say "tords"'. Wellington, Lloyd James, and Simond decided that this new policy should be explained at the next meeting of the Main Committee through a written statement by Reith (28 June 1936; R6 / 196 / 9).

The history of Reith's statement is a telling one. The draft in the Advisory Committee files, which was written by Lloyd James, differs with respect to a very important point from Reith's actual statement which was read out by R. C. Norman, the Chairman of Governors, to the Main Committee on 29 January 1937. On the question of publishing alternative pronunciations, the draft reads:

> It has been suggested that possibly it is inadvisable to publish one agreed alternative, but rather to publish in each case such alternatives as are current, possibly in order of preference, with the general understanding that Announcers shall be instructed to use the first. If the Corporation should decide that this course is to be followed, then it becomes clear that the function which the first committee was called upon to perform—that is to choose one alternative only—will have ceased to exist; and that further reconstruction and modification of procedure may be necessary. (R6 / 196 / 9)

This paragraph was substituted by the following one in the actual statement, which was attached to the minutes in the Advisory Committee minute books; the new paragraph clearly indicates that Wellington got his way in terms of suspending routine publication as well as shifting the weight of decision-making away from the Main Committee to the Experts and the BBC:[5]

> The Corporation has given serious thought to this problem [majority votes and alternative pronunciations] and now proposes that, since the public persistently misunderstands its motive in publishing a list of pronunciations recommended for the use of Announcers, it should no longer necessarily publish them in the 'Radio Times' and in the daily Press as a matter of routine. Acceptance of this proposal would involve a slight change of procedure, whereby the report of the smaller Committee, together with the main Committee's comments on it, would be passed to the Corporation by the Secretary. The Corporation would then give private instruction to Announcers in the light of the advice contained in these reports. The Corporation hopes that it may have the Committee's assistance in the future as it has in the past. (R6 / 201 / 2)

The problem of announcers' needs not really being met by the existing Committee system was aired in a host of documents, some by Wellington, dating from the autumn of 1936. A five-page memo of unknown provenance observes that '[n]o Committee system can be adequate to the day-to-day needs of Announcers'. More to the point, the announcer, when 'faced with a word whose pronunciation is in doubt, needs guidance at extremely short notice—at most a matter of hours, sometimes of minutes'. It goes on to say that '[s]uch guidance can only be given by a competent consultant, attached to the B.B.C. staff and therefore on the spot'. It was recognized that such a linguistically competent consultant needed executive powers, powers to advise, and the freedom to consult other language experts. The Advisory Committee would only review the consultant's work two or three times per year.[6] The obvious candidate for the task was Lloyd James. And another anonymous memo states that, while the BBC ascribed 'considerable importance to this question of the English language', the anticipated remuneration in excess of £1,000 a year was perceived to be a luxury, which required careful deliberation (R6 / 196 / 9).

Not surprisingly, Lloyd James's work was paralysed by the uncertainty. In December 1936, he asked 'what the future procedure will be with regard to the working of the Committee', so that he and Miss Simond could prepare for the January meeting. In particular, he wanted clarification on three points. First, as 'there will be no further publication of lists of pronunciations in the Daily Press or in the B.B.C. Press', he needed to know whether the intention was to carry on publishing further editions of *Broadcast English I*. Secondly, he asked whether alternative pronunciations were to be considered or not. If so, 'consultant members at their last meeting took notice of alternatives, and several are contained in their last Report, which is to be considered at the next meeting'. And finally, he wanted to know whether the two booklets now in preparation on the pronunciation of foreign and English personal names would still be published in the *Broadcast English* series. Wellington replied coldly and factually:

(a) No publications, but booklets to be printed for private circulation within the Corporation.

(b) Alternative pronunciations not to be considered. The suggestion to consider them was, as I remember it, a device to mitigate criticism of the published lists and is no longer necessary if publication is to cease.

(c) The two booklets should go forward with the object of being printed for private circulation (see a.)

He added that Lloyd James's memorandum 'did in fact form the basis of the draft which has gone to Shaw' but added, ominously as we saw, that 'it was altered in the sense of conveying decisions rather than inviting discussion in Committee' (11 and 15 December 1936; R6 / 196 / 9).

Indeed, Reith wrote to Shaw on 4 December 1936 that he was now 'able to answer definitely the points you raised in your letter to me in November of last year'. He enclosed a draft of the statement and invited Shaw's comments—which he received one and a half months later. Shaw called the draft statement 'admirable', but then raised a procedural question as to what would happen after the statement had been read out: 'I shall have to invite the meeting to discuss it; and they will talk all over the place until the discussion is adjourned to leave time for the ordinary business.' But more importantly, he raised a fundamental question—and an observation that reflects the hard linguistic lessons learned by the Committee over the years:

> Have the Governors made up their minds whether it is worth while going on with the Committee—whether its value as window dressing is worth its refreshments and travelling expenses and the time the staff has to waste on it? Except as window dressing the big Committee has reduced itself to absurdity: their discussions can have no value unless they are unanimous or very nearly so; but they usually divide 50–50 or thereabouts, and do not even agree with themselves; for when the consultant members make a recommendation they as often as not vote against it when it comes up at the full committee. *All that they have established is that there is no standard pronunciation of the English language*, and that if an announcer can produce a general impression that he is a gentleman he can pronounce as he pleases. If they are in doubt there are the pronouncing dictionaries, which are more authoritative than we can pretend to be. Daniel Jones is publishing a new one next month. (21 January 1937; R6 / 196 / 10; my emphasis)

Importantly, Shaw implies—in his own inimitable style—that there is no 'incorrect' or 'correct' pronunciation of the English language; spoken English mirrors dialects and accents, including RP, and the interplay of class, race, gender, and nationality.

Reith naturally was glad to know that Shaw agreed with the draft statement. He wrote to Shaw that the BBC was prepared to follow Shaw's initial suggestion to stop publishing recommendations, but, he added, 'we do not care to force the issue against the wishes of the Committee. As regards procedure, therefore, we shall do as you suggest and ask the Committee to discuss our proposal to cease publication, postponing decision until the next meeting, if that discussion looks like being protracted, but hoping that this will not be necessary.' As for the Committee's survival, Reith outlined the BBC's position as follows: 'So far as the Corporation is concerned there is no question of disbanding the Committee' (26 January 1937; R6 / 196 / 10).

All this activity, consultation, drafting, and re-drafting finally culminated in the fourth meeting of the reconstituted Committee on 29 January 1937. The minutes record that Norman, the Chairman of Governors, opened his statement by 'outlining the history of the Committee and suggesting that the time had come for a change of policy'. It continued that, although not all publication of the Committee's research results should be abandoned ('He had no hesitation in saying that the Governors would agree to the publication of such booklets as "Broadcast English VI"—the booklet dealing with the pronunciation of foreign place names—which was before the Committee'), 'publication in the daily Press as a matter of regular routine should be suspended'. A copy of the actual four-page statement, attached to the minutes, is more explicit and explains why this decision had been reached. It reads:

the reason that led the Corporation in 1926 to seek advice was first and foremost their desire to give authoritative rulings to Announcers on words of doubtful pronunciation, and particularly on those for which alternatives existed. The use of different alternative pronunciations by different Announcers was in the early days the cause of much public criticism, and listeners, who were naturally not familiar with the intricacies of English pronunciation, constantly sought advice as to which was the 'right' pronunciation of this word or that. The Corporation formed the view that it was advisable to ensure, as far as possible, that all Announcers should use one agreed alternative, not so much because greater merit might attach to that alternative as merely that there should be uniformity of practice. It was repeatedly stated, in the public Press, in Corporation publications, and in the first publication of the Committee itself, 'Broadcast English I', that these recommendations were for the benefit of the Announcers alone, that no special merit attached to the alternative selected, and that it was not the intention of the Corporation to endeavour to impose its views on pronunciation upon the public.

This is obviously a palliated account (see, for example, Sections 2.2 and 2.3), mitigated with the benefit of hindsight, particularly with respect to some very controversial decisions, such as *garage* or *ski* or *margarine*, which 'were so violently criticised in the Press when they were publicly announced, that they were withdrawn'. One could also ask why, if the sole purpose of the Committee had been to achieve consistency among announcers—surely a BBC-internal role—were decisions subsequently published in the first place, not just in *Broadcast English I* but also in the press? The blunt facts are that, as we have already seen (Chapter 2), one of the early intentions of the Committee was to *standardize*, to *fix* the pronunciation of (educated Southern) English; in that they failed, and should have admitted so after more than ten years of trying. Instead, Norman's statement shifted the blame to the public, which 'persistently misunderstands' the work, purpose, and decision-making processes of the Committee. Therefore, routine publication of the Committee's findings in the *Radio Times* and daily papers was to stop; instead, the BBC would advise its announcers 'after considering the recommendations in the reports [i.e. the report by the Sub-committee, along with the Main Committee's comments]'.[7]

After Norman had delivered Reith's statement, according to the minutes 'the question of dealing with the serious differences of opinion as to which of two or more pronunciations was to be recommended, was debated at some length'. It was then agreed that

> the previous practice, whereby decisions were frequently arrived at by a very small majority, was undesirable. It was resolved:
>
> > that before a pronunciation could be recommended to the Corporation, a two-thirds majority of the full Committee was necessary. Where this majority was not attained the word in question should be referred back to the Consultant Members for further recommendation.

The minutes record laconically that, with a few emendations, 'the Committee adopted the B.B.C.'s statement'. One such modification was that the passage originally reading 'The Corporation... now proposes that, since the public persistently misunderstands its motive in publishing a list of pronunciations recommended for the use of Announcers, it should publish them no longer'. The final clause now read: 'it should no longer necessarily publish them in the "Radio Times" and in the daily Press as a matter of routine' (R6 / 201 / 2). This wording, basically, left the door open a little at least—as we shall see later on.

The meeting on 29 January 1937 still was not the end of the matter; there remained the issue of the equally controversial decision that recommended pronunciations had to have passed by a two-thirds majority. There was also a certain degree of confusion among Committee members as to which publication activities would continue and which would be stopped. As to the former, a memo from the Programmes Controller to Reith states that, after the meeting, Lloyd James had been instructed to 'sort out the whole business about the two-thirds majority' because 'every single word that was voted on should have been referred back to the specialists because it did not have a two-thirds majority' (1 February 1937; R6 / 196 / 10). As for the latter issue, Norman's statement must have perplexed the Committee members a great deal. George Gordon, for example, reflected on Norman's statement in a letter to Lloyd James where he advocated not abolishing publication in the press as, on balance, the topic was of such public interest that it would benefit the BBC (1 February 1937; R6 / 196 / 10). Lloyd James agreed that there was 'a great deal of misunderstanding at the meeting' but thought that 'the minutes are fairly clear—and I am afraid it is not unusual that the minutes are clearer than the events they record'. He then continued with his interpretation of Reith's statement, downplaying the end of the routine publication of recommendations and basically blaming Shaw:

> With regard to publication, there was never any idea in the minds of anyone in the Corporation, not in my mind, that publication by pamphlet should be discontinued. These decisions might very well be published in the 'Listener'. We agree with you that one of the most useful functions which the Committee serves leads up in fact to publication in pamphlet form. [The Corporation's] attitude was determined, largely if not entirely,

out of courtesy (perhaps mistaken) to the former Chairman, your predecessor.

As we saw, this was clearly not what the senior people within the BBC thought—quite the opposite: they felt that publication in the daily press should *definitely and irreversibly* stop, and any new booklets should primarily be circulated within the Corporation for the benefit of announcers. Nonetheless, Lloyd James told Gordon that 'we propose at the next meeting of the Committee to have this point raised specifically:—Would the Committee, in fact, like Press and "Radio Times" publication to ensue or not? We feel tolerably certain that the great majority of the Committee will be in favour of such regular publications' (11 February 1937; R6 / 196 / 10).[8] Gordon seemed satisfied, as he felt that Lloyd James's letter was very clear and complete (17 February 1937; R6 / 196 / 10). At the next meeting, the crucial phrase 'in pamphlet form' was deleted from a sentence that now read: 'They [Governors] would also consider the publication [deleted 'in pamphlet form'] of the recommended pronunciations of ordinary words, in "The Listener"' (7 December 1937; R6 / 201 / 2). The protracted discussion thus demonstrates the refusal by the Full Committee to recognize public exposure simply was a thing of the past.

Although a memo to Miss Simond indicated that 'Sanction has now been given for the compilation of books on foreign personal names and foreign expressions' and that 'Authorisation now exists for all publications contemplated at the moment', for which 'the services of Miss Henderson shall be retained on the present conditions' (18 June 1937; R6 / 196 / 10), the foreign personal names project was in fact stopped by the Deputy Director General in a memo addressed to Lloyd James and marked Private:

> I reported to the Board of Governors at their meeting yesterday the discussion which took place at the last Spoken English Advisory Committee, and they were of opinion that the Corporation could not accept the suggestion that you should undertake the publication of a standard work of reference on the pronunciation of foreign personal names, as this was outside the scope of the Corporation's work.

But he added that 'naturally they were anxious that the pamphlet which you have prepared in proof should be made available for the use of the announcers' (28 July 1938; R6 / 196 / 10). This, as we saw in Chapter 2, is precisely what happened.

The fourth meeting of the reconstituted Advisory Committee on Spoken English, which took place on 29 January 1937, was therefore to prove to be the beginning of the end. Although publication of the foreign place name pamphlet (*Broadcast English VI*, 1937) was approved by R. C. Norman, the Chairman of the Governors, at that very same meeting ('in view of the very extensive research that had been carried out'), and *Broadcast English VII*, which dealt with the pronunciation of British family names and titles, did appear in 1939, the Committee had its wings seriously clipped: the routine publication of its findings in the daily press was halted and, generally, the emphasis was moved away from a very public and visible role for the Committee to a BBC-internal function primarily for the benefit of the people behind the microphone. After almost eleven years, the BBC realized the futility of their attempt to standardize spoken English and RP; the best that could be hoped for was some sort of relative consistency among announcers and newsreaders, if not for words in common parlance, at least for place names and proper names.

5.2 Suspension

During the first half of 1939, everything had the appearance of perfect normality. In February, for example, one of the usual requests was sent to all the Committee members and regional directors 'for any proposed additions or alterations', as 'the next work to be undertaken by the Committee will be in connection of the publication of a Fourth Edition of Broadcast English No. I'. And some of the usual suggestions and corrections were sent back, such as the following one by Andrew Stewart, the Scottish Programme Director:

The final 'th' in 'tollbooth' is shown as 'smooth'. Surely the 'th' should be as in 'truth'. It certainly is in Scotland. Since I am writing on the theme it might be as well to mention one or two mispronunciations of Scottish place names in the News recently:—

1. Dálry, instead of Dalrý
2. Cromárty, instead of Crómarty
3. Whittingehame—the 'g' is soft
4. Viscount Tra I práin—the accent is on the second syllable and not as in a device for catching rain water. (R6 / 196 / 11)

Also a sign of normality was the regular re-surfacing of the alternative pronunciations issue. Wyld wrote to Lloyd James (18 February 1939) that he had always been of the opinion 'that variant pronunciations should be included, a view [he believed was] shared by all the members of the Consultants' Committee'. Lloyd James, once more, consulted widely (Orton apparently had 'a great deal of sympathy' with Wyld's point of view), but he replied to Wyld that the new Director General, Professor F. W. Ogilvie

(Reith had left the Corporation on 30 June 1938), had revisited this point, and had 'decided to continue the *existing* policy and not to publish alternative pronunciations' (R6 / 196 / 11).

The reason was the same as given before, namely 'that if we were to publish alternatives, then a Committee is not necessary'. Wyld accepted 'the decision as final', though of course regretted that his proposal had been turned down (18 February 1939; 13, 15, 21, 24 March 1939; R6 / 196 / 11).

The air of normality also included preparations for a Consultants' Meeting in Oxford on 3 July 1939, a request for words for discussion to be sent in (Kenneth Barnes suggested *cucümber* vs. *cücumber* as this had not been addressed before),[9] and Wyld's usual worries about money ('I understand that the question of an increase... is under consideration')[10] (R6 / 196 / 11).

But the political clouds over Europe darkened rapidly, and at the outbreak of war the Committee was suspended.[11] Lloyd James, however, 'made a strong request that the Advisory Committee on Spoken English should continue its work'. J. M. Rose-Troup, the Director of Programme Administration, informed Lloyd James of the Home Service Board's decision against continuation. This meant suspension for the duration of the war, and he added that the 'honoraria of the consultants has, of course, been paid in advance and covers the period up to 1st June next, but the honoraria will not be paid thereafter'. J. M. Rose-Troup did not show himself unappreciative, but he saw the obligation 'to subordinate many of our normal activities to the pressing requirements which war-time broadcasting makes upon the whole of our organisation' (18, 29 December 1939; R6 / 196 / 11).

The fees were duly paid,[12] and instructions were issued to 'take definitive steps to see that the specialist consultants, including Lloyd James, are wound up and their fees stopped'.

A memo marked Private and Confidential states: 'Advisory Committee on Spoken English: To be left dormant. Honoraria of specialist advisers to be suspended after May 1940.' Lloyd James said that he understood the situation, but wistfully added that he 'shall regard publication [of the 4th edition of *Broadcast English I*] merely as interrupted by the war, & hope the interruption will not be long'. Lloyd James finally suggested 'that the members of the committee be written to: and that the specialists be informed of your decision' (19 December 1939, 3 January 1940; R6 / 196 / 11).

On 22 February 1940, Ogilvie, the new Director General, wrote to the Specialist Consultants as well as to all the other members of the Main Committee. 'Owing to the pressure of war-time conditions', opens his short and rather sad letter, which continues:

> it has been found necessary to curtail many of our ordinary activities, and I am writing to say that, after most careful consideration, we feel that the meetings of the Advisory Committee on Spoken English must unhappily be suspended for the duration of the war.
>
> May I take this opportunity of thanking you most warmly for your services on this Committee? We look forward to the continuance of its very important work in happier times. (R6 / 196 / 11)

Over the next ten days or so the replies poured in: Daniel Jones thanked Ogilvie in particular for his 'very kind remarks about our work'; Greg Gordon expressed his full comprehension that committee work was not essential now and therefore would be discontinued during the war; Rose Macaulay found that 'it has been a very amusing & interesting committee to be on' and expressed her hope that 'it may revive in happier times'; Kenneth Barnes (Royal Academy of Dramatic Art) was also delighted to continue working for the Committee in the hopefully not too distant future. Harold Orton was not surprised at all at the cessation of the Committee's activities. He recognized that the Committee had not only served admirably well the internal purposes of the BBC, but importantly the BBC had also raised public awareness of the evolution of spoken language. The BBC, he added, had created a platform accessible to a very wide audience where spoken English was addressed from a linguistic point of view. Hence, he recommended the Committee should be continued after the war (R6 / 196 / 11).

Alas, all of them were to be proved wrong on both counts; not only would the war last a great deal longer than the three years that Churchill mentioned in his 'The First Month of War' speech on 1 October 1939 (Churchill 1974: 6160–4), but the Advisory Committee on Spoken English would never be reactivated again.

Four days later, Rose-Troup, the Director of Programming Administration, wrote to Consultant Members Jones, Wyld, and Orton quashing any hope of a quick re-activation of the Committee and, therefore, a continuation of their honoraria (16 February 1940; R6 / 196 / 11).

Wyld replied to Ogilvie that he 'rather feared that such would be your decision, & I quite understand it'. He then added:

> I have been wondering whether there is any way in which I could serve the B.B.C. in the meantime. I have much enjoyed my association with the Corporation, & should be very sorry to sever my connections altogether. Is there not some aspect of Broadcasting—Pronunciation or Accentuation—on which I could usefully report . . . each week, or each month as might be desired? (13 March 1940; R6 / 196 / 11)

Wyld was obviously worried about the loss of his income. A BBC internal memo sarcastically, but succinctly, remarks that 'Dr. Wyld only means... that he would like to do something in order to be able to draw an honorarium'. The reply that was sent to him speaks of the BBC's appreciation of his 'kind wish' to 'continue to help us with advice on pronunciation and accentuation'; however, 'this work is in the hands of Mr. Lloyd James, but should there be any need to extend it we shall not, of course, forget that we may call upon you' (19, 21 March 1940; R6 / 196 / 11).

The Sub-Committee on Words had not even been officially suspended but had died a natural death, as we saw in Chapter 4. In January 1943, Pearsall Smith asked Mary Somerville, who by then had been Director of School Broadcasting for thirteen years, when exactly his suggestions on various aspects of the English lexicon had been put before the Committee, as 'the Oxford Press wants to publish this plan or project of mine for the S.P.E. [Society for Pure English]'. Somerville found or remembered the date, 28 November 1935, and reminded him:

> A special sub-committee was set up to consider it, you remember, but we are not certain what happened to it. A lot of the records dealing with this period were lost in one of the blitzes. The Spoken English Committee itself was suspended for the duration of the war with a number of other committees, but I imagine that it will be revived afterwards. I, too, miss our pleasant meetings.

This was not to be. One of many reasons was that Lloyd James, the pivotal force behind the Committee and its activities, was 'not very well', as Somerville remarked in that same letter. 'His mind clears from time to time but I believe he is subjected to relapses.… The whole business was an appalling tragedy' (R6 / 196 / 11). Lloyd James, not only the Committee's Honorary Secretary but also its driving force, had suffered from 'depressive insanity' due to 'stress and anxieties of war' and committed suicide in 1943 (*ODNB* 2004–13).

It was obvious that as much as possible of the work carried out by the Advisory Committee should be safeguarded and continued to be made available to announcers and newsreaders. At an announcers' meeting in December 1939, attended by Lloyd James and Miss Miller, the Assistant Secretary, it was decided that all information on pronunciation—ranging from the reference libraries for Home and Empire Announcers to 'the more academic Committee work'—should be pooled together. The new scheme would thus have

> **1)** A central reference library of pronunciations (on the Fourth Floor) for the benefit of Home and Empire Announcers (and, where it can be of assistance to them, for foreign Announcers), containing as wide a range as possible of British, Empire and foreign personal and place names; names of naval craft, which would be obtained from the Admiralty; the Committee's recommendations on English words of doubtful pronunciation; the pronunciation of various musical terms; the pronunciation of song titles in other languages, etc. etc.
> **2)** A complete duplicate set of cards with all pronunciations necessary for News, in the Home News Library on the Fifth Floor, as at present.
> **3)** A similar duplicate set in the Empire News Room on the Second Floor. (BBC internal document, 21 December 1939; R6 / 196 / 11)

Lloyd James, until his death in 1943, and Daniel Jones remained as advisers to the BBC. But the day-to-day work was taken over by two Assistant Secretaries to the former Committee, both trained in phonetics at University College London and now carrying the newly created title of Pronunciation Assistants.

In the early 1940s, this 'gang of four' became known as the *BBC Pronunciation Research Unit*, whose brief it was to provide guidance to newsreaders and announcers on the pronunciation of place names and personal names. After the war, neither the Advisory Committee on Spoken English nor the Specialist Sub-committee were reactivated.

John Reith's original idea of fixing English pronunciation could not be realized. Although the early BBC announcers and newsreaders were from the upper class or upper middle class, had attended university, and spoke RP, it was soon realized that there were variations even within RP—as one would expect from a focused but not fixed accent. Even more relevant was the recognition that class, age, gender, and nationality were the primary factors that are the cause of variability of spoken language. Failure was predestined, as diversity was simply not represented in the Full Advisory Committee, even though the Specialist Sub-Committee, first and foremost Lloyd James, Daniel Jones, and G. Bernard Shaw, had recognized these sociolinguistic factors. In other words, the quest for a standard of English pronunciation was abandoned.

NOTES

1. Interestingly, two days before the meeting, W. W. Greg, representing the British Academy on the Committee, made the suggestion to keep a record of alternative pronunciations. In particular, he assumed that the public want to be informed about alternative pronunciations. The Committee should therefore first list the pronunciation recommended to the BBC's announcers; then, similarly to recommendations regarding place names, should follow alternative pronunciations (26 November 1935; R6 / 196 / 8).
2. Modern estimates are that somewhere around 3 to 5 per cent of the population speak RP (Trudgill 2002: 171–2).

3. An interesting observation is that almost every university in the country had a chair of English literature, but that there were only two chairs of phonetics, both in London. Lloyd James makes similar remarks in a paper entitled 'The Spoken Word', published in 1936 in *The Magazine of the English Association*, a paper whose ideas are very much based on his letter to Graves. 'It is towards the written word that the main burden of teaching has for centuries been directed.... [But] until we build up a tradition in Speech education that will raise the level of relevant criticism..., we shall...fail to contribute to the ideal now held before us—an enlightened democracy capable of expressing itself freely in speech' (R6 / 196 / 9). Leaving the pathos of the last sentence aside, Lloyd James made a valuable point; in fact, the grammatical differences between spoken and written Standard English are a source of confusion and misunderstanding even today (see e.g. Carter 1999 and Section 1.2)
4. Lloyd James wrote to Reith on board the *Aquitania* on his way back to Britain: 'At N.B.C. I gave three talks in their weekly Speech Programme, and gave an hour's talk to the Announcing & Talk Staff on the linguistic problems involved in Broadcasting. At C.B.C. I gave a special talk on the work of our Pronunciation Committee and stressed the importance of a similar committee for America.' The letter continues with a list of talks he gave in Boston and to the Rockefeller Fellows, 'twelve interviews to the press...three public lectures...attended 24 lunches and 26 dinners! I hope it has not all been in vain' (1 April 1936; R6 / 196 / 9).
5. Lloyd James's draft of the statement was sent by Miss Simond to Wellington, who added that Lloyd James 'would be grateful if you would amend this draft in any way you think necessary: he is not quite sure whether it expresses the case quite strongly enough' (28 September 1936; R6 / 196 / 9).
6. Another copy of the same document recommending the new procedure appears in R6 / 196 / 10, the files for 1937 and 1938, as part of the frantic flurry of correspondence, draft statements, etc. immediately before the 29 January 1937 meeting. In the R6 / 196 / 10 version, which shows corrections by hand, possibly by Reith himself, the words 'executive power to decide pronunciation' were replaced by 'power to advise'.
7. The Statement by the Chairman of Governors is printed in its entirety in Appendix III.
8. In a letter to Kenneth Clark, Reith equally downplayed the consequences of Norman's statement and claimed that 'surely the decision of the meeting left full liberty for publication, either in the press or in pamphlets, providing only for sensible flexibility of practice' (18 February 1937; R6 / 196 / 10).

9. Miss Miller (Assistant Secretary) to Kenneth Barnes (10 July 1939): 'Thank you for your letter of July 7th, suggesting the addition of "cucumber" to our list. Miss Simond, I am afraid, left the Committee last July [= 1938], at the same time as Miss Henderson, and I now combine the two rôles' (R 6 / 196 / 11).
10. Wyld was informed that an increase of £25 was granted and a cheque was sent to him.
11. For the BBC's wartime preparations, see Briggs 1995b: chapter VI.
12. A memo, dated 19 December 1939, states that 'we have paid fees in advance for one year from 1st June, 1939 until 30th May, 1940 to the following persons who form the Advisory Committee on Spoken English:—

Prof. A. Lloyd James	£ 105. 0. 0.
Prof. H. C. K. Wyld	131. 5. 0.
Prof. Daniel Jones	105. 0. 0.
Harold Orton	52.10. 0.

These cheques were sent on the 1st June, 1939' (R6 / 196 / 11).

Chapter 6
Legacies and Conclusion

The BBC Advisory Committee on Spoken English has a mixed legacy, both domestically (the Home Service) and internationally (Empire Broadcasting), as will be sketched out in this chapter. Its successor, the BBC Pronunciation Unit,[1] advises, and *only* advises, on personal and geographical names in a pragmatic and differentiated manner. As late as the 1980s, it was more prescriptive, although the BBC had abandoned the idea of delivering rulings on general vocabulary. The work of the Pronunciation Unit is related to the burgeoning of radio and TV stations that not only broadcast nationally but now also cater to local, target audiences; thus, local accents and a wide choice of vocabulary used in 'on-the-spot' reporting are now a common feature of broadcasts. Internationally, however, the BBC World Service is still perceived as presenting a 'model of spoken English'. But even there, stereotypes are being abandoned in favour of 'natural voices', and the use of a wide variety of second and foreign language accents is on the rise.

Despite its legacy, the BBC Advisory Committee on Spoken English was a failure. The Committee's work is thus a particularly

Dictating to the Mob. First edition. Jürg R. Schwyter

instructive example of the futility of attempting to standardize and regulate spoken language.

6.1 Legacy: The Home Service

At the outbreak of the Second World War, the Advisory Committee on Spoken English was formally suspended. Tellingly, it was not reactivated after the war ended in 1945. Instead, the BBC-internal Pronunciation Unit eventually emerged in the 1940s, with Daniel Jones as Chief Pronunciation Advisor, a role he kept until his death in 1967 (*ODNB* 2004–13). The Unit's much-reduced responsibility was, and still is, 'to give guidance to news-readers and announcers on the pronunciation of place and personal names' (McArthur 1992: 110).

Reflecting on the history of the BBC's language policy in general, Leitner (1979: 24) identified two periods, one from *c.*1924 to the early 1950s, which he describes as the period of 'strong conformity', and a second, since the early 1950s, one of 'limited variation'. Notably, during the latter years of the Second World War he identified a process of 'relativization of conformity', marking a departure from a strict pronunciation standard. Even in the 1970s and 1980s, the booklet *BBC Pronunciation Policy and Practice* (1974) had a stated purpose of encouraging conformity: 'This document is a guide to the pronunciation adopted in English language programs broadcast by the BBC. It is based on the work of the BBC Pronunciation Unit, [which] grew out of the Advisory Committee on Spoken English.' A telex from the BBC Pronunciation Unit in London was received by newsreaders throughout the country every day which was 'effectively the ruling on how to pronounce the difficult names in the day's news' (private communication, Jim Latham, News Editor,

BBC Radio Humberside, 7 April 1981). To illustrate this, on 3 April 1981 the telegram read:

JODI FOSTER	JOH'DI
HANS DIETRICH GENSCHER	HANSS' DEET'RIKH GEN'SH@R
DENG XIAOPING	DUNG' SHI-OW' PING'

. . .
' FOLLOWS STRESSED SYLLABLE(S)
@ INDETERMINATE VOWEL,
AS IN 'A', 'THE', VARIOUSLY SPELT A, E, O, U.

As far as personal and place names are concerned, the Unit's policy has basically covered two areas: names from English-speaking countries and those from other languages. To quote from *BBC Pronunciation: Policy and Practice* (1974: 10): 'For British personal names and titles, the BBC uses the pronunciation adopted by the individual concerned. For British place-names, the BBC follows local educated usage.' Note the phrase 'local educated usage'—a clear vestige of the Advisory Committee's 'country-vicar campaign' in the late 1920s. Country vicars at the time were perceived to be beacons of local knowledge and propriety. In particular, poorly educated people would consult and seek advice from them. The pre-war *Broadcast English* pamphlets have, of course, long been out of print, but in 1971 Oxford University Press published its 'Bible', the *BBC Pronouncing Dictionary of British Names* (ed. G. M. Miller; 2nd edition, enlarged, 1983). This work incorporates information from most of the earlier pamphlets. For foreign personal names, the BBC uses as close an approximation to the native pronunciation as possible. For foreign place-names the BBC uses an established anglicisation [e.g. *Geneva* rather than *Genève*]. Where none exists, the Pronunciation Unit makes a recommendation based on the native pronunciation [e.g. *Lausanne*]. (*BBC Pronunciation: Policy and Practice* 1974: 10)

Again, and I cannot stress this enough, this is very much in agreement with the Advisory Committee's 1926 guidelines.

How did this procedure work in the 1970s and 1980s? As mentioned, a list of current pronunciations of names, places, etc. likely to crop up in the news was telexed from the Pronunciation Unit on a daily basis to each BBC station. And for personal and place names in the UK there was, of course, the BBC 'Bible'. For local pronunciations—as a regional presenter from BBC North in Leeds put it (Brian Baines, private communication, 3 April 1981)—'we rely on local knowledge, information from the source of the story, or, as a last resort, an educated guess! We do try, of course, to be as accurate as possible. For a person's name we frequently contact them personally.'

Generally speaking, this system worked quite well, and, again, was first and foremost meant to achieve consistency rather than standardization. However, even today, after almost ninety years of guidelines on pronunciation, inconsistencies do, of course, occur (BBC announcers and newsreaders are, after all, only human). Here is a small list of examples:

Basle /bɑːl/—Basel /bɑːzl̩/ (both used in Sports Roundup, BBC World Service, 5 Oct. 1997, 9.45 GMT)

Montenegro /e/—/ɪ/ (both in Newsdesk; BBC World Service, 5 Oct. 1997, 10.00 GMT)

Scálfaro—Scalfáro (BBC World Service News, 10 Oct. 1997, 06.00 GMT)

Prodi: /o/—/au/ (BBC World News, BBC World TV, 10 Oct. 1997, 20.00 GMT)

Budapest /s/—/ʃ/ (BBC World News, BBC World TV, 10 Oct. 1997, 20.00 GMT).

But what about general English language use and pronunciation—the /r/ in all its forms, schwa /ə/, WH /hw/, and all those words in common parlance—*ski*, *garage*, *again*, *zoology*, and so on—that kept the pre-war Advisory Committee so busy? To quote again from *BBC Pronunciation: Policy and Practice* (1974), the BBC Pronunciation Unit

> normally does not step outside its role to lay down the law on the pronunciation of individual words from the general vocabulary stock; but occasionally, after pressure has been exerted from outside, it issues reminders about this or that 'desirable' [!] pronunciation. Some phoneticians might be inclined to consider even this as misguided. (pp. 6–7, my exclamation mark)

But what *was* expected of newsreaders and announcers in the 1970s and 1980s? What amount and type of pressure came from outside, and what exactly was 'desirable' pronunciation? First, newsreaders and announcers did not necessarily have to speak in what was referred to earlier as Standard Received Southern English. As we saw, this *had been* expected of them, at least at the southern stations, from the earliest days of the BBC until the mid-to-late 1950s; this changed quite suddenly, not least under the influence of Independent Television. (The advent of Independent Television was important: ITV was and is a great deal more populist and less stuffy than the 'Beeb'.) Since then, basically, some regional accents which are not too strong (or stigmatized) have become acceptable—and the public seem to go along with that. The key requirement is that the speaker is intelligible to all listeners; clarity, competence, and comprehensibility are by far the most important criteria. Consequently, complaints—or 'pressure from outside', as the Pronunciation Unit called it—are commonly received about the pronunciation of individual words rather than about accents in general (though complaints about accents do, of course, also come in).

Today, the BBC Pronunciation Unit consists of three full-time linguists, all of whom are academically trained phoneticians with extensive knowledge of modern languages (Sangster 2008: 252). Unlike the pre-war Advisory Committee, they do not come up with mandatory rulings on pronunciations, but instead research and merely *advise* BBC staff on words, names, or phrases from any language that may come up in broadcasts. To do this successfully, the Unit works within a clear set of policies. Catherine Sangster, a former member of the team of three linguists comprising the BBC's Pronunciation Unit, elucidates these:

- For place names in English-speaking countries, we recommend a standardized version of the local pronunciation.
- For place names in non-English-speaking countries, we usually also recommend a standardized version of the local pronunciation. However, if there is an established English form of a place name such as *Florence* or *Munich*, then we recommend this rather than the local form *Firenze* or *München* ... For place names which have sounds which would

cause difficulties of production or comprehension, we devise an anglicized form which is as close as possible to the native pronunciation.

- For people's names, we recommend the pronunciation that the individual concerned prefers. . . . In the case of personal names of people from non-English-speaking countries, as with place names, we consult native speakers and reference works, and devise an anglicized pronunciation which is as close as possible to the original.
- If people's names, place names or words are fictional and the intended language or etymology is unclear or itself fictional, we consult the author directly. If this is not possible, we talk to the agent or publisher or to serious fans. . . .
- When it comes to specialist vocabulary—medical, pharmacological, zoological, botanical, etc.—we consult published sources and expert informants.
- For words and phrases in languages other than English, we make recommendations based on our own linguistic knowledge, a wide range of reference works, and (in the case of living languages) consultation with native speakers and other experts. . . . (Sangster 2008: 252–3)

The Unit's findings and recommendations on pronunciations are then made available to BBC staff through an on-line pronunciation database, complete with speech synthesizer, which currently includes over 200,000 entries; typically, an entry 'shows the headword, the pronunciation written in BBC Modified Spelling (with keywords), a description, notes on the source of the pronunciation, an IPA transcription and a range of metadata' (Sangster 2008: 255–6).[2] The database is regularly updated whenever new pronunciations are researched, a process which results in roughly 50–100 new entries per week (Catherine Sangster, BBC Pronunciation Research Unit, 18 November 2004, private communication).

Besides a daily list of news-related items—'names, places and phrases which are likely to feature in the day's news broadcasts across the BBC's networks'—the Pronunciation Unit prepares 'themed lists for major sports events that the BBC is covering, such as Wimbledon, the World Cup, etc., and for major news and political events such as the general elections or the war in Iraq' (Sangster 2008: 259–60).

Roach (2009: 5) remarks with respect to the BBC's 'excellent Pronunciation Unit' that 'most people are not aware that it has no power to persuade broadcasters to use particular pronunciations: BBC broadcasters only use it on a voluntary basis.' The role of the present-day BBC Pronunciation Unit is solely to advise and recommend for the sake of (as far as this is achievable) accuracy and consistency, rather than to impose and prescribe in the name of a 'standard form of pronunciation'. In other words, only the Advisory Committee's work on personal and place names, British as well as foreign, survives into the twenty-first century. One final area that can be seen as a continuation of the Advisory Committee's *Broadcast English* pamphlets is the BBC Pronunciation Unit's occasional collaboration with Oxford University Press on the compilation of reference works that draw on the Unit's pronunciation database, such as Miller (1971), Pointon (1990), or Olausson and Sangster (2006) (Sangster 2008: 260).

The BBC also had to respond to the external pressures resulting from the dramatic changes of Britain's media landscape after 1945. The beginning of commercial television (ITV) in 1955, 'pirate' radio stations such as Radio Caroline, which started broadcasting in 1964,[3] and even the BBC's own re-launch of the Home Service as Radio Four in 1967, with the simultaneous introduction of Radio One, Two, and Three as well as its first local stations, were all major contributing factors. Although the

BBC held on to its policy of using RP well into the 1970s, particularly for reading the news on the national networks, the emergence of independent as well as local radio and TV stations provided additional pressure to eventually admit a larger variety of accents. A further important development in the 1970s was the introduction of new programme and reporting formats, ranging from the 'on-the-spot' reporter to a variety of phone-in programmes (see Leitner 1983; Hendy 2007: 70–3). This created a much greater sense of closeness, linguistic and otherwise, between broadcasters and their audiences. In the 1970s, the BBC thus hovered between what it saw as maintaining standards of language as well as content, on the one hand, and increasingly reflecting the voices and opinions of 'ordinary people', on the other.

Complaints about language were frequent. Particularly vocal was the BBC Radio Four audience, which 'included a great many people who had been listening to the BBC since the War, or earlier', so that to them 'any slip by the BBC was not just a fall from the glory days of Reith but easily regarded as an index of the nation's decline' (Hendy 2007: 88). Phone-in programmes could be a particularly tricky affair, not only with regard to *what* a particular caller said live on air but also *how*. Even among BBC staff, opinions on phone-in programmes were divided. For example, Martin Esslin, the BBC's Head of Radio Drama, described callers' views expressed in a 1974 edition of *Voice of the People* about Rhodesia as nothing more than 'a collection of untested and untestable old wives' tales' (Hendy 2007: 72).

The 'language problem' manifested itself on two levels. First, there was the issue of 'bad' language. Although the word *fuck*[4] was uttered on air for the first time in 1965, it took the BBC six years to produce a formal policy paper which stated that swear-words were acceptable only on artistic grounds (Hendy 2007:

101–17); today, the most offensive swearwords 'must be referred and approved by a senior editorial figure' (*BBC Editorial Guidelines* 2005: 81). Secondly and more importantly, there was the 'accent question', and the BBC also initially struggled to find a viable compromise about this issue. While non-RP accents were acceptable in drama and phone-ins, they were still not used for reading the news and presenting programmes. However, as Hendy (2007: 126) noted, on the one hand 'there was constant sniping from the growing number of BBC local station managers faced with commercial competitors who were busy adopting a colloquial—if rather mid-Atlantic—style of address', and on the other, there were 'those for whom "Received Pronunciation" was still the gold standard'. It was a double bind: either alienate the majority of the audience, particularly young listeners, by ignoring modern usages, or alienate those who still looked upon the BBC as the guardian of spoken English.

These debates continued throughout the 1970s and led in 1979 to the Burchfield Report after public complaints in *The Listener* by a well-known newsreader about widespread linguistic distortions from a perceived standard in the news. Burchfield reassured the nation that there was 'abundant evidence that the standard of spoken English broadcast on the BBC radio networks is in broad terms acceptable', mostly even 'pleasantly presented in a variety of styles, and frequently with excellent regional or modified standard accents'; the problem therefore lay more with 'those who express concern about the state of the English language', as they 'fail to recognise that more grievous or more fundamental changes to the language have occurred at various periods since it was first recorded' (Burchfield et al. 1979: 9). Burchfield's two co-authors, by contrast, were somewhat more critical: Denis Donoghue, an Irish literary critic, insisted that 'the BBC should be slow to enforce linguistic change', and Andrew Timothy, a BBC radio announcer, recommended 'regular and *continuing* critical listening by members of management staff' (Burchfield et al. 1979: 18, 23). A later pamphlet, *The Spoken Word: A BBC Guide* by Burchfield (1981), reminded broadcasters of some of the most frequent causes of complaint and made recommendations for, particularly, formal programmes. The guide consisted of three sections—pronunciation, vocabulary, and grammar.

In the pronunciation section, Burchfield 'assumed that the speaker uses Received Standard English in its 1980s form': 'The form of speech recommended is that of a person born and brought up in one of the Home Counties, educated at one of the established southern universities, and not yet so set in his ways that all linguistic change is regarded as unacceptable' (Burchfield 1981: 9). Paragraphs on various specific points follow, such as what is expected in 'formal presentation of the news or of other scripted speech', including admonitions such as: 'Avoid the intrusive *r*', 'Be careful not to garble words like *deteriorate*..., *government, library*..., *secretary*', and 'Avoid the use of reduced forms like "gunna, kinda, sorta, wanna"' (Burchfield 1981: 10–11). Then comes a list of 'preferred' pronunciations, such as:

acoustic	-coo- (*not* -cow-)
adults	stress on 1st syllable
government	1st n fully pronounced (*and never* guv-ment)
research	stress on 2nd syllable (noun and verb)
zoology	(zo-*ol*-ogy), 1st syllable with long o as in *zone*
	(Burchfield 1981: 11–16)

Burchfield further added: 'All pronunciation problems may be referred to the BBC Pronunciation Unit' (Burchfield 1981: 10).

With respect to vocabulary, Burchfield recommended the avoidance of clichés (such as *at the end of the day*, *at this moment in time*, *in this day and age*, *you name it*), as well as what he called 'modishness of diction' (for example, *affluent* instead of the preferred *rich*; *draconian* instead of the preferred *severe*, *harsh*, *cruel*; *gay* instead of the preferred *homosexual*; and *utilize* instead of the preferred *use*) (Burchfield 1981: 17–18). He added a list of individual words with their preferred usage, such as:

	Acceptable in formal broadcasts	***Avoid if possible***
aggravate	To make worse or more serious	To annoy
decimate	To destroy one tenth of	To destroy a large proportion of
hopefully	In a hopeful way	It is hoped (that); let us hope
pristine	Ancient, primitive, old and unspoilt	Fresh as if new
transpire	(Of information, etc.) leak out, to become known	To happen

(Burchfield 1981: 19–25)

The grammar section draws a threefold distinction in usage—unacceptable, informal only, and debatable; below is a small set of examples:

1. Unacceptable usages in any circumstances[5]

—*False concord*	*There's two* birds in the nest.
	Someone has left *their* umbrella behind.

—Failure to use oblique case of pronouns	He will give another chance to you and *I* (correctly *me*)
—Confusion of 'less' and 'fewer'	We need *less* workers.

2. Usages registered by listeners but permissible in informal English

—Use of 'like' as a conjunction	They didn't talk *like* other people talk (Martin Amis [source])
—Verbless sentences	*Still no letters* (Iris Murdoch [source])
—Emphasis on minor words, esp. indefinite and definite article	*A* 16-year-old boy . . . They are standing *by* their threat . . .

3. Debatable features: preferences provided

—Use of 'who' and 'whom'	Preference: 'who' and 'whom' should be carefully distinguished
—different/from/to/than	Preference: Use *different from* whenever possible
—split infinitive	Preference: Avoid split infinitives whenever possible but do not suffer undue remorse if a split infinitive is unavoidable for the natural and unambiguous completion of a sentence already begun. (Burchfield 1981: 32–6)[6]

Although throughout the 1980s the most frequent complaints to the BBC continued to be related to pronunciation, and to a lesser extent vocabulary and grammar, the decade saw two important developments: first, a kind of de-focusing of RP into 'modified

RP' or, as Crystal (2002: 65) suggests, into 'modified RPs, as in each case the kind of modification stems from a person's regional background', which obviously varies. With this, secondly, RP lost the pre-eminent position it had in the first half of the twentieth century and became only 'one among several accents used on the BBC... along with others which carry the unmistakable mark of regional origin' (Quirk et al. 1985: 22).

Nowadays, the BBC uses 'a wide range of accents, depending on the type of station and target audience': local stations might foster the local accents of the community or county to which they are broadcasting, while even more serious or highbrow stations such as BBC Radio Three or BBC Radio Four would use RP as well as educated Scottish, Northern Irish, and Welsh accents. In short: 'The trend is away from elitist speech on all British broadcasting networks and local stations towards an increased cherishing of the riches of local speech accents and dialects' (Herbert 1997: 19).

David Crystal (2012: 510) gives the example of Susan Rae who, in the early 1980s, had to give up her job as a newsreader because of widespread antagonism to her Scottish accent, 'but she was back reading the news on Radio 4 at the end of 2003. [This is because] the BBC opened their doors to regional speech partly as a reaction to the emergence of independent local radio and television stations.'

There is also a kind of hierarchical order within individual programmes with respect to accents: 'the main newsreaders... read in standard English, with a mainstream RP accent; while the accents of specialist reporters outside the studio "at the scene" are much less constrained and may sometimes be regionally marked...' (Thornborrow 2004: 67).

Over the last ninety years, the BBC has thus moved from the ideal of a single, 'fixed' standard accent on air to a plurality of accents; it has moved from a backward-looking model of pronunciation heavily influenced by spelling to accepting linguistic variation and change; and it has abandoned mandatory pronunciations of common words that have 'rival pronunciations'. The only aspect of early BBC pronunciation policy that has survived into the twenty-first century is the recommendations for proper names, though even for these the current Pronunciation Unit advises and no longer prescribes. Finally, as to the Reithian view of the BBC as a model of 'correctness', Richard Sambrook, the one-time Director of the BBC World Service and Global News, stated unequivocally: 'Being a guardian of the language is not a responsibility that I want to take upon my shoulders' (quoted by Thompson 2005: 13).

6.2 Legacy: Empire Broadcasting

Two very important developments in terms of English as used on the radio took place in the 1930s. The first was Empire Broadcasting.[7] In the late 1920s, other countries had already been using shortwave technology in order to keep in touch 'with outlying nationals' and ensure 'the world-wide presentation of the national viewpoint' (Briggs 1995b: 347), but the BBC only started its first regular transmissions on 19 December 1932. 'There would have been Empire broadcasting long before', Briggs (1995b: 343) observed, 'had it not been for technical and, even more important, financial limitations.' The former obstacle was overcome by building a new shortwave station at Daventry, utilizing a completely new concept that would allow for world-wide coverage:

It had two transmitters which could operate on eight wavelengths and numerous aerials—some directional and some omni-directional. The Empire was divided into five 'zones', each zone being served by directional aerials. Programmes were 'beamed' to Australia, India, South Africa, West Africa, and Canada, the centres of the five zones. The six omni-directional aerials were designed for transmitting special programmes which Empire listeners could receive at any hour in any part of the world. (Briggs 1995b: 353)

The second problem, the financing of the new service, was overcome by the BBC's agreement 'to carry the cost of Empire broadcasting', basically through the licence fee paid by British listeners (Briggs 1995b: 352).[8] Today, the UK domestic services and World Service (called the Empire Service before 1965) are largely financed through licence fees paid by British TV owners. The World Service had been funded by the Foreign and Commonwealth Office (FCO) from the Second World War until 1 April 2014 through grants-in-aid.

It is important to note that not only were British programmes broadcast to the Empire, but programmes produced overseas were also sent back to Britain, though to a rather modest degree at first. Following tours of the Empire by BBC representatives, the South African Broadcasting Company arranged an Empire-wide broadcast in March 1933 from Table Mountain at Cape Town. The broadcast was received in London 'by Post Office beam telephone service, electrically recorded and rebroadcast by the BBC to Canada and other parts of the Empire. The first programme from India to be treated in this way was broadcast in December 1933' (Briggs 1995b: 355–6).

Foreign language programmes were introduced gradually, beginning with Arabic broadcasts to the Middle East in January

1938, followed two months later by Spanish and Portuguese services for South America, and German, Italian, and French later in the same year as the clouds of war gathered over Europe (following the Munich Crisis, when Nazi Germany was permitted to annex Czechoslovakia's bordering territories, which were mainly inhabited by German speakers). However, in government circles and BBC-internally, 'South America was mentioned before the Middle East, certainly as a cover'; for it was primarily Middle Eastern audiences who were seen as 'a "vulnerable" target for Russian, German, and Italian propaganda—particularly Italian propaganda from the short-wave station at Bari' (Briggs 1995b: 371). 'By the end of 1940, the BBC was broadcasting in 34 languages.... By the time Germany was defeated in 1945, the BBC was broadcasting in 45 languages and was the biggest international broadcasting organisation in the world.' By 2006, the World Service had 163 million listeners, and it currently broadcasts in 27 languages. Reading through the timeline that was created to celebrate 75 years of Empire/World Service broadcasting, one major recurring theme stands out: various government reports that demand further cuts and/or a re-allocation of resources.[9]

The modern BBC World Service was born in May 1965. More emphasis was put on broadcasting to Asia and Africa, as well as helping newly independent countries set up their own broadcasting services (which were often modelled on the BBC). It was important to see foreign language broadcasts and those in English as complementary, because: '[b]y far the largest part of the BBC's world audience was to be found in countries where English was either the official language or one of the customary languages. There were 350 million people in the world who spoke English' (Briggs 1995c: 697).

In fact, as Crystal (2002: 241) makes clear, the 'proportion of native speakers of English to the total of world speakers of English has been steadily falling for sometime', so that 'for every one native speaker there are now three non-native speakers'. Graddol (1997: 46) also points out the importance of this vast group of listeners abroad:

> Until the 1990s, the BBC World Service was one of the few broadcasting institutions with worldwide reach. Its coverage today spans Europe, the Americas, Asia and the Pacific, Africa, the former USSR and South-west Asia. In 1996 to 1997 its weekly audience was 143 million listeners with the majority in Asia . . . , a presence supported by BBC English, offering teaching programmes and materials to many local broadcasters. The BBC World Service share is, however, a small part of a massive industry . . .

Although the BBC had been broadcasting English language teaching programmes since 1939, education was given a higher priority in the 1950s and 1960s, since English had been gaining a dominant role in business. Briggs remarked that 'Mueller's *The World's Living Languages* (1964) put the total number of people who had acquired English as a foreign language at 240 million, while Max Adler [in his *The Business Languages of the World*] estimated in 1965 that 54 per cent of the world's population used English as the first foreign language in business' (Briggs 1995c: 697).

In broader terms, too, English language broadcasting for listeners in other countries became 'another important area of influence [i.e. for the "march of Modern English"]'. Not only did the BBC Empire and World Services have a very large audience, but also since the Second World War the Voice of America has 'broadcast English-language programmes to audiences of millions, with the American English services developing the most far-reaching network of stations throughout the world' (Davies 2005: 36).[10]

Hamish Norbrook, who has worked for the BBC's English Language Teaching Unit for more than thirty years, has illustrated in a recent article (Norbrook 2008) how the news, arguably the most important output of any international broadcaster, can be used successfully to help non-native speakers maintain or improve their level of English. News bulletins are particularly suitable for this task because of their structural predictability and controlled language use. The BBC undertook various initiatives to this end. In the 1960s, for example, its English language teaching unit transmitted news bulletins at the speed of dictation (Norbrook 2008: 271). Later on in 1989, modelled largely on the Voice of America's News in Special English, the BBC World Service began its Slow Speed News, a lexically and syntactically simplified version of the day's news read at approximately three-quarters of the normal speed.[11] Here is an example from the BBC World Service's 15.00 hours GMT bulletin on 16 September 1994:

Original format

1. Officials from North Korea and the United States have ended several days of talks in Germany with North Koreans still refusing to bow to American pressure to buy nuclear reactors from South Korea.

2. Both sides described the talks as 'full and frank'.

3. The Americans are pressing North Korea to replace its existing reactors, because they produce plutonium which could be used for nuclear weapons.

4. The head of the North Korean delegation, Kim Jong U, said the United States would have to finance the changeover, but his country reserved the right to find its own suppliers. [95 words]

Slow News format

1. Officials from North Korea and the United States have ended several days of talks in Germany.
2. The North Korean officials still refuse to listen to American demands to buy nuclear reactors from South Korea.
3. Officials from both countries said that the talks were 'full and frank'.
4. The Americans are insisting that North Korea replace its existing nuclear reactors, because they produce plutonium which could be used for nuclear weapons.
5. The head of the North Korean delegation, Kim Jong U, said that the United States would have to finance the changeover, but that North Korea felt it should be allowed to find its own suppliers. [104 words] (Norbrook 2008: 272)

Various tests of these Slow News bulletins showed that, in addition to obvious lexical and syntactic simplifications, the reading out in full of certain abbreviations like GCHQ, the avoidance of metonymies like *Number 10*, the insertion of *that* to introduce complement clauses, and chunking ('not so much the length of pauses between sections, but where they were split up') all helped to improve listener comprehension (Norbrook 2008: 273–4).

One important audience can be found in the anglophone countries of Africa. Adekunle (1995: 64) has observed: 'It is an open secret that, in recent years, the BBC, the Voice of America and CNN broadcasts in English have become sources of daily news and of valuable information to thousands of Nigerians.' And Schmied (1991: 41) reports regular use of English on the radio for the following East African states: Zambia, Zimbabwe, Malawi, Uganda, Kenya, Seychelles, Somalia, Tanzania, and Ethiopia. More specifically, the language-teaching department of the

World Service, BBC English, has developed 'a variety of programmes on different subjects, in different formats and at different levels', which include, for example, programmes for teachers as well as programmes focusing on literature and comprehension skills; 'the aim is to enable learners to pursue their English studies independently and at no more cost than the price of batteries for their radios' (Norbrook and Ricketts 1995: 304).

In terms of 'accent of preference', even the BBC World Service has evolved radically over the last few years:

> women are now being used extensively; the male-voice stereotypes have changed to a lighter, more natural voice quality, giving in all a younger, more neutral accent and sound; and different accents are much more common, including Welsh, Scottish, Northern Irish, and the Indian subcontinent. (Herbert 1997: 20)

'Overseas', Thompson (2005: 13) states, 'it seems clear that the BBC is still regarded as the model of spoken English'; and he is seconded by McArthur (2012: 465), who says that 'by 1999 BBC-style English had kept much of the social gloss, including among admiring middle-class Americans'. Bell (1983: 29–31) discusses in some detail the function of a standard broadcast language in a variety of speech communities: in multilingual contexts (e.g. Amharic in Ethiopia), in diglossic situations (e.g. Standard German in German-speaking Switzerland), and in multidialectal societies (e.g. BBC English and Network English in Britain and the United States). He explains 'that broadcasting adopts the standard language because of its social prestige' but admits: 'It is less obvious why broadcast news then becomes identified as a standard by which the standard itself is measured' (Bell 1983: 37).

As we can see, the BBC World Service also adopts changes in pronunciation, albeit at a somewhat slower pace than the BBC's domestic services. Accents now reflect the diversity of ethnicity and gender—highly relevant, of course, for a service catering to a wide range of audiences across the world. But by assuming a didactic role as well, the BBC World Service is perceived as a model of spoken English and thus confers a kind of social prestige on the varieties of English used in its broadcasts.

6.3 Conclusion, or what came of it

What can we conclude about the BBC's Advisory Committee on Spoken English? The existence of the Committee may be viewed as a relic of a nineteenth-century attempt to establish a rigid and fixed standard of pronunciation. At first it followed a strict and dogmatic type of prescriptivism. The original intention was not only to achieve consistency among BBC announcers and newsreaders but also to educate the public through notions of what was—or was not—'good and correct English'; in short, to find and define the 'best' pronunciation, to fix and diffuse it, and thus create a uniform standard—modelled after (upper-class) RP. Herein lies the fundamental dilemma of a top-down, elitist approach to language versus language as an ever-changing, dynamic, and self-regulating system. One simply cannot prescribe how to pronounce 'correctly'.

This realization gradually helped the development of a 'listening BBC', which regarded its decisions on pronunciation as largely provisional until appropriate feedback from an ever-increasing circle of Committee members, advisers, and the public was received. Additionally, there was a slow but steady trend towards what could be called linguistic professionalization: the weight of decision-making clearly shifted towards the Specialist

Sub-Committee; alternative pronunciations were admitted and eventually deemed to be ‘equally good’; the International Phonetic Alphabet (IPA) was used routinely, though not consistently. For example, the Card Index (Appendix IV) featured Modified Spelling only, whereas the *Broadcast English* booklets feature both the IPA and Modified Spelling (starting with *Broadcast English II: English Place Names*). The dogmatic press releases giving the Committee’s rulings were stopped.

Was it all a failure then? Yes and no. Yes, in the sense that the Advisory Committee’s goals as set out in its early mission statements—to fix and thus standardize spoken English by finding the ‘best’, ‘most correct’ pronunciation of ‘doubtful words’ and then, through the BBC’s ‘powerful example, endeavour to stem modern tendencies to inaccurate and slurred speech’—simply could not be fulfilled; phonology, as Lesley Milroy (1999: 173) has observed, is ‘particularly resistant to standardisation’. To give just one example, that of unstressed vowels: the Advisory Committee could not stop ‘the loss of a post-tonic secondary stress in words such as *territory*, *adversary*, *ceremony*, with a consequent weakening of the vowel to /ə/ and its frequent elision’[12] (Gimson 1984: 47); though in 1981, as we saw, Burchfield still advised announcers to ‘be careful not to garble’ words like *library* or *secretary*; nor could it prevent the change from /ɪ/ to /ə/ in weak syllables, particularly after /l/ and /r/, as in *angrily* or *merrily* (Gimson 1994: 83, 99–100). Wells (1982: 296) lists *merrily* among various types of words ‘where RP speakers differ from one another, some using /ɪ/ and some using /ə/’. Twenty years on, Hughes, Trudgill, and Watt (2005: 48) wrote that ‘in general, younger people are more likely to have /ə/, upper-class speakers are more likely to have /ɪ/’. Language variation and change are undeniable facts, as is the focused (rather than fixed) nature of even a reference accent such as RP—something the Advisory Committee only gradually came to terms with. Trudgill (2002: 177) noted, for instance, that 'RP now admits certain types of /t/-glottaling[13] which were formerly associated with local accents only'.

The Committee's process of widening its membership in 1929 and 1934 also failed because, far from removing pressure on individual members to attend, this did little more than convert the Committee into a mere talking shop. The Onions affair certainly did not help, nor did the lack of a well-formulated mandate by the BBC for the Sub-Committee for the Invention of New Words. Unsurprisingly, the Sub-Committee, with missionary zeal, went far beyond their task to establish a lexicon related to television, and tried to reform and regulate the English lexicon as a whole. Corpus planning on this scale is, of course, highly problematic to begin with (one need think only of the *Académie française,* whose 'forays into corpus planning' Sue Wright (2004: 55) has described as 'largely unsuccessful'), but even more so when the planning body has no legal, educational, or regulatory mandate and is restricted to the spoken medium, as was the case with the BBC. By contrast, Phillipson (2003: 14–15) gives the example of Denmark, where a Language Board was created and its functions defined by an Act of Parliament. Now Danish state employees 'are expected to follow [the Board's] prescriptions in any official correspondence or documents'. Nothing, however, is said about spoken Danish or the Danish speech community at large which, most likely, would not have been affected at all. Any wider success that corpus planning policies may have had in the past was usually not due to the pronouncements of academies or language boards but 'has come about through trained social behaviour, particularly that instilled by the long and effective educational policy of the nineteenth century' (Ager 1996: 204). In Great Britain, the BBC's Advisory Committee only painfully and slowly recognized that its attempt at prescriptive linguistic legislation outside its Charter was oblivious and ignorant to actual language practice.

Furthermore, the sociology of the Advisory Committee, and particularly its Sub-Committee on the Invention of New Words, was riddled with notions of snobbery and propriety—hallmarks of an elitist and paternalistic view of the world, social class, and language. Inherent in the Committee's set-up was the initial failure of members to recognize language evolution and change. This became manifest in the tensions between linguists such as Lloyd James and Daniel Jones, and some of the very prescriptive and purist members such as Kenneth Clark and, particularly, Logan Pearsall Smith. The conservative members took the Advisory Committee's mandate to heart to counter 'the modern tendency of slovenly speech', especially as John Reith wanted the BBC not to broadcast 'lower class usage' such as Cockney (unless when heard in comedies) or the 'appalling travesties of vowel pronunciation'. The committees only slowly came to terms with a necessary shift from prescriptivism rooted in snobbery and 'old dons' attitudes' to a treatment of spoken language which was free of value judgements—that is, descriptive.

Which brings me to the final point, namely that in its early days, the BBC was deliberately vague about the role of the Advisory Committee on Spoken English, and with it the Specialist Sub-Committee and the Sub-Committee on Words, vis-à-vis the general public. Were these committees meant merely to ensure consistent usage amongst announcers and newsreaders, or were they supposed to act like a language academy and attempt to regulate the wider language and influence its users through publication of their decisions in the press and the *Broadcast English* series? This uncertainty was finally resolved by R. C. Norman, the BBC's Chairman from 1935 to 1939, who wanted the BBC to be more of a broadcaster and less an enforcer of language 'standards'. The BBC needed concrete and specific advice especially on the pronunciation of proper names and phrases, from any language, that their staff needed to say on air. Thus, the Reithian idea from the 1920s that the 'best' linguistic variants could be identified and a linguistic standard could be determined by the BBC was abandoned; regular publication of the committees' findings in the press was also halted. Instead, the BBC was only to 'give private instruction to announcers' (29 January 1937; R6 / 201 / 2).

However, the Advisory Committee was not a failure in three other meaningful senses. First, it played an important role in the emergence of a kind of 'broadcast English' or 'broadcast style' which—though allowing for some variability—nonetheless conveyed and still conveys a sense of objectivity and authority which reaches far beyond the UK, particularly when it comes to news broadcasts. The link between accent and certain stereotypes has been amply documented, with RP consistently scoring high on factors relating to competence and status such as intelligence, education, hard work, self-confidence, and ambition (Giles 1970 and 1971, cited in Wells 1982: 30). The other, darker, side of the coin is that non-RP speakers may be systematically disadvantaged, particularly so in professional and institutional contexts (e.g. job interviews, education, medical consultations, and the law) (Kalin 1982, quoted by Dixon et al. 2002: 162). In a recent matched-guise study,[14] Dixon et al. (2002: 162) found that a 'suspect' was 'rated as significantly more guilty when he employed a Birmingham rather than a standard [RP] accent'. The Advisory Committee's influence can be felt up to this day, most clearly when it comes to the generally 'correct', and therefore respectful, treatment of domestic as well as foreign place and personal names. Thus, the early and pioneering work of the BBC in defining a style appropriate for broadcasting may be seen as somewhat parallel to the influence of printing on the written language, though the analogy is, of course, only a superficial one and therefore should not be pushed too far.

Secondly, the Specialist Sub-Committee formed a cornerstone of the BBC's professionalization and led, after the Second World War, to the formation of the BBC Pronunciation Unit, staffed by trained phoneticians. Organizationally, the Specialist Sub-Committee comprising linguistics experts moved into a central role by filtering discussion before it reached the Main Committee and, importantly, by recommending pronunciations. Thus the Sub-Committee laid the groundwork for the general acceptability of *alternative* pronunciations; but it, too, had to learn not to concern itself with general parlance.

Finally, the Advisory Committee on Spoken English succeeded in raising awareness of language issues among the general population, as this early radio address from 1931 shows:

Dialects *not* ignorant English.
I hope that none of you fall into the vulgar error of looking on dialect as mispronounced and ignorant English; the real dialects of England [i.e. traditional local dialects as opposed to social dialects] are the foundations of our speech, and what we shall call Standard English is only one of them that has been adopted by the majority.—*From a talk by Miss Mary Kelly* (*Radio Times*, 14 August 1931)

True, every variation in pronunciation (or grammar, for that matter) triggered and still triggers up to this day a flood of letters by the 'language mavens', as Steven Pinker (1994: 370–403) has famously called them, but at the same time, the various discrepancies in pronunciation—be it between two newsreaders, or a newsreader's pronunciation and our own—has made us think more than ever before about notions such as 'standard', focused versus fixed varieties, RP, 'correctness', and written versus spoken English. And this, I believe, is the other lasting legacy of John Reith and his BBC Advisory Committee on Spoken English.

NOTES

1. Its full name is the BBC Pronunciation Research Unit.
2. The BBC Modified Spelling table is available to the public on: <bbc.co.uk/blogs/magazinemonitor/phonetics.doc> (last accessed on 11 February 2013) and in the preliminary matter of this book.
3. See <http://www.radiocaroline.co.uk/#history.html> (last accessed on 11 February 2013).
4. On 13 November 1965 Kenneth Tynan, a theatre critic and writer, used the word 'fuck' on the late-night television show *BBC-3* in connection with theatre plays: 'I doubt if there are very many rational people in this world to whom the word "fuck" is particularly diabolical or revolting or totally forbidden.'
5. False concord, as well as the confusion between *I* and *me,* were issues that had created a lot of anxiety as early as five or six decades ago. Here are two older letters from the *Radio Times*:

   A question of Grammar.

   Dear Sir,—I do not think the announcers of the B.B.C. will be perturbed by the attack on their English by 'D.G.T.' He says that band, orchestra, choir, etc., are singular, and that it is incorrect to say 'The band *are* going to play.' He is wrong. Band, orchestra, choir, and similar words are not singular nouns. They are known as collective nouns. . . . Yours, etc., A.E.H., Plumstead S.E. (*Radio Times*, 9 January 1925)

Grammarian Protests.
Please, couldn't they croon
'I can see you and me
In days that used to be'
instead of
'I can see you and I
As in the days gone by'?
Equally banal, I admit. But at least my version is grammatical!—
D. S. Petrie, Kirkcaldy. (*Radio Times*, 26 August 1938)

6. For some of the most common language complaints, past and present, see Crystal (1981), Zimmermann (1982), Crystal (2002: 59–63), Allen (2003: 8), and <http://www.bbc.co.uk/complaints/reports/> (last accessed on 11 February 2013).
7. English language broadcasting started in Canada, Australia, and New Zealand in the early 1920s, and the Indian Broadcasting Company was established in 1927 (Crystal 2003b: 96).
8. Reith's inauguration of the Empire Service on 19 December 1932 at 9.30 a.m. can be heard on the BBC World Service web-page, which also provides a convenient summary of the history of this global broadcaster from its beginnings to the present (<http://www.bbc.co.uk/worldservice/history/>, last accessed on 11 February 2013).
9. <http://www.bbc.co.uk/worldservice/history/story/2007/02/070122_html_40s.shtml> (last accessed on 11 February 2013).
10. For a background on the various domains covered—commerce, science, international and 'global English'—see Bailey (2012: 429–42).
11. This idea actually goes back to the Voice of America's launch in 1959 of Special English programmes, which still exist today. Special English has three characteristics: a core vocabulary of not more than 1,500 words, the use of simple sentences in the active voice, and a slower reading pace (<http://learningenglish.voanews.com>, last accessed on 11 February 2013).
12. That is, in addition to the main stressed syllable, there is a syllable with minor stress which is then either weakened to schwa /ə/, i.e. it becomes an unstressed vowel, or is lost completely; for example *adversary* can be pronounced /ˈadvəsərɪ/ or /ˈadvəsrɪ/.
13. That is, a glottal stop, produced by closing or narrowing the glottis.
14. The matched-guise technique obtains 'information about language attitudes.... The output of one person capable of speaking in two "guises" (authentically sounding alternative...dialects) is presented to listeners who rate the speech in terms of such scales as intellectual capability and social solidarity' (Crystal 1997: 235).

Appendix I
Members of the BBC Advisory Committee on Spoken English

(a) Original Advisory Committee on Spoken English

The July 1926 committee comprised the following six members including the Honorary Secretary (all information has been taken from the *Oxford Dictionary of National Biography* [*ODNB* 2004–13] unless stated otherwise):

Dr Robert Bridges: Born in 1844, an eminent poet and founding member of the Society for Pure English, he was appointed Poet Laureate in 1913, a position which he held until his death in 1930.

Mr Logan Pearsall Smith: A Philadelphian (1865–1946) who had spent most of his life in Britain as an English language and literary scholar, and was, together with Bridges, one of the founding members of the Society for Pure English.

Mr G. Bernard Shaw: Born in Dublin in 1856 and the winner of the Nobel Prize for Literature in 1925; he wrote nearly sixty plays, among them *Pygmalion*, and a host of essays and was active in journalism. He was a lifelong socialist and member of the Fabian Society.

Mr Daniel Jones: A phonetician at University College, London and most famous for his *English Pronouncing Dictionary* (1917), he worked for the Simplified Spelling Society and the International Phonetic Association. He studied the non-regional variety of educated British English which he termed 'Received Pronunciation'. In addition to the regular work at the BBC Committees ('full' and 'permanent specialist'), he also was, from 1942 to 1967, chief pronunciation adviser to the BBC.

Sir Johnston Forbes-Robertson: An actor and theatre manager (1853–1937), he was highly regarded in his time as a very fine actor and an impeccable speaker of Public School English or Received Pronunciation. He was also a moderately successful painter.

Mr A. [Arthur] Lloyd James: Born in 1884, he was a phonetician at the School of Oriental Studies, University of London. Trained in phonetics by Daniel Jones, he joined the BBC as a language adviser even before the Advisory Committee on Spoken English was set up in 1926, of which he became Honorary Secretary. Undoubtedly the driving force in the Committee, he published its findings for the BBC (*Broadcast English* booklets) and was also member of the Philological Society, the Modern Languages Association, and the International Phonetic Association. He committed suicide in 1943 because of the stress and anxiety of war.

For the BBC, **Sir John Reith** (1889–1971) was the first Director General and ultimately responsible for the BBC Advisory Committee on Spoken English. And **Mary Somerville**, 'a very clever and self-confident young lady', according to Reith (Briggs 1995a: 231), was the Committee's then Assistant Secretary and as such responsible for the everyday running of the Committee (correspondence, setting up meetings, etc.).

(b) Changes to the Advisory Committee on Spoken English and its structure

The changes in 1934 came in two important steps. First, a Permanent Specialist Sub-Committee (see also 'Naming Conventions' in the preliminary matter) was created whose paid members—Professors

Daniel Jones (see above) and Lloyd James (see above), Henry Cecil Kennedy Wyld, Merton Professor of English Language at Oxford University, and Mr Harold Orton, a dialectologist from King's College, Newcastle, and former pupil of Wyld (*ODNB* 2004–13)—would make recommendations before the word-lists were put before the Full Committee. An example of a list of recommendations can be seen in the facsimile of 20 September 1934 in Chapter 3 (Figure 8).

Secondly, after its reconstitution in 1934 and other smaller changes, the composition of the Advisory Committee on Spoken English, that is, the Full or 'Main' Committee, looked as follows by the winter of 1938: besides Lloyd James (still the Committee's Honorary Secretary), Daniel Jones, George Bernard Shaw, Logan Pearsall Smith, H. C. K. Wyld, and Harold Orton the membership consisted of[1]

Professor George Gordon (Chairman) [a literary scholar, President of Magdalen College, Oxford, and Vice-Chancellor of Oxford University];

The Lady Cynthia Asquith [writer of memoirs and diaries; admired at the time primarily for her 'unique blend of intelligence and playfulness', social background, and beauty; friendships with D. H. Lawrence, who depicted her in some of his works, and the playwright J. M. Barrie (*ODNB* 2004–13)];

The Lord David Cecil [a literary biographer and critic, former fellow of Wadham College, Oxford];

Sir Kenneth Clark [art historian, director of the National Gallery, and surveyor of the king's pictures];

Alistair Cooke [BBC Film Critic 1934–7, he was suggested by Lloyd James as he is 'a very brilliant man who did English at Cambridge, got a Commonwealth Fellowship and did work on Dramatic Criticism for three years at Harvard and Yale. He is an excellent phonetician, and very familiar with modern educated American usage' (Lloyd James to

Reith, 31 March 1935; R6 / 196 / 7); Cooke's weekly 'Letter from America' could be heard on the BBC until just before his death in March 2004];

Professor Julian S[orell] Huxley [zoologist, formerly professor of zoology at King's College, London; Secretary of the Zoological Society, popular science writer];

F[rank] L[aurence] Lucas [author and classical scholar, fellow of King's College, Cambridge];

P[ercy] H[ugh] B[everly] Lyon [Headmaster of Rugby School (*Who Was Who* 1991)];

Miss Rose Macaulay [novelist and essayist, Macaulay was also the author of *Catchwords and Claptrap* (1926), 'which reflected the pleasure she derived from the English language and her insistence on verbal precision' (*ODNB* 2004–13)];

Sir Edward Marsh (Representing Royal Society of Literature) [retired civil servant, who had closely worked with Winston Churchill in various Departments; patron of the arts, chairman of the Contemporary Art Society, and council member of the Royal Society of Literature];

Emeritus Professor Sir H[erbert] J[ohn] C[lifford] Grierson [literary critic and scholar, formerly Professor of English at the universities of Aberdeen and Edinburgh];

S[amuel] Ratcliffe [a journalist and lecturer, suggested by Shaw as he is 'very sensitive to shades of pronunciation, and he does a lot of lecturing in America and comes up against all the differences between spoken English and Spoken American' (19 June 1934; R6 / 196 / 5)];

Dr I[vor] A[rmstrong] Richards [lecturer in English at Cambridge University, later professor at Harvard, well known to linguists for his collaboration with C. K. Ogden on *The Meaning of Meaning* (1923) and, in the 1930s, on 'Basic English' (acronym for British American Scientific International Commercial)];

Dr W[alter] W[ilson] Greg (Representing British Academy) [independent literary scholar and biographer, fellow of the British Academy since 1928];

The Revd Canon H[arold] Costley-White (Representing English Association) [when nominated by the English Association, Costley-White was Headmaster of Westminster School; he later became Dean of Gloucester (*Who Was Who* 1979)];

Sir Kenneth R[alph] Barnes (Representing Royal Academy of Dramatic Art) [head of the Royal Academy of Dramatic Art, knighted in 1938 'at the insistence of George Bernard Shaw, a firm friend and generous benefactor' (*ODNB* 2004–13)]. (Memo, 31 October 1938; R6 / 196 / 10)

NOTE

1. All biographical information, unless stated otherwise, has been taken from the *Oxford Dictionary of National Biography* (*ODNB* 2004–13).

Appendix II
Minutes of the Reconstituted Advisory Committee on Spoken English, 20 September 1934

Parts of the First Meeting of the reconstituted Advisory Committee on Spoken English, 20 September 1934, include an Introductory by Colonel Dawnay (a), the Standing Orders (b), and, in Enclosure A, the history of the Advisory Committee on Spoken English by Lloyd James (c) (BBC Advisory Committee on Spoken English Minutes, Minutes; R6 / 201 / 2):

(a) Introductory

Colonel Dawnay, speaking on behalf of the Director-General, who was out of the country, welcomed the new members, outlining briefly the early history of the committee, and explaining the reasons that had led to the Corporation in 1934 to review the constitution and future procedure of the committee. The Corporation had decided that in view of the varied nature of the work involved, calling as it did for a very wide body of expert opinion, the original committee should be considerably expanded; that for members, academic experts of acknowledged standing in linguistic science, should be called Consultant Members; and that the Corporation should in future submit all words in the first instance to the Consultant Members. These members would prepare a report, having in mind the relevant considerations concerning past and present usage, making recommendations as to pronunciations to be adopted for the purposes of broadcasting. The Corporation would then submit this report to the full committee, asking them to make such recommendations as they thought fit.

The following had been invited by the B.B.C. to act as Consultant Members: Professor H. C. K. Wyld, Professor Daniel Jones, Professor Lloyd James and Mr. Harold Orton.

Colonel Dawnay expressed the sense of the Corporation's appreciation of the great services rendered by the Committee, and especially of their indebtedness to Mr. Bernard Shaw for acting as Chairman. He stated that Mr. Shaw had felt it his duty, upon the reconstruction of the committee, to offer to resign from the Chair, but that he had consented meanwhile to act as Chairman on consideration that a definite term should be set to the period for which he, or any subsequent Chairman, should hold office.

Mr. Bernard Shaw said that he was prepared to continue in office provided that the committee would agree to the inclusion in the standing orders of the provision that the chair should go to election after four meetings, the retiring Chairman being eligible for re-election once only.

(b) Standing orders

1. The Committee shall consist of a number of persons representative of many aspects of intellectual and artistic activity, together with certain consultant members who are recognised academic experts in phonetics, and one representative of each of the following associations:—
   1) The British Academy
   2) The Royal Society of Literature
   3) The English Association
   4) The Royal Academy of Dramatic Art.

2. The Committee shall meet not less than twice per annum, and a quorum shall consist of not less than seven members.

3. The Chair shall go to election after four meetings, the retiring Chairman being eligible for re-election once only.

4. The Honorary Secretary of the Committee shall be one of the consultant members.

5. The Honorary Secretary shall have the assistance of an Assistant Secretary, who shall be an employee of the B.B.C., responsible, on the one hand to the Committee through the Honorary Secretary, and on the other hand to the B.B.C., for all executive work arising from the Committee.

6. Certain members of the B.B.C. staff shall have the right to attend meetings of the Committee and to take part in discussions, but shall have no power to vote in divisions.

7. The B.B.C. shall submit the words to be discussed in the first instance to the consultant members, asking them to report as expert phoneticians on the pronunciation of each word. This report shall take past and present usage into consideration and may admit of accepted alternative pronunciations.

8. The B.B.C. shall submit the consultant members' report to the full Committee, which shall consider the pronunciations recommended therein in relation to broadcasting, and shall make recommendations as to the pronunciations to be adopted by the announcers of the Corporation.

9. Pronunciations recommended by the full Committee shall be published provisionally in the Press.

10. Such recommendations shall from time to time be revised in the light of correspondence or further evidence regarding modern usage.

11. The Committee shall authorise publication of booklets and reports dealing with all matters of pronunciation.

12. The B.B.C. shall reserve the right to exercise its discretion as to adopting the recommendations of the Committee.

13. Members of the Committee shall have the right to bring forward work for discussion or to make any proposals relevant to the function of the Committee.

(c) Enclosure A—Statement by Professor A. Lloyd James, Hon. Sec.

The history of the B.B.C. Advisory Committee on Spoken English is given in very brief outline in the Forewords to the three editions of Broadcast English I.

It may be desirable, at this stage of the Committee's history, to restate briefly some of the general principles laid down in the early days, mainly under the guidance of Mr. Bridges, the first chairman.

At its first meeting in July, 1926, it was decided that recommendations should be in three classes—

(1) Place Names
(2) Words that had not yet been encountered what Bridges called 'speech rub' (literary words, etc.)
(3) Words in common speech use.

It was decided that the Place Names required separate consideration; and that, with regard to the other two classes of words, it was advisable that the announcers should all be required to use a uniform pronunciation. The pronunciations recommended were to pay due regard to derivation and traditional usage.

The question of publishing alternative pronunciations was discussed at length in the early days, and it was generally agreed that nothing would be gained by so doing. It was pointed out that the dictionaries gave the alternatives, and that the function of the Committee was to advise the B.B.C. as to which alternative was to be preferred for the specific purpose of broadcasting. . . .

The question of representing pronunciation in print was considered, and it was decided to use the modified spelling system, with diacritical marks.

The Committee's recommendations were to be published under two heads:—

(i) Those definitely recommended for use by announcers.
(ii) Those only suggested, to be reviewed after the publication in the Press, and after further evidence concerning usage.

It was agreed that Latin words were to be pronounced according to the principles laid down by the Classical Association, except in the case of the long-established English pronunciations used in the Law Courts, etc.

Foreign place names were to be pronounced as far as possible according to the lists of the Royal Geographical Society.

At all meetings, the leading English and American dictionaries were consulted, every member being provided beforehand with the pronunciations recorded in all these dictionaries.

It has not proved expedient to act in accordance with all these principles, and there have been modifications. Southern announcers cannot treat the r̲ sound in the Northern manner, and very few English born speakers give to the unaccented vowels the flavour that Mr. Bridges recommended. But the B.B.C. very definitely concerns itself with checking ultra-modern tendencies in the language, and in carrying out the injunctions of the Committee with regard to the so-called 'purity' of English vowels.

The early recommendation to record pronunciations only in the modified spelling system proved unsatisfactory, and a strictly phonetic pronunciation (using the International Phonetic Alphabet) was adopted in addition. This was first used in Broadcast English II.

In 1930 the suggestion was made that certain eminent scholars and artists should be invited to act as Honorary Advisers with regard to words coming within the special sphere of their practice. This suggestion was adopted, but never put into practice.

In 1933 tentative steps were taken to set up cooperation with the U.S.A. and correspondence with two American scholars has taken place. The suggestion that corresponding committees in the Dominions would serve a useful purpose was made, but no action has been taken.

In 1934 the Committee was reconstituted as explained in the preface to the third edition of Broadcast English I.

This brief memorandum may serve to bring before the new members of the Committee some of the general considerations discussed in the early days. It need not in any way be regarded as a list of principles to be followed in the future. The committee dealing with questions of English pronunciation is an innovation in the history of our language, and consequently it has no precedents to guide it. The difference between such a Committee and a dictionary is hard to define. Possibly the only truth that has emerged in the course of the last ten years of broadcasting is that the dictionary is not enough.

Appendix III
Statement by the Chairman of Governors, BBC, to the Advisory Committee on Spoken English, 29 January 1937 (R6 / 201 / 2, pp. 42–5)

Statement by Chairman of Governors, B.B.C., to the Advisory Committee On Spoken English—January 29th, 1937

It is now more than ten years since the Corporation decided to seek advice on pronunciation of the English language, and to invite a small body of scholars to determine the pronunciation to be used by Announcers of the countless words the pronunciation of which was doubtful. The original committee was composed of Mr. Robert Bridges, by whom the idea of establishing such a Committee had been enthusiastically supported, Mr. Bernard Shaw, Mr. Logan Pearsall Smith, Sir Johnston Forbes Robertson, Professor Daniel Jones and Mr. Lloyd James; and later (in 1930) Professor Lascelles Abercrombie and Dr. C. T. Onions also joined the Committee. Mr. Bridges was the first Chairman, and the Corporation will always have cause to be grateful to him for his wise counsel in those early days. On his death in 1930 Mr. Shaw was unanimously elected to succeed him in the Chair, and it gives us great pleasure to express the high appreciation which the Corporation has of this service so willingly rendered by one so eminently fitted to render it.

We do not propose to review the history of the Committee in detail; but it is, however, necessary that the story be brought briefly up to date.

In 1934 the Corporation felt that the time had come for the Committee to be reconstituted to include a larger body of authoritative opinion over a wider range of scholarship. At the same time a revision of procedure was made, by which the preliminary research conducted before each meeting was entrusted to four specialists, who would submit the results of their enquiries, with further suggestions, to the larger Committee.

This enlarged Committee has been in existence now for two years, and has held four meetings. We welcome this opportunity of expressing to all of you the Corporation's gratitude for the valuable work you have done.

Now the reason that led the Corporation in 1926 to seek advice was first and foremost their desire to give authoritative rulings to Announcers on words of doubtful pronunciation, and particularly on those for which alternatives existed. The use of different alternative pronunciations by different Announcers was in the early days the cause of much public criticism, and listeners, who were naturally not familiar with the intricacies of English pronunciation, constantly sought advice as to which was the 'right' pronunciation of this word or that. The Corporation formed the view that it was advisable to ensure, as far as possible, that all Announcers should use one agreed alternative, not so much because greater merit might attach to that alternative as merely that there should be uniformity of practice. It was repeatedly stated, in the public Press, in Corporation publications, and in the first publication of the Committee itself, 'Broadcast English I', that these recommendations were for the benefit of the Announcers alone, that no special merit attached to the alternative selected, and that it was not the intention of the Corporation to endeavour to impose its view on pronunciation upon the public. These decisions were published, said the Corporation, in order that people might know that the pronunciation used by the Announcers had been approved by a body of scholars fully competent to collect evidence of usage and to make such recommendations.

In the early days the responsibility of collecting evidence rested with the Secretary: the Committee then discussed the evidence and made its decisions usually without very much difference of opinion. But even then, in the days of the small Committee, there were cases where it was almost impossible to agree on any one alternative, and the question had to be put to the vote. Some decisions, e.g. 'garage', 'Conduit' (St.), were so violently criticised in the Press when they were publicly announced, that they were withdrawn.

Nothing that the Corporation did could prevent the idea growing up that these recommendations were national injunctions rather than domestic regulations; and it became evident that the responsibility thrown upon the Committee by the public was far greater than that with which it had been invested by the Corporation.

It was the realisation of this fact that led to the expansion of the Committee in 1934, and to the reform of its procedure. The collection of evidence was entrusted to four experts, and the assessing of such evidence to a wider body of experienced scholars. But whatever have been the advantages of the new system, there has emerged one fact: it is that unanimity of opinion upon the choice of pronunciation for the purposes of broadcasting is no more easily attained under the new dispensation than under the old. Decisions have often to be arrived at by majority vote, even the casting vote of the Chairman having at times to be used. Moreover, many scholars have had to confess that, whatever their competence in other fields, the spoken word is a matter of human behaviour in which few have had that scientific training that alone makes possible calm and dispassionate judgments. The larger committee is naturally more swayed by diversity of opinion than the smaller committee, merely because it is more widely representative of current thought. The question arises, and has indeed been put very pertinently by the Chairman, as to how far the Corporation is entitled to publish as recommendations—in view of the importance attached to them by the public—the decisions that often hang upon a small majority vote. It is for this reason that the recommendations made at the last meeting have not yet been published.

The Corporation has given serious thought to this problem and now proposes that, since the public persistently misunderstands its motive in publishing a list of pronunciations recommended for the use of Announcers, it should no longer necessarily publish them in the 'Radio Times' and in the daily Press as a matter of routine. Acceptance of this proposal would involve a slight change of procedure, whereby the report of the smaller Committee, together with the main Committee's comments on it, would be passed to the Corporation by the Secretary. The Corporation would then give private instruction to the Announcers in the light of the advice contained in these reports. The Corporation hopes that it may have the Committee's assistance in the future as it has in the past.

The Corporation has also read with interest the minutes of the Sub-Committee appointed to make recommendations as to the framing of new words. It feels that it must define more closely the extent to which it can accept the advice of the Sub-Committee. Such advice will be sought by the Corporation when new words have to be found for its own purposes—as in the creation of vocabulary of television terms. The Sub-Committee, however, has recommended the introduction to the public of new words for general use (e.g. 'halcyon', 'stop-go'). This responsibility for modifying the English vocabulary is one which the Corporation feels it cannot accept.

Appendix IV
A Sub-set of Words Discussed by the BBC Advisory Committee on Spoken English

The sub-set of words comprises the words discussed for the 3rd edition of *Broadcast English I* in addition to words discussed since. The index with words discussed comes in two volumes: Spoken English Advisory Committee, Index of Words Discussed, Vol. 1 A–N, Vol. 2 O–Z and Index of Proper Names A–Z (R6 / 199 / 1 & 2). The words were written on colour-coded paper slips, namely—

- white: Ordinary words, included in the 3rd edition of *Broadcast English I*
- pink: Foreign words, included in 3rd edition of *Broadcast English I*
- yellow: Words discussed since 3rd edition of *Broadcast English I*
- blue: Deferred words, or NOT FOR PUBLICATION.

[A–N]

white	ALLY	(a) noun: ăllý (b) verb: ăllý
	Date discussed	Comments
	20.9.34	Added on recommendation of Broadcast English I
white	ALLIES	ălliés
	Date discussed	Comments
	5.7.26	'ălliés'

	20.9.34	Consultants asked for alterations to 'állies', recommendation not accepted
white	ALLIED Date discussed 10.7.30	ălliéd, but 'állied fórcĕs'
blue	AGAIN Date discussed 9.6.27	ăgáyn, this is ăgén Comments Not for publication The last syllable may rhyme with <u>rain</u> or with <u>then</u>. The Committee recommends the latter pronunciation
yellow	ADVERSE Date discussed 29.1.37	ádverse Comments Not published in 'Radio Times' etc.
white	ADULT Date discussed 9.6.27 20.9.34	(a) noun: áddult (b) adjective: áddult Comments Noun only Adjective added at recommendation of Consultants for third edition of Broadcast English I
white	ACOUSTIC Date discussed 5.7.26 20.9.34	ăcówstic Comments ăcóostic Added to 'ăcówstic'. (Consultants asked for reconsideration after collection of evidence on modern usage)

pink	A PRIORI	áy prī-ór-ī
	Date discussed	
	20.11.30	
yellow	AMEN	(a) Liturgical usage: aamén
		(b) Non-liturgical usage: aymén
	Date discussed	Comments
	28.11.35	Not published in 'Radio Times' etc.
white	AMATEUR	ámmăter
	Date discussed	Comments
	9.6.27	Last syllable rhymes with 'fur'
	20.9.34	Consultants asked for reconsideration after collection of evidence as to modern usage, but no alteration made
white	AUTOMOBILE	áwtomobeel
	Date discussed	Comments
	9.6.27	
pink	ATELIER	áttĕlliay
	Date discussed	Comments
	30.11.33	
blue	ASS	ass ('a' as in 'man')
	Date discussed	Comments
	25.7.29	Not for publication
		To rhyme with 'lăss'
yellow	ASIATIC	ayshiáttic
	Date discussed	Comments
	28.11.35	Not published in 'Radio Times' etc.
yellow	ARMADA	armáydă
	Date discussed	Comments

	9.1.35	Deferred by Consultants for further inquiries
	28.3.35	See result of same, all in favour of 'arma'adă'
	28.11.35	Committee confirmed 'armáydă', in spite of criticism received
yellow	BOYCOTT	(a) Verb: bóycŏt (b) Noun: bóycŏt
	Date discussed	Comments
	28.3.35	Consultants recommended 'bóycott' (verb and noun) but not accepted by Committee
yellow	BOER	bṓer
	Date discussed	Comments
	28.3.35	Consultants recommended 'báwer', but not accepted by Committee
white	BANAL	băna'al
	Date discussed	Comments
	2.6.27	Deferred. 'báynăl' recommended
	10.7.30	Still further deferred
	20.11.31	Decided 'băna'al'
pink	BUFFET	(a) blow: búffĕt (b) refreshment bar: bo͞offay
	Date discussed	Comments
	1.12.27	(a) blow: 'búffĕt' (b) refreshment bar: as in French
	20.9.34	(b) expanded to 'bo'offāy' on recommendation of Consultants
white	BROME-GRASS	brṓme-grass
	Date discussed	Comments

	22.6.34	Recommendation by Consultants: 'brōme'
	20.9.34	Altered to 'broo' by Committee
	Jan. 35	Altered to 'brōme' by Secretary for 3rd edition of Broadcast English I, after consultation with botanists
white	CELTIC	séltic
	Date discussed	Comments
	9.6.27	The pronunciation 'kéltic' is recommended for Wales
white	CASUALTY	cázzewăłty
	Date discussed	Comments
	9.6.27	not 'cázhewălty'
white	CAISSON	cáyssŏn
	Date discussed	Comments
	9.6.27	Cässo'on
	20.9.34	Altered to 'cáyssŏn' on recommendation of Consultants
white	CINEMA	sínnĕma
	Date discussed	Comments
	9.6.27	'sínnimaa'
	20.11.30	Altered to 'sínnĕmă'
white	CHIROPODY	kīróppŏdy
	Date discussed	Comments
	25.7.29	'kīróppŏdy'
	20.9.34	Consultants asked for recommendation but no alteration made
yellow	CHARABANC	shárrăbang
	Date discussed	Comments

	28.3.35	Consultants recommended 'shárră-bang' but Committee decided upon 'As in French'
	28.11.35	Recommendation reversed to 'shárrăbang' as result of criticism received
white	COMRADE	cómrăd
	Date discussed	Comments
	9.6.27	Recommended first syllable to rhyme with 'Tom', but deferred
	10.7.30	Finally recommended first syllable to rhyme with 'Tom'
yellow	CODIFY	cŏ́dify
	Date discussed	Comments
	29.1.37	Not published in 'Radio Times' etc. Consultant members suggested: 1. codify; 2. coddify. But asked for reference to lawyers for legal usage
white	CONTROVERSY	cóntrŏversy
	Date discussed	Comments
	9.6.27	
white	CONDUIT (tubing and London Street)	cúndit
	Date discussed	Comments
	19.1.33	Deferred for further inquiries
	30.11.33	'cóndewit'
	20.9.34	Altered to 'cúndit' (Consultants asked for reconsideration)
pink	CUL DE SAC	cŏ́ol-dĕ-sac
	Date discussed	Comments

	29.11.28	Preferably 'blind alley'
	20.9.34	Above comment to be omitted on recommendation of Consultants
blue	CROSS	
	Date discussed	Comments
	9.6.27	Not for publication This, with other words like 'off', 'frost', 'cough', and 'loss', is pronounced either with a short vowel as in 'boss', or with a long vowel as in 'all'. The Committee suggested the former pronunciation
white	DEMONETIZE	deemúnnĕtīze
	Date discussed	Comments
	20.9.34	Consultants recommended 'deemónnĕtīze', but not accepted
blue	DEFEATIST	
	Date discussed	Comments
	24.6.32	The Committee discussed this word but decided that the pronunciation was too obvious to adjudicate
pink	DEBRIS	dáybree
	Date discussed	Comments
	29.1.37	Gave rise to considerable discussion and referred to Consultant Members for final decision
	7.12.37	As below [i.e. dáybree]. Not printed in the 'Radio Times' etc.
blue	DIRECTIONAL	
	Date discussed	Comments

	24.6.32	Decided not to adjudicate upon this word, as the Committee could not come to an agreement
white	DIRECT	(a) Verb: dirréct (b) Adjective: dirréct
	Date discussed	Comments
	9.6.27	'Dirréct'
	20.9.34	Expanded to verb and adjective
blue	DRASTIC	drásstic
	Date discussed	Comments
	1.12.27	'Drass-' not 'draas-'. Published as such in the 2nd edition of Broadcast English I
	20.9.34	Omitted by Secretary from 3rd edition as being inconsistent with the Committee's policy
white	ELUDE	illéwde
	Date discussed	Comments
	9.6.27	'eeléwd'
	20.9.34	Altered by Secretary to 'illéwde'
blue	EITHER	īther, e'ether
	Date discussed	Comments
	9.6.27	Not for publication. Either pronunciation is correct
white	EXPIRATION	expīráyshŏn
	Date discussed	Comments
	1.12.27	Recommended vowel in 2nd syllable short. Deferred
	10.7.30	Recommended vowel in 2nd syllable long

yellow	FINANCIAL	finnánshăl
	Date discussed	Comments
	28.11.35	Not published in 'Radio Times' etc.
white	FINANCE	finnánce
	Date discussed	Comments
	8.11.26	
pink	FIANCÉ	as in French
	Date discussed	Comments
	20.11.31	As in French, but preferable 'engaged' or 'betrothed'
	20.9.34	Above remark omitted at suggestions of Consultants
blue	FEBRUARY	fébroŏăry
	Date discussed	Comments
	9.6.27	The first 'r' is often omitted (probably on the analogy of January). The Committee recommended the pronunciation of this 'r'. Deferred
	20.11.31	Decided not to adjudicate upon this word, as the alternative 'fébuăry' is definitely a mistake and not an alternative pronunciation
blue	FAULT	fawlt
	Date discussed	Comments
	9.6.27	Long vowel as in 'fall'. Published as such in the 1st and 2nd edition of Broadcast English I
	20.9.34	Omitted by Secretary from 3rd edition as being inconsistent with the Committee's policy

white	FASCIST	fásh-ist
	Date discussed	Comments
	19.1.33	
white	FASCISM	fásh-izm
	Date discussed	Comments
	19.1.33	
white	FUSELAGE	féwzĕlĕdge
	Date discussed	Comments
	17.1.30	'féwzĕlaazh' (French '-age') is the usage of the Air Ministry, but the man in the street, who is the majority, uses 'féwzĕlĕdge'
	20.9.34	Consultants asked for a reconsideration after collection of evidence as to modern usage, but no alteration made
yellow	FORMAT	fórmatt
	Date discussed	Comments
	28.11.35	Not published in 'Radio Times' etc. Consultant Members recommended 'fórmaa'
yellow	GOVERNMENT	gúvvernmĕnt
	Date discussed	Comments
	7.12.37	Not published in 'Radio Times' etc. The Consultant Members stated that the omission of the first 'n' was admissible
white	GIBBERISH	gíbberish
	Date discussed	Comments

	9.6.27	Recommended 'g' soft as in 'ginger'. Deferred
	10.7.30	'g' as in 'get'
white	HOTEL	hotél
	Date discussed	Comments
	9.6.27	'h' to be sounded
blue	HYSTERICS	
	Date discussed	Comments
	24.6.32	The mispronunciation 'histírrics' is so obviously wrong that the Committee decided not to adjudicate
white	HUMOUR	héwmŏr
	Date discussed	Comments
	5.7.26	'h' to be sounded
	20.9.34	Consultants ask for reconsideration after attention of evidence as to modern usage, but no alteration made
white	INFINITE	ínfinnit
	Date discussed	Comments
	9.6.27	Not 'in-fine-ite' except where metrical considerations require this pronunciation
	20.9.34	Above remarks omitted from 3rd edition of Broadcast English I
white	ISSUE	íssew
	Date discussed	Comments
	1.12.27	
blue	IRON	íĕrn
	Date discussed	Comments

	9.6.27	Deferred
	20.9.34	'ī́ĕrn' suggested by Consultants, but not included in 3rd edition of Broadcast English I
white	IODINE	ī́odeen
	Date discussed	Comments
	9.6.27	'ī́odīne'
	20.11.30	Altered to 'ī́odeen'
white	INTUIT	intéwit
	Date discussed	Comments
	19.1.33	Deferred for further inquiries
	30.11.33	'intéwit'
white	JUNTA	júntă
	Date discussed	Comments
	24.6.32	
white	JOULE (scientist and unit of electricity)	jool
	Date discussed	Comments
	24.6.31	Deferred for further inquiries
	30.11.33	'jool'
pink	KURSAAL	ko͝órzaal
	Date discussed	Comments
	25.7.29	'As in German'
	20.11.30	Simplified to 'ko͝órzaal'
white	KORAN	kora'an
	Date discussed	Comments
	9.6.27	
white	KILLOMETRE, KILLOMETER	kíllomeeter

	Date discussed	Comments
	19.1.33	
yellow	LANDSCAPE	lánskayp
	Date discussed	Comments
	9.1.35	Deferred by Consultant Members for further inquiries
	28.3.35	Committee recommended 'lánskip'
	28.11.35	Recommendation reversed to 'lánskayp' as a result of criticism received
	29.1.37	Brought up again for reconsideration. Gave rise to considerable discussion and was referred back to the Consultant Members for final decision
	7.12.37	As below [i.e. 'lánskayp']
white	LUXURY	lúckshŭry
	Date discussed	Comments
	1.12.27	'lúcksŭry'
	20.11.30	Altered to 'lúckshŭry'
white	MEMOIR	mémwaar
	Date discussed	Comments
	29.11.28	'mémwăr'
	20.11.30	Altered to 'mémwaar'
yellow	MARYLEBONE (Rd, Church, etc.)	márribŏn; but 'the district, church, etc. of Saint Máry-lĕ-bōne'
	Date discussed	Comments
	9.1.35	Deferred by Consultants for further inquiries
	28.3.35	See result of same

	28.11.35	Reconsideration confirmed
white	MARGARINE	marjăre'en
	Date discussed	Comments
	29.11.28	'márjăreen'
	20.9.34	Altered to 'marjăre'en'
	7.12.37	Word reconsidered at request for Unilever Ltd. (manufacturers of product), who stated that g was required by derivation and usage. Committee did not feel justified in reversing previous recommendation
white	MANKIND	(a) in general: mankínd (b) opposed to womankind: mánkīnd
	Date discussed	Comments
	20.9.34	
yellow	MALL (The)	mal
	Date discussed	Comments
	28.3.35	
white	MISCHIEF	míschiff
	Date discussed	Comments
	20.9.34	Added to 3rd edition of Broadcast English I at suggestion of Consultants
white	MINIATURE	mínnicher
	Date discussed	Comments
	9.6.27	'mínniătŭre'
	20.9.34	Altered to 'mínnicher' at suggestion of Consultants

white	METALLURGY	méttălurjy
	Date discussed	Comments
	9.6.27	'méttălurjy'
	29.1.37	Brought up for reconsideration. Gave rise to considerable discussion and was referred back to Consultant Members for final decision
	7.12.37	Decided not to reverse original recommendation

white	NESCIENCE	néssiĕnce
	Date discussed	Comments
	1.12.27	Recommended 'ne'essiĕnce'. Deferred
	10.7.30	Recommended 'néssiĕnce'

white	NEITHER	nī́ther, ne'ether
	Date discussed	Comments
	9.6.27	Either pronunciation is correct

[O – Z]

white	ORDEAL	orde'eăl
	Date discussed	Comments
	9.6.27	'orde'el' not 'orde'eăl'
	20.9.34	Altered to 'orde'eăl' at suggestion of Consultants

blue	ORATIO OBLIQUA	
	Date discussed	Comments
	20.9.34	Deferred by Consultants and Committee until publication of handbook on foreign words

blue	OFTEN	óffen
	Date discussed	Comments
	5.7.26	Not for publication The 't' is not sounded. Value of first vowel optional
blue	OFF	'o' as in 'not'
	Date discussed	Comments
	25.7.29	Omitted from 2nd and 3rd edition of Broadcast English I as being inconsistent with Committee's policy
yellow	OASIS	Sing.: ō-áyssiss Plur.: ō-áysseez
	Date discussed	Comments
	7.12.37	Not published in 'Radio Times' etc.
white	OVERLAP	(a) Noun: ṓverlap (b) Verb: ōverláp
	Date discussed	Comments
	19.1.33	
white	ORGANISATION	orgănīzáyshŏn
	Date discussed	Comments
	1.12.27	Recommended third syllable short. Deferred
	10.7.30	Recommended third syllable long
white	PATRIOT	páttriŏt
	Date discussed	Comments
	8.11.26	
white	PATENT	páytĕnt
	Date discussed	Comments

	8.11.26	Except in 'Letters Patent' and 'Patent Office' which have 'páttěnt'
white	PASHA	păsha'a
	Date discussed	Comments
	20.11.31	'Páshă' first 'a' as in 'man'
	20.9.34	Altered to 'păsha'a' on recommendation of Consultants
white	PARQUET	párkay
	Date discussed	Comments
	30.11.33	Deferred for further inquiries
	20.9.34	As below [i.e. párkay]
yellow	PALL MALL	péll méll
	Date discussed	Comments
	28.3.35	Consultants recommended on 2nd syllable, but Committee recommended double stress
	28.11.35	Committee confirmed recommendation
yellow	POIGNANT	póynyănt
	Date discussed	Comments
	29.1.37	Not published in 'Radio Times' etc. Consultant Members recommended 'póynyănt'
white	PIANO	(a) instrument: piánnō (b) musical term: pia'anō
	Date discussed	Comments
	20.9.34	
white	PRIVACY	prī́văcy
	Date discussed	Comments
	5.7.26	

blue	PRIMA FACIE	prī́mă fáyshiee
	Date discussed	Comments
	20.7.34	'prī́mă fáyshiee' recommended by Consultants, but deferred by Committee until publication of handbook on foreign words
white	PREMATURE	pre'emătéwer
	Date discussed	Comments
	9.6.27	'prémmătewer'
	20.9.34	Altered to 'pre'emătéwer (Consultants recommended: (a) Attributive: prémmătewer (b) Predicative: premmătéwer Recommendation not accepted by Committee)
white	PROTOCOL	prṓtŏcoll
	Date discussed	Comments
	10.7.30	prṓtŏcoll
	20.9.34	Altered by Secretary to 'prṓtŏcoll' for 3rd edition of Broadcast English I
yellow	QUININE	kwinne'en
	Date discussed	Comments
	28.3.35	Pronounced 'kwinne'en' by the Royal Pharmaceutical Society Pronounced 'kwī́nīne' in America
pink	QUESTIONNAIRE	kwestiŏnnáire
	Date discussed	Comments
	10.7.30	Recommended the use of the English word 'questionary'

	20.9.34	Above remark to be omitted on recommendation of Consultants
white	RELAY	(a) of horses, etc. Noun: re'elay Verb: rěláy (b) to lay again: re'eláy (c) broadcasting sense Noun: re'eláy Verb: re'eláy
	Date discussed	Comments
	20.11.31	
white	REFECTORY	rěféctŏry
	Date discussed	Comments
	17.1.30	The usage in monasteries is 'réffěctŏry'
white	REVERBERATORY	rěvérberatŏry
	Date discussed	Comments
	9.6.27	Principal stress on 2nd syllable, secondary on 4th syllable
	20.9.34	Altered by Secretary to 'rěvérber-atŏry' for 3rd edition of Broadcast English I
white	RESTAURANT	réstărong
	Date discussed	Comments
	20.11.31	réstărănt
	20.9.34	Altered by Secretary to 'réstărong'. Consultants asked for reconside-ration
white	RESEARCH	rěssérch
	Date discussed	Comments

	9.6.27	
	28.11.35	Confirmed
white	RÖNTGEN	rúntgĕn
	Date discussed	Comments
	19.1.33	Deferred for further inquiries
	30.11.33	Deferred for further inquiries
	20.9.34	As below [i.e. rúntgĕn]; 'g' as in 'get'
yellow	SCONE	skon
	Date discussed	Comments
	28.11.35	Not published in 'Radio Times' etc.
white	SACHEM	sáychem
	Date discussed	Comments
	20.9.34	'ch' as in 'chin'
yellow	SHORTCOMINGS	shortcómings
	Date discussed	Comments
	7.12.37	Not published in 'Radio Times' etc. The Consultant Members recommended stress on first syllable
white	SKI	shee
	Date discussed	Comments
	17.1.30	'skee'
	20.9.34	Altered to 'shee' on recommendation of Consultants
white	SUBSIDENCE	súbsiddĕnce
	Date discussed	Comments
	17.1.30	'subsídĕnce'
	20.9.34	Altered to 'súbsiddĕnce' on recommendation of Consultants

white	SWASTIKA	swóstikkă
	Date discussed	Comments
	30.11.33	
white	TRAIT	tray
	Date discussed	Comments
	8.11.26	'trayt'
	20.9.34	Altered to 'tray'. (Consultants asked for reconsideration)
blue	TOWARD	tŏwárd
	Date discussed	Comments
	9.6.27	Not for publication. Two syllables
white	TELEVISOR	téllĕvīzŏr
	Date discussed	Comments
	19.1.33	
white	UKULELE	ewkĕláyly
	Date discussed	Comments
	20.11.31	'ewkĕle'ely'
	20.9.34	Altered to 'ewkĕláyly' on recommendation of Consultants
white	VEHEMENT	ve'eĕmĕnt
	Date discussed	Comments
	9.6.27	've'ehĕmĕnt'
	20.9.34	Altered to 've'eĕmĕnt' on recommendation of Consultants
yellow	VASE	vaaz
	Date discussed	Comments
	28.11.35	Not published in 'Radio Times' etc.

yellow	VITUPERATION	vītewperáyshŏn
	Date discussed	Comments
	8.11.26	'vittewperáyshŏn'
	29.1.37	Brought up for reconsideration. Gave rise to considerable discussion, and referred back to Consultant Members for final decision
	7.12.37	Decision reversed as below [i.e. vītewperáyshŏn]
white	VITAMIN	vī́tămin
	Date discussed	Comments
	29.11.28	
yellow	WEDNESDAY	wénzday (see note)
	Date discussed	Comments
	28.3.35	
	28.11.35	The Committee confirmed recommendation but added the following note: 'Similarly, the word '-day' should be pronounced '-dy' in unstressed positions; e.g. 'Sátturdy', 'yésterdy', etc.'
white	WESLEYAN	wéssliăn
	Date discussed	Comments
	9.2.27	wéssliăn
	20.9.34	Consultants asked for reconsideration, but no alteration made
yellow	WAISTCOAT	wéss-cŏt
	Date discussed	Comments
	29.1.37	Not published in 'Radio Times' etc.

yellow	XYLOPHONE	zílŏphōne
	Date discussed	Comments
	28.3.35	
white	ZOOLOGY	zō-óllŏjy
	Date discussed	Comments
	9.6.27	
yellow	ZOOLOGICAL	zō-ŏlojjicăl
	Date discussed	Comments
	8.6.27	'zō-ŏlojjicăl', but 'Zoolójjicăl Gárdĕns'
	29.1.37	Emended to 'zoo-ŏlójjicăl', with consent retained
	7.12.37	Emended to 'zō-ŏlójjicăl', with comment deleted. This emendation not published in 'Radio Times' etc.

[O – Z]

Index of Proper Names A-Z (R6 / 199 / 2). The words were also written on colour-coded paper slips, namely—

- green: All foreign place names
- pink: All foreign names of persons
- white: All English words and names
- blue: Deferred words, or 'NOT FOR PUBLICATION'

green	ASIA	áyshă
	Date discussed	Comments
	17.1.30	
white	ARMADA	armáydă
	Date discussed	Comments

	9.1.35	Deferred by Consultants for further inquiries
	28.3.35	See result of same, all in favour of 'arma'adă'
white	BOER	bő́er
	Date discussed	Comments
	28.3.35	Consultants recommended 'báwer', but not accepted by Committee
white	CONNECTICUT	connéttikut
	Date discussed	Comments
	8.11.26	
white	CONDUIT (Street, London)	cúndit
	Date discussed	Comments
	30.11.33	'cóndewit'
	20.9.34	Altered to 'cúndit'
green	CARIBBEAN	carribe'eăn
	Date discussed	Comments
	17.1.30	
pink	EROS	e'eross
	Date discussed	Comments
	10.7.30	
white	HUGUENOT	héwguĕnott
	Date discussed	Comments
	9.1.35	Deferred by Consultants for further inquiries
	28.3.35	See result of same, all in favour of 'héwguĕnō'
white	HARTLEPOOL	hártlipool or hártlĕpool

	Date discussed	Comments
	8.11.26	Either pronunciation
pink	JOULE	jool
	Date discussed	Comments
	30.11.33	
green	KENYA	ke'enyă
	Date discussed	Comments
	20.11.30	
green	LOS ANGELES	loss ángĕlez
	Date discussed	Comments
	17.1.30	'g' as in 'get'
white	LONDONDERRY	(a) Lord: lúndŏndry
		(b) Place: lúndŏndérry
pink	MOHAMMED, MAHOMET	măhómmet
	Date discussed	Comments
	25.7.29	
white	NORTHAMPTON	north-ámtŏn
	Date discussed	Comments
	5.7.26	
green	NEWFOUNDLAND	(a) Country: accent on 3rd syl.
		(b) Dog: accent on 2nd syl.
	Date discussed	Comments
	17.1.30	
white	OGILVIE	ógle-vy
	Date discussed	Comments
	17.1.30	
white	PALL MALL	péll méll
	Date discussed	Comments

	28.3.35	Consultants recommended stress on second syllable
green	RHEIMS	reems
	Date discussed	Comments
	5.7.26	
white	SYNGE	sing
	Date discussed	Comments
	29.11.28	
white	ST. JOHN ERVINE	sínjŏn-érvin
	Date discussed	Comments
	28.11.29	
green	ST. HELENA	saint hĕle'enă
	Date discussed	Comments
	8.11.26	
white	SOUTHAMPTON	south-hámptŏn
	Date discussed	Comments
	5.7.26	
pink	SEIDLITZ	sédlits
	Date discussed	Comments
	10.7.30	
pink	SALOME	sălómy
	Date discussed	Comments
	20.11.31	
pink	TRAFALGAR	trăfálgăr
	Date discussed	Comments
	8.11.26	
white	TOWCESTER	tṓster
	Date discussed	Comments
	5.7.26	

white	WROTHAM	ro'otăm
	Date discussed	Comments
	8.11.26	
green	YOSEMITE	yōssémity
	Date discussed	Comments
	10.7.30	

It should be mentioned that the Proper Names Index in particular appears very sketchy and incomplete. Considering the various Foreign Names and Place Names booklets, one would expect many more words to have been discussed. However, the General Word Index, that is, the 3rd edition of *Broadcast English I* plus the words discussed since ('yellow' paper slips), appears more complete, but not even there all words discussed between 1936 and 1939 seem to have been included.

Acknowledgements

This volume incorporates material from a number of research papers that I have written over the years, in particular 'The BBC Advisory Committee on Spoken English or How (not) to Construct a "Standard" Pronunciation' (2008a), 'Setting a Standard: Early BBC Language Policy and the Advisory Committee on Spoken English' (2008b), both of which have been used in part for Chapter 2; 'How not to Do Things with Words: The BBC Sub-Committee for the Invention of New Words (1935–1937)' (2009), which comprises Section 4.2; and 'English and the Media: Radio' (2012), which forms part of Section 6.1.

The book draws upon a wealth of primary sources made available by the BBC Written Archives Centre (Caversham). The Centre houses a formidable collection of documents that serve as the foundation of the book. The Centre's staff have been exceptional in their support and I would like to acknowledge the BBC for giving me permission to quote from their copyrighted material. I should also like to gratefully acknowledge the Society of Authors, on behalf of the Bernard Shaw Estate, for giving me permission to quote from G. B. Shaw's numerous letters and postcards to the BBC; my thanks go to Sarah Baxter in particular.

I am greatly indebted to Laura Forbes, the granddaughter and copyright holder of Daniel Jones, who allowed me generously and kindly to quote from Daniel Jones's unpublished writings and letters. Inger Mees very helpfully made that contact possible.

I am grateful to the copyright holders for allowing me to use the following unpublished BBC archive material: Jeff Cooper, for the use of the letters of Lascelles Abercrombie; The London Library, for the letters of Logan Pearsall Smith; Dr S. O. Lucas for the letters of Frank Laurence Lucas; Richard Luckett, for the letters of Ivan Armstrong Richards; Susan Pares, for the letters of Bernard Pares; the family of S. K. Ratcliffe, for S. K. Ratcliffe's letters; The Society of Authors as the Literary Representative of the Estate of Rose Macauley, for Rose Macauley's letters; John Swire and Sons for the letters of Edward Manico Gull; and Colin Webb, for the letters of Alistair Cooke.

The quotes by Kenneth Clark are from a letter dated 15 February 1937 and reproduced by permission of the Estate of Kenneth Clark c/o The Hanbury Agency Ltd, 28 Moreton Street, London SW1V 2PE. Copyright © 1937 Kenneth Clark. All Rights Reserved.

The book has benefited greatly from a number of professional colleagues. Peter Jackson made available and passed on to me his source material on the topic. Fellow researchers and experts on Broadcast English—Lynda Mugglestone, Catherine Sangster, Hamish Norbrook, Jennifer Price, and Didier Maillat—shared many of their insights and provided valuable input. Discussions with Hans Frede Nielsen and the late Horst Weinstock over the course of a Broadcast English conference, and with Charlotte Brewer about a number of research projects, proved highly valuable, too. Also, the book has benefited greatly from comments and suggestions made by the reviewers. I would also like to express my heartfelt gratitude to Julia Steer, the editor at OUP, and her colleague, Céline Louasli, editorial administrator at OUP, who have so wonderfully supported and encouraged me in all the work leading to publication of the book. I would have not accomplished this without their engaging and enthusiastic backing.

Not only did Peter Trudgill share his vast knowledge on all linguistic matters, but he and Jean Hannah also read and made substantial improvements to this book. Their help has been most valuable during the recovery period from my stroke. I owe them a lasting and deep debt of gratitude.

In the course of carrying out research for this book, my home institution, the University of Lausanne, helped me to organize a conference on Broadcast English held in 2006. Above all, however, I would like to express my gratitude to the Warden and Fellows of Robinson College, Cambridge. Their hospitality and support during the Easter Term 2013 at Robinson College have provided me with the ideal setting for finishing this book.

Finally I would like to thank my partner, Gunter Siddiqi, for helping me all along.[1]

NOTE

1. Due to partial paralysis of my right arm, the book was dictated using a speech recognition programme, *Dragon Dictate* for Mac OS X, and was then automatically typed into the file.

Bibliography

1. Unpublished files from the BBC Written Archives Centre, Caversham

R6 / 196 / 1: Advisory Committee Spoken English, File 1, 1926–1927.

R6 / 196 / 2: Advisory Committee Spoken English, File 2, 1928.

R6 / 196 / 3: Advisory Committee Spoken English, File 3, 1929.

R6 / 196 / 4: Advisory Committee Spoken English, File 4, 1930–1933.

R6 / 196 / 5: Advisory Committee Spoken English, File 5, January–June 1934.

R6 / 196 / 6: Advisory Committee Spoken English, File 6, July–December 1934.

R6 / 196 / 7: Advisory Committee Spoken English, File 7, January–June 1935.

R6 / 196 / 8: Advisory Committee Spoken English, File 8, July–December 1935.

R6 / 196 / 9: Advisory Committee Spoken English, File 9, 1936.

R6 / 196 / 10: Advisory Committee Spoken English, File 10, 1937–1938.

R6 / 196 / 11: Advisory Committee Spoken English, File 11, 1939–1943.

R6 / 199 / 1: Advisory Committees, Spoken English Advisory Committee, Index of Words Discussed, Vol. 1: A–N.

R6 / 199 / 2: Advisory Committees, Spoken English Advisory Committee, Index of Words Discussed, Vol. 2: O–Z, A–Z Index of Proper Names.

R6 / 201 / 1: Advisory Committees, Spoken English Advisory Committee, Minute Book: 1926–1933.

R6 / 201 / 2: Advisory Committees, Spoken English Advisory Committee, Minute Book: 1934–1938.

2. *Broadcast English* pamphlets

Broadcast English I: Recommendations to Announcers Regarding Certain Words of Doubtful Pronunciation. With an Introduction by A. Lloyd James. 1st edn 1928; 2nd edn 1932; 3rd edn 1935. Savoy Hill, London: The British Broadcasting Corporation.

Broadcast English II: Recommendations to Announcers Regarding the Pronunciation of some English Place Names. Collected and Transcribed for the B.B.C. Advisory Committee on Spoken English by A. Lloyd James. 1930. Savoy Hill, London: The British Broadcasting Corporation.

Broadcast English III: Recommendations to Announcers Regarding the Pronunciation of some Scottish Place Names. Collected and Transcribed for the B.B.C. Advisory Committee on Spoken English by A. Lloyd James. 1932. Savoy Hill, London: The British Broadcasting Corporation.

Broadcast English IV: Recommendations to Announcers Regarding the Pronunciation of some Welsh Place Names. Collected and Transcribed for the B.B.C. Advisory Committee on Spoken English by A. Lloyd James. 1934. Savoy Hill, London: The British Broadcasting Corporation.

Broadcast English V: Recommendations to Announcers Regarding the Pronunciation of some Irish Place Names. Collected and Transcribed for the B.B.C. Advisory Committee on Spoken English by A. Lloyd James. 1935. Broadcasting House, London: The British Broadcasting Corporation.

Broadcast English VI: Recommendations to Announcers Regarding the Pronunciation of some Foreign Place Names. Collected and Transcribed for the B.B.C. Advisory Committee on Spoken English by A. Lloyd James. 1937. Broadcasting House, London: The British Broadcasting Corporation.

Broadcast English VII: Recommendations to Announcers Regarding the Pronunciation of some British Family Names and Titles. Collected and Transcribed for the B.B.C. Advisory Committee on Spoken English by A. Lloyd James. 1939. Broadcasting House, London: The British Broadcasting Corporation.

3. Published and electronic sources

Adekunle, Mobolaji (1995). 'English in Nigeria: Attitudes, Policy and Communicative Realities', in Ayo Bamgbose, Ayo Banjo, and Andrew Thomas (eds), *New Englishes: A West African Perspective.* Trenton, NJ and Asmara, Eritrea: Africa World Press, 57–86.

Ager, Dennis (1996). *Language Policy in Britain and France: The Processes of Policy.* Open Linguistics Series. London: Cassell.

Aitchison, Jean (1997). *The Language Web: The Power and Problem of Words.* Cambridge: Cambridge University Press.

Aitchison, Jean (2001). *Language Change: Progress or Decay?* 3rd edition. Cambridge: Cambridge University Press.

Algeo, John (1998). 'Vocabulary', in Suzanne Romaine (ed.), *The Cambridge History of the English Language. Volume IV: 1776–1997.* Cambridge: Cambridge University Press, 57–91.

Allen, John (2003). *The BBC News Styleguide.* London: BBC Training and Development. <www.bbctraining.com/pdfs/newsstyleguide.pdf> (last accessed 26 January 2009).

Andersson, Lars-Gunnar and Peter Trudgill (1992). *Bad Language.* Harmondsworth: Penguin.

Bailey, Richard W. (2012). 'English among the Languages', in Mugglestone 2012b: 415–45.

Barber, Charles (1997). *Early Modern English.* 2nd edition. Edinburgh: Edinburgh University Press.

Barbour, Stephen and Patrick Stevenson (1990). *Variation in German: A Critical Approach to German Sociolinguistics.* Cambridge: Cambridge University Press.

BBC Complaints =<bbc.co.uk/complaints/reports/> (last accessed on 11 February 2013).

BBC Editorial Guidelines 2005 = <www.bbc.co.uk/guidelines/editorialguidelines/> (last accessed 26 January 2009).

BBC Entertainment = <bbcentertainment.com> (last accessed on 26 April 2013).

BBC iPlayer Radio = <bbc.co.uk/radio> (last accessed on 26 April 2013).

BBC One, Two, Three, Four = <bbc.co.uk/tv> (last accessed on 26 April 2013).

BBC Phonetic Respelling = <bbc.co.uk/blogs/magazinemonitor/phonetics.doc> (last accessed on 11 February 2013).

BBC World News TV = <bbc.co.uk/news/world_radio_and_tv> (last accessed on 26 April 2013).

BBC World Service History: 75 Years = <bbc.co.uk/worldservice/history/> (last accessed on 11 February 2013).

BBC World Service History: The 1940s = <bbc.co.uk/worldservice/history/story/ 2007/02/070122_html_40s.shtml> (last accessed on 11 February 2013).

Bell, Allan (1983). 'Broadcast News as Language Standard', *International Journal of the Sociology of Language 40: Language and Mass Media*, ed. Gerhard Leitner: 29–42.

Bex, Tony (1996). *Variety in Written English: Texts in Society—Societies in Text*. London: Routledge. Ch. 1: 'Variety and "Standard English"', 8–29.

Bex, Tony and Richard J. Watts (eds) (1999). *Standard English: The Widening Debate*. London: Routledge.

Briggs, Asa (1995a). *The History of Broadcasting in the United Kingdom. Volume I: The Birth of Broadcasting 1896–1927*. First published 1961, reissued 1995. Oxford: Oxford University Press.

Briggs, Asa (1995b). *The History of Broadcasting in the United Kingdom. Volume II: The Golden Age of Wireless 1927–1939*. First published 1961, revised 1995. Oxford: Oxford University Press.

Briggs, Asa (1995c). *The History of Broadcasting in the United Kingdom. Volume V: Competition.* First published 1961, revised 1995. Oxford: Oxford University Press.

British Broadcasting Corporation Pronunciation Unit (1974). *BBC Pronunciation Policy and Practice.* London: BBC.

British Broadcasting Corporation Pronunciation Unit, Telegram, 3 April 1981.

Burchfield, Robert (1981). *The Spoken Word: A BBC Guide.* London: British Broadcasting Corporation.

Burchfield, Robert, Denis Donoghue, and Andrew Timothy (1979). *The Quality of Spoken English on BBC Radio.* London: British Broadcasting Corporation.

Burnley, David (2000). *The History of the English Language: A Source Book.* 2nd edition. London: Longman.

Carey, John (1992). *The Intellectuals and the Masses.* London: Faber and Faber.

Carter, Ronald (1999). 'Standard Grammars, Spoken Grammars: Some Educational Implications', in Bex and Watts 1999: 149–66.

Churchill, Winston (1974). *Winston S. Churchill: His Complete Speeches 1897–1963.* Ed. Robert Rhodes James. Volume VI: *1935–1942.* New York and London: Chelsea House Publishers.

Clyne, Michael (1995). *The German Language in a Changing Europe.* Cambridge: Cambridge University Press.

Crowley, Tony (1999). 'Curiouser and Curiouser: Falling Standards in the Standard English Debate', in Bex and Watts 1999: 271–82.

Crystal, David (1981). 'Language on the Air—Has it Degenerated?' *The Listener* 9 July 1981.

Crystal, David (1997). *A Dictionary of Linguistics and Phonetics.* 4th edition. Oxford: Blackwell Publishers.

Crystal, David (2002). *The English Language.* 2nd edition. London: Pelican.

Crystal, David (2003a). *The Cambridge Encyclopedia of the English Language.* 2nd edition. Cambridge: Cambridge University Press.

Crystal, David (2003b). *English as a Global Language*. 2nd edition. Cambridge: Cambridge University Press.

Crystal, David (2012). 'Into the Twenty-First Century', in Mugglestone 2012b: 488–513.

Davies, Diane (2005). *Varieties of Modern English*. Harlow: Pearson Longman.

Dixon, John A., Berenice Mahoney, and Roger Cocks (2002). 'Accents of Guilt: Effects of Regional Accent, Race, and Crime Type on Attributions of Guilt', *Journal of Language and Social Psychology* 21: 162–8.

Dobson, E. J. (1955). 'Early Modern Standard English', *Transactions of the Philological Society* 1955 [no vol.]: 25–54.

Drabble, Margaret (2000). *The Oxford Companion to English Literature*. 6th edition. Oxford: Oxford University Press.

Duden, Band 1: Die deutsche Rechtschreibung (2006). 24th edition. Ed. Dudenredaktion. Mannheim: Bibliographisches Institut.

Ferguson, Charles A. (1959). 'Diglossia', *Word* 15: 325–40.

Garvin, P. L. and M. Mathiot (1956). 'The Urbanisation of the Guaraní Language: A Problem in Language and Culture', in A. F. C. Wallace (ed.), *Men and Cultures*. Philadelphia: University of Pennsylvania Press, 783–90; also in J. A. Fishman (1968). *Readings in the Sociology of Language*. The Hague: Mouton.

Gimson, A. C. (1984). 'The RP Accent', in Peter Trudgill (ed.), *Language in the British Isles*. Cambridge: Cambridge University Press. 45–54.

Gimson, A. C. (1994). *Gimson's Pronunciation of English*. 5th edition, revised by A. Cruttenden. London: Arnold.

Gneuss, Helmut (1972). 'The Origin of Standard Old English and Æthelwold's School at Winchester', *Anglo-Saxon England* 1: 63–83.

Görlach, Manfred (1991). *Introduction to Early Modern English*. Cambridge: Cambridge University Press.

Graddol, David (1997). *The Future of English?* London: British Council.

Gretsch, Mechthild (1999). *The Intellectual Foundations of the English Benedictine Reform.* Cambridge Studies in Anglo-Saxon England 25. Cambridge: Cambridge University Press.

Haugen, Einar (1966). 'Dialect, Language, Nation', *American Anthropologist* 68: 922–35; also in J. B. Pride and J. Holmes (eds) (1972). *Sociolinguistics.* London: Penguin, 97–112.

Hendy, David (2007). *Life on Air: A History of Radio Four.* Oxford: Oxford University Press.

Herbert, John (1997). 'The Broadcast Voice', *English Today* 50.13.2: 18–23.

Hofstetter, W. (1988). 'Winchester and the Standardization of Old English Vocabulary', *Anglo-Saxon England* 17: 139–61.

Honey, John (1997). *Language Is Power: The Story of Standard English and its Enemies.* London: Faber and Faber.

Hughes, Arthur, Peter Trudgill, and Dominic Watt (2005). *English Accents and Dialects: An Introduction to Social and Regional Varieties of English in the British Isles.* 4th edition. London: Hodder Arnold.

Jones, Daniel (1924 and 1937). *English Pronouncing Dictionary.* 2nd and 4th editions. London: Dent.

Jones, Daniel (1972). *The Pronunciation of English.* 4th edition. Cambridge: Cambridge University Press.

Labov, William and Wendell A. Harris (1986). 'De Facto Segregation of Black and White Vernaculars', in David Sankoff (ed.), *Diversity and Diachrony.* Philadelphia: John Benjamins, 1–24.

Leitner, Gerhard (1979). *BBC English und der BBC: Geschichte und soziolinguistische Interpretation des Sprachgebrauchs in einem Massenmedium.* Linguistische Berichte 60. Wiesbaden: Vieweg.

Leitner, Gerhard (1983). *Gesprächsanalyse und Rundfunkkommunikation: Die Struktur englischer phone-ins.* Hildesheim: Georg Olms Verlag.

McArthur, Tom (ed.) (1992). *The Oxford Companion to the English Language.* Oxford: Oxford University Press.

McArthur, Tom (1998). *The English Languages*. Cambridge: Cambridge University Press.

McArthur, Tom (2012). 'English World-Wide in the Twentieth Century', in Mugglestone 2012b: 446–87.

McGill, Steven (1998). 'Double Standard English', *English Today* 53: 6–12.

Miller, G. M. (1971). *BBC Pronouncing Dictionary of British Names*. 2nd edition, enlarged, 1983. London: Oxford University Press.

Milroy, James (1999). 'The Consequences of Standardisation in Descriptive Linguistics', in Bex and Watts 1999: 16–39.

Milroy, Lesley (1999). 'Standard English and Language Ideology in Britain and the United States', in Bex and Watts 1999: 173–206.

Mugglestone, Lynda (2003). *'Talking Proper': The Rise of Accent as Social Symbol*. 2nd edition. Oxford: Oxford University Press.

Mugglestone, Lynda (2012a). 'English in the Nineteenth Century', in Mugglestone 2012b: 340–78.

Mugglestone, Lynda (ed.) (2012b). *The History of English*. Updated edition. Oxford: Oxford University Press.

Norbrook, Hamish (2008). 'The English of Broadcast News: When English is Not the First Language of the Audience', in Jürg Rainer Schwyter, Didier Maillat, and Christian Mair (eds), *Broadcast English Past, Present and Future*. Arbeiten aus Anglistik und Amerikanistik 33, Special Issue. Tübingen: Narr, 263–83.

Norbrook, Hamish and Keith Ricketts (1995). 'Broadcasting and English', in Ayo Bamgbose, Ayo Banjo, and Andrew Thomas (eds), *New Englishes: A West African Perspective*. Asmara: Africa World Press, 300–6.

ODNB 2004–13 = *The Oxford Dictionary of National Biography* online: <http://www.oxforddnb.com>, accessed 25 April 2013.

OED = *Oxford English Dictionary*, 2nd edition 1989 and online draft revisions: <http://www.oed.com>, accessed 25 April 2013.

Olausson, L. and C. Sangster (2006). *Oxford BBC Guide to Pronunciation*. Oxford: Oxford University Press.

Phillipson, Robert (2003). *English-Only Europe? Challenging Language Policy*. London: Routledge.

Pinker, Steven (1994). *The Language Instinct: How the Mind Creates Language*. New York: William Morrow & Co.

Pointon, G. (1990). *BBC Pronouncing Dictionary of British Names*. 2nd edition. Oxford: Oxford University Press.

Pullum, Geoffrey K. and William A. Ladusaw (1996). *Phonetic Symbol Guide*. 2nd edition. Chicago and London: University of Chicago Press.

Puttenham, George (1589). *The Arte of English Poesie*. Ed. Gladys Doidge Willcock and Alice Walker (1936). Cambridge: Cambridge University Press.

Quirk, Randolph, Sidney Greenbaum, Geoffrey Leech, and Jan Svartvik (1985). *A Comprehensive Grammar of the English Language*. London: Longman.

Radio Caroline History = <radiocaroline.co.uk/#history.html> (last accessed on 11 February 2013).

Radio Times: 18 January 1924; 20 June 1924; 9 January 1925; 16 April 1926; 16 July 1926; 30 July 1926; 16 September 1927; 18 January 1928; 29 March 1929; 12 April 1929; 3 May 1929; 24 May 1929; 28 June 1929; 15 November 1929; 14 August 1931; 6 November 1931; 12 February 1932; 29 December 1933; 19 April 1935; 26 August 1938.

Reith, J. C. W. (1924). *Broadcast over Britain*. London: Hodder and Stoughton.

Roach, Peter (2009). *English Phonetics and Phonology: A Practical Course*. 4th edition. Cambridge: Cambridge University Press.

Sangster, Catherine (2008). 'The Work of the BBC Pronunciation Unit in the 21st Century', in Jürg Rainer Schwyter, Didier Maillat, and Christian Mair (eds), *Broadcast English Past, Present and Future*. Arbeiten aus Anglistik und Amerikanistik 33, Special Issue. Tübingen: Narr, 251–61.

Schmied, Josef (1991). *English in Africa*. London: Longman.

Schwyter, Jürg Rainer (2008a). 'The BBC Advisory Committee on Spoken English or How (not) to Construct a "Standard" Pronunciation', in Miriam Locher and Jürg Strässler (eds), *Standards and Norms in the English Language*. Berlin: Mouton de Gruyter, 175–93.

Schwyter, Jürg Rainer (2008b). 'Setting a Standard: Early BBC Language Policy and the Advisory Committee on Spoken English', in Jürg Rainer Schwyter, Didier Maillat, and Christian Mair (eds), *Broadcast English Past, Present and Future*. Arbeiten aus Anglistik und Amerikanistik 33, Special Issue. Tübingen: Narr, 217–50.

Schwyter, Jürg Rainer (2009). 'How *not* to Do Things with Words: The BBC Sub-Committee for the Invention of New Words (1935–1937)', *Neuphilologische Mitteilungen* 2 CX: 159–74.

Schwyter, Jürg Rainer (2012). 'English and the Media: Radio', in Alex Bergs and Laurel Brinton (eds), *English Historical Linguistics: An International Handbook*. HSK 34.1. Berlin: Mouton de Gruyter, 1089–104.

Smith, Jeremy J. (1992). 'The Use of English: Language Contact, Dialect Variation, and Written Standardisation During the Middle English Period', in W. Machan and Ch. T. Scott (eds), *English in its Social Context: Essays in Historical Sociolinguistics*. Oxford Studies in Sociolinguistics. Oxford: Oxford University Press.

Smith, Jeremy (1996). *An Historical Study of English: Function, Form and Change*. London: Routledge.

Smith, Jeremy (2012). 'From Middle to Early Modern English', in Mugglestone 2012b: 147–79.

Steinberg, Jonathan (1996). *Why Switzerland*. 2nd edition. Cambridge: Cambridge University Press.

Stuart-Smith, Jane (2007). 'The Influence of the Media', in Carmen Llamas, Louise Mullany, and Peter Stockwell (eds), *The Routledge Companion to Sociolinguistics*. London: Routledge.

The Spectator: 12 March 1988.

The Times: 14 January 2002.

Thompson, Rick (2005). *Writing for Broadcast Journalists*. London: Routledge.

Thornborrow, Joanna (2004). 'Language and the Media', in Linda Thomas, Shân Wareing, Isthla Singh, Jean Stillwell Peccei, Joanna Thornborrow, and Jason Jones (eds), *Language, Society and Power: An Introduction*. 2nd edition. London: Routledge, 55–74.

Tieken-Boon van Ostade, Ingrid (2012). 'English at the Onset of the Normative Tradition', in Mugglestone 2012b: 298–339.

Trask, Robert Lawrence (2000). *The Penguin Dictionary of English Grammar*. London: Penguin.

Tristram, Hildegard L. C. (2001). 'Sprache und Identität in Minoritätensprachen. Zwei Fallbeispiele: Irisch und Bretonisch', in Gerda Hassler (ed.), *Sprachkontakt und Sprachvergleich*. Münster: Nodus, 9–37.

Trudgill, Peter (1986). *Dialects in Contact*. Oxford: Blackwell.

Trudgill, Peter (1999). 'Standard English: What it Isn't', in Bex and Watts 1999: 117–28.

Trudgill, Peter (2000). *Sociolinguistics: An Introduction to Language and Society*. 4th edition. London: Penguin Books.

Trudgill, Peter (2002). *Sociolinguistic Variation and Change*. Edinburgh: Edinburgh University Press.

Trudgill, Peter (2003). *A Glossary of Sociolinguistics*. Oxford: Oxford University Press.

Variantenwörterbuch des Deutschen (2004). Ed. Ulrich Ammon et al. Berlin: Walter de Gruyter.

Verstegan, Richard (1605). *Restitution of Decayed Intelligence, in Antiquities: Concerning the Most Noble and Renovvmed English Nation / by the Studie and Trauaile of R.V. Dedicated vnto the Kings most Excellent Maijestie*. Printed at Antvverp: by Robert Bruney. And to be sold at London: by Iohn Norton and Iohn Bill.

Voice of America Learning English = <learningenglish.voanews.com> (last accessed on 11 February 2013).

Watts, Richard J. (1999). 'The Social Construction of Standard English: Grammar Writers as a "Discourse Community"', in Bex and Watts 1999: 40–68.

Wells, J. C. (1982). *Accents of English.* 3 vols. Cambridge: Cambridge University Press.

Wright, Sue (2004). *Language Policy and Language Planning: From Nationalism to Globalisation*. Basingstoke: Palgrave Macmillan.

Write-On, BBC World Service, 17 February 2003, 18.45 GMT.

Zimmermann, Gerhard (1982). 'Sprachkritik des Englischen am Beispiel der BBC', *Die Neueren Sprachen* 81: 419–38.

Index

Index